# Life under British Colonial Rule: Recollections of an African and a British Administrator in Tanganyika and Southern Rhodesia

## Godfrey Mwakikagile

Life under British Colonial Rule: Recollections of an African and a British Administrator in Tanganyika and Southern Rhodesia

First Edition

ISBN 978-9987-16-042-6

New Africa Press
Dar es Salaam, Tanzania

TUNISIA

CAPE VERDE ISLANDS
MOROCCO

ALGERIA

LIBYA

EGYPT

WESTERN SAHARA

MAURITANIA

MALI

NIGER

CHAD

SUDAN

ERITREA

DJIBOUTI

SOMALIA

SENEGAL

GAMBIA

GUINEA BISSAU

GUINEA

BURKINA FASO

NIGERIA

CENTRAL AFRICAN REPUBLIC

ETHIOPIA

SIERRA LEONE

COTE D'IVOIRE

LIBERIA

BENIN

TOGO

GHANA

EQUATORIAL GUINEA

CAMEROON

UGANDA

KENYA

SAO TOME AND PRINCIPE

GABON

CONGO

DEMOCRATIC REPUBLIC OF CONGO

RWANDA

BURUNDI

TANZANIA

CORMOROS

ANGOLA

ZAMBIA

MOZAMBIQUE

ZIMBABWE

MADAGASCAR

NAMIBIA

BOTSWANA

MALAWI

SWAZILAND

SOUTH AFRICA

LESOTHO

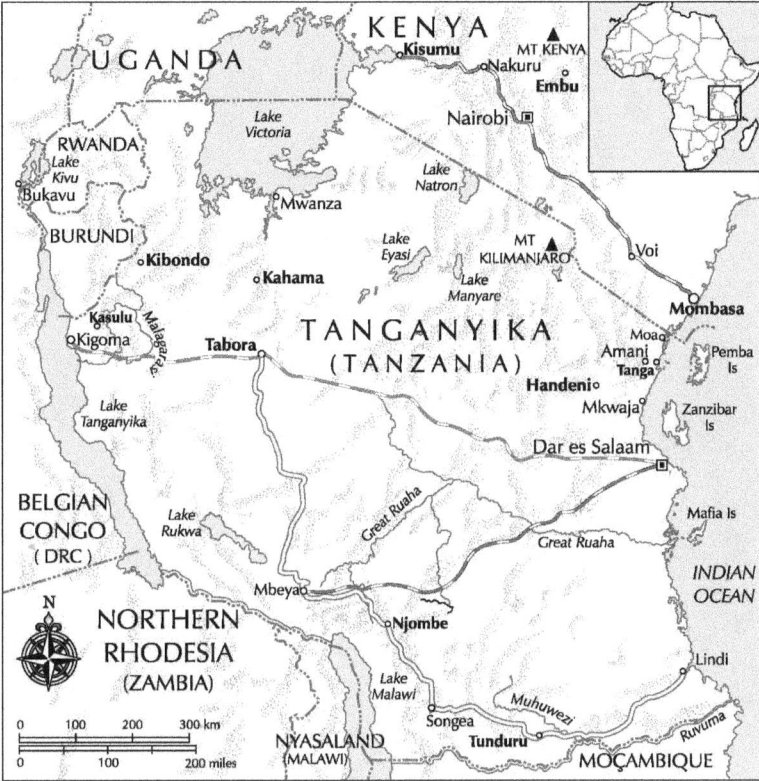

# Contents

Formation of Tanganyika

Colonial federations

Racial cooperation

Dream shattered

Good life for the colonial rulers and settlers

My childhood
in the Southern Highlands Province

From Tanganyika to South Africa:
Working in the mines

Whites I saw in the fifties:
My perception

Quest for independence
on multiracial basis

More than a dog bite:
Reflections

Kyimbila Moravian Church

My father:
victim of racism

Racial incidents and injustices

My early political awakening

# Chapter Four
# Campaign for independence

## Part Two:

## Conclusion:
## Our colonial experience
## and our destiny

## Part Three

## Administrator in Africa

## 1951 – 1956: Tanganyika

## Tanganyika, 1950s

### Kahama

### Kasulu

### Safari

### Malagarasi safari

### Kibondo

### Handeni

### Tanga

### Meeting my destiny

# Introduction

THIS WORK focuses on life under British colonial rule in Tanganyika and Southern Rhodesia.

I was born in colonial Tanganyika and spent my early years under colonial rule. When I was growing up, I witnessed some of the events which took place during that important period in the history of my country, now known as Tanzania. I am glad to share some of my memories of that bygone era.

As a witness to some of the historical events which took place in pre-independence Tanganyika, I feel that I have a responsibility, especially as a Tanzanian, to share with my readers the memories I have of those days as well as the memories of other people who lived in Tanganyika during that period. I hope that my reflections on those days will play a role, however small, in providing a better picture and understanding – from the perspective of the colonised – of how life was during colonial rule.

I wish to express my profound gratitude to Dr. David Warwick Brokensha, professor emeritus in the department of anthropology at the University of California-Santa Barbara, whose areas of specialisation included Africa. He taught there from 1966 to 1989 when he retired.

When I asked him in November 2016 for permission to use some of his material, he kindly agreed and said I could use whatever I wanted to use in my book. Unfortunately, he passed away not long after that, on 15 June 2017, at his home in Fishoek, South Africa.

He worked for the colonial government in Tanganyika from 1951 to 1956. I have included in my book the material about his work in Tanganyika. It is a treasure trove on life in Tanganyika in those days from the perspective of a British colonial administrator.

I hope hope both perspectives, his and mine, complement each other to shed some light on how life was in colonial Tanganyika for the indigenous people and for the British settlers and colonial rulers.

It was a critical period in the history of Tanganyika and for the future of the country which came to be known as Tanzania after uniting with Zanzibar in April 1964 when I was a 14 years-old student in a boarding middle school in Rungwe District in the Southern Highlands Province.

I am also very grateful to Stephen Luscombe of britishempire.co.uk for giving me permission to use the material provided by him and his colleagues on their website. I have not used it in this book but intend to do so in my forthcoming works on life in Tanganyika and other parts of Africa which were also under British colonial rule during my lifetime and before then.

I bear full responsibility for whatever mistakes and shortcomings students and members of the general public may find in my book. It is a work of a mere mortal with frailties.

# Chapter One

# Born in Tanganyika

THE PERIOD in which I was born witnessed some of the most important events and changes in the history of Tanganyika, the land of my birth, and indeed of the entire African continent. It was the dawn of a new era.

It was only a few years after the end of the Second World War in which many Africans, including one of my maternal uncles, fought and in which many of them died. Fortunately, my uncle, who fought in Burma, survived and returned safely to Tanganyika after the war.

It was also a period of political ferment in which the campaign for independence started in earnest in Tanganyika – the largest British possession in East Africa – and in other colonies on the continent.

## Kigoma
## My birthplace

I was born at 6 a.m. on Tuesday, 4 October 1949, in Kigoma, a port town on the eastern shore of Lake Tanganyika in what was then the Western Province of Tanganyika.

It was during British colonial rule. Tanganyika in those days had seven provinces: Western, Central, Lake, Northern, Coast, Southern and Southern Highlands. The capital of the Western Province was Tabora.

13

My parents came from Rungwe District in the Southern Highlands Province which was also simply known as the Southern Highlands.

Rungwe District is in the Great Rift Valley and is ringed by misty blue mountains. It is close to the border with Malawi and is home to the Nyakyusa, my ethnic group, one of the largest in Tanzania. South of Rungwe is Kyela District which borders Malawi. It was once a part of Rungwe District.

My father worked as a medical assistant during British colonial rule. That is how he and my mother ended up in Kigoma. My parents also lived in other parts of Tanganyika where my father worked before I was born.

I am the first-born in my family. I was born at Kilimani Hospital and lived with my parents in one of the government houses for government employees in an area known as Mwanga and on a street with the same name in the town of Kigoma. My father worked as a medical assistant at the same hospital. It was a government hospital. I was born four months after my parents moved from Tanga to Kigoma in June 1949.

My parents and I later moved to Ujiji, about six miles south of Kigoma, where my sister Maria was born at a Roman Catholic hospital on Sunday, 1 April 1951.

Ujiji is one of the oldest towns in Tanzania and the oldest in the western part of the country. It is also of historical significance as the starting point of the main slave trade route from the western part of the country to the east coast on the Indian Ocean.

It was also in Ujiji where Henry Morton Stanley found Dr. David Livingstone on 10 November 1871. When he first saw him, he reportedly asked: "Dr. Livingstone, I presume?"

Dr. Livingstone was presumed to be missing – he had been "missing" for three years – and the Royal Geographical Society sponsored an expedition to look for him in Africa.

Stanley was sent to East Africa to look for the Scottish missionary doctor who in the African hinterland and uttered those words which became famous in the history of African exploration. Exploration eventually led to the conquest and colonisation of Africa which came to be described as the white man's burden in fulfillment of three C's: Christianity, Civilisation, and Commerce.

Dr. Livingstone himself helped to pave the way for the colonisation of Africa. It is true that he campaigned against the slave trade that was going on before and when he went there. But his activities were also an invitation to the imperial powers to invade and colonise Africa. They had to do so ostensibly to end the slave trade.

The area that came to be known as the Western Province of Tanganyika was one of the most fertile grounds for the slave trade conducted by Arabs and their African collaborators.

Besides my sister Maria who was born in the same province I was, the rest of my siblings were also born in different parts of Tanganyika. Most of us were born during colonial rule when our father worked as a medical assistant for the colonial government. Three were born after independence: one when the country was still Tanganyika and two after it became Tanzania.

It was my father who filled out my birth certificate. And it was he who always reminded me of my birthday every morning when I was growing up. My mother also reminded me of that, but not as much as my father did, and was not as punctual. As soon as I woke up in the morning on October 4th when I lived at home before going to boarding school in 1963 when I was 13 years old, my father would tell me it was my birthday.

I was named Godfrey by my aunt, Isabella, one of my father's younger sisters, and lived in different parts of Tanganyika in my early years: Western, Coast, and Southern Highlands provinces.

I also lived in what was once the Southern Province

when I was a teenager. That was when I was a student at Songea Secondary School from 1965 to 1968 in Songea, the capital of Ruvuma Region.

Ruvuma Region was once a part of the Southern Province until 1963 when the seven provinces – Western, Central, Coast, Northern, Southern Highlands, Lake, and Southern – were divided into regions.

My father was one of the few Africans in Tanganyika in those days who had secondary school education. It was considered to be high education for Africans. And they played a critical role in the provision of vital services for the country during the early years of independence.

My father's assignment to Kigoma after working in other parts of the country turned out to be one of the most important events in my life because that is where I was born. And it will always remain an important part of my life as my birthplace more than anything else.

Unfortunately, in all the years I lived in Tanganyika, later Tanzania, I never got the chance to visit Kigoma as a youngster or as an adult. And I still have not been able to.

My parents never went back to Kigoma either. And I did not get the chance to go there even when I was a news reporter in Tanzania, a job which could have provided me with an opportunity to do so.

I was never assigned to cover Kigoma. I worked in Dar es Salaam most of the time except once when I was sent to Zanzibar in January 1972 and stayed there for several days during the eighth anniversary of the Zanzibar revolution. I went to Zanzibar with Juma Penza, my fellow news reporter at the *Daily News*. We were assigned to cover the anniversary of the revolution in the former island nation which became an integral part of the United Republic of Tanzania when Tanganyika and Zanzibar united in April 1964 to form one country.

The president of Zanzibar who was also the first vice president of Tanzania, Abeid Karume, was assassinated about three months later, on 7 April, after the eighth anniversary of the revolution.

Years later, Juma Penza served as press secretary to Tanzania's vice president, John Malecela. He later became deputy publicity secretary of the ruling party, CCM (Chama Cha Mapinduzi – Party of the Revolution or Revolutionary party), and served as the party's assistant secretary general.

Much as I liked going to Zanzibar, I also wished I had been sent to Kigoma as one of my assignments when I was a reporter at the *Daily News*.

But I have two very important items which always remind me of Kigoma as my birthplace.

One is my photograph taken when I was one year and three months old. It also has my father's handwriting on it in black ink, still legible almost 70 years later. He wrote in English: "Fifteen months old."

In this photograph, I'm standing looking at the camera, chubby and wide-eyed. My father is holding my right hand in front of the house in which we lived. It was a wooden house with a grass-thatched roof.

When I look at the picture, I can see how much I have changed through the years. I was chubby when I was a baby less than two years old. Yet, when I was growing up, I never gained much weight and was always slim. Many people said I was very thin. I thought my weight was in proportion to my frame. And I have always been that way, slim.

Another item I cherish so much is my birth certificate which my father gave me when I was a teenager and a student at Mpuguso Middle School in Rungwe District in the Southern Highlands Province from 1961 to 1964.

Also on my birth certificate are reminders of two other important events in my life: when I was baptised, by whom, and in what church.

I was baptised by Reverend Frank McGorlick on Christmas day, 25 December 1949, two months and three weeks after I was born. My birth certificate also bears his name in his own handwriting. It was issued by CMS, the Church Missionary Society, which did a lot of missionary work spreading Christianity in Tanganyika and in many other parts of Africa.

Reverend McGorlick came from Victoria, Australia. Decades later, I was able to get in touch with his wife, Barbara, in Australia, who told me they lived in Tanganyika, later Tanzania, until the early 1990s and that her husband died in 1993. I got in touch with her in 2005, as I did with their son Richard who also lived in Victoria, Australia. He grew up in Tanganyika, later Tanzania, as did the other children.

I remember when I was growing up that my parents used to tell me I was baptised as a CMS member. That was also the church my parents attended when they lived in Kigoma even before I was born until they returned to Rungwe District in the Southern Highlands Province years later as members of the Moravian Church which was well-established in the district. They were members of the same church before they left Rungwe District.

The Moravian Church in Rungwe District was first established in the 1890s by the Germans who were also the first colonial rulers of Tanganyika, what was then was known as Deutsch-Ostafrika or German East Africa which, together with what is now Rwanda and Burundi, constituted one colony.

The missionaries played a very important role in the development of the district in terms of education including vocational training. They laid the foundation. And there is a very interesting history about their activities in the district which had a lasting impact.

The Church Missionary Society (CMS) in which I was baptised was British in origin. It was founded in 1799 by a group of activist evangelical Christians.

One of the founders was William Wilberforce, a prominent leader of the movement which was launched to abolish slavery. He was asked to be the first president of this missionary organisation but declined to take the offer and instead became its vice president.

CMS was also supported by another prominent abolitionist, Dr. David Livingstone of the London Missionary Society, who was Scottish himself like Reverend McGorlick who baptised me.

Years later, when I became familiar with some Scottish names, I came to the conclusion that the minister who baptized me, Reverend McGorlick, was probably Scottish. And I was right. Before I found out about him, I didn't know if he spent the rest of his life in Tanganyika, later Tanzania, or "returned to Britain" since I assumed that's where he came from. I was wrong. But there is no question that he left an indelible mark on me as the one who baptised me.

The Church Missionary Society of Australia effectively dates from 1916 when the individual CMS associations in the Australian states were amalgamated into a national organisation. CMS had sent missionaries to many countries by that time, including China, India, Palestine and Iran, but by 1927 they had particular interest in North Australia and Tanganyika.

Although I never got the chance to visit Kigoma and see the place of my birth, my sister Maria ended up living in Kigoma years later with her husband who was sent by his church to work there as a Seventh-Day Adventist pastor while she worked as a nurse. And I have always been interested in learning as much as I can about Kigoma not only because it is my birthplace but also because it is an integral part of my home country Tanzania. But because it is my birthplace, there is no question that I have special interest in – and attachment to – Kigoma in a way I don't other parts of the country.

And the place has an interesting history. For example, not many people in Tanzania know that Kigoma was once a part of the Belgian colony of Ruanda-Urundi. Had it remained under Belgian control, my history would have been different. My father would never have been sent by the British colonial government to work in Kigoma, since it would not have been a part of their territory of Tanganyika. And I would not have been born in Kigoma.

But obviously, that was not my destiny. And Kigoma always brings back memories of my childhood in the fifties because that is where it all began, this short journey of mine into this world where we are mere mortals and which reminds me of one song by Jim Reeves, also sung by others, I used to listen to when I was a teenager in Tanzania in the sixties: "This world is not my home, I'm just passing through, my treasures are laid up, somewhere beyond the blue..."

But short as our presence is, in this world, we have to make the best of it. And in my case, my early life in Tanganyika played a critical role in determining what type of person I came to be years later.

It is this land which I love from the very depth of my being, heart and soul, which shaped my character. And it is this land that I will always love for the rest of my life. It determined my destiny.

It was in Tanganyika where I was born, and it was in Tanganyika where I was brought up. And it reminds me of another song we sang in Kiswahili in school and sometimes during national celebrations: *Tanganyika, Tanganyika, nakupenda kwa moyo wote*. In English it means: "Tanganyika, Tanganyika, I love you with all my heart."

It was also in Tanganyika where I spent one of the most important decades of my life and in the history of the my country and my continent: the fifties.

## Race and racism
## from my perspective as a child

The fifties were my formative years. They were also

20

the years when Tanganyika began its peaceful transition from colonial rule to independence.

I witnessed some of those events during the transitional period especially in the late fifties. But I was still too young to understand exactly what they meant. I looked at things from a child's perspective. Simply having fun – chasing grasshoppers and butterflies – was more important to me than politics. That is what I remember most.

Even if they told me, I don't know if I would have been able to fully understand what was meant by *siasa*, which is a Swahili word meaning "politics."

When I saw white people as child in the mid- and late fifties, I saw them just as people. Yes, they looked different in terms of skin colour; and yes, they lived better than we did. But I still saw them as people, nonetheless; not as our rulers or anything else.

Difference in skin colour meant absolutely nothing to me and other children in terms of an individual's worth as a human being, although even at that young age we noticed that white people had material things we didn't have. But we did not associate that with power, skin colour or racial injustice.

If someone tried to explain to me and other children the connection between skin colour and wealth or social status, we would not have been able to understand. We would have been confused. We just didn't understand why white people had things we didn't have, or why they lived in better houses than we did. Colonialism meant nothing to us at that age when we were under 10 years old.

Yet we were subjected to the same racial injustices our parents and other Africans were because were black even though we didn't understand what "racism" or "racialism" meant.

All we knew was that we lived differently. It was not until years later when I became a teenager that I came to identify that with racial injustice.

And I had no reason to ask why white people were

21

there, in Tanganyika, or where they came from, or why they had a different complexion. After all, there were Arabs and Indians in Tanganyika who also had a light complexion and even some black Africans who had a light brown complexion.

Even my own mother had a light brown complexion; so did my brothers, some of my sisters, cousins, uncles and aunts; not white-looking or light-complexioned like the Indians and the Arabs we saw around when we were growing up but not dark-skinned either.

Still, all that meant nothing to me.

I even remember my mother telling me when I was under ten years old in the late fifties and even in my early teens in the early sixties that when we lived in Mbeya in 1954, a British couple used to give me some cake and sweets and other things now and then whenever we passed by their house. And that only reinforced – even if not consciously – whatever notions I had, as a child, of a colour-blind society; which was, of course, not entirely the case as older people of all races knew very well.

As a colony, Tanganyika – a UN Trust Territory, but a colony, nonetheless, in terms of imperial rule – was a colour-conscious society. Yet to a child, such colour consciousness meant something different, if anything at all, even though it was a fact of life for all of us since our status was defined by racial identity.

Still, in spite of all that, there were people of all races who got along very well. They got along well at work; many white families and their African servants were on very good terms and even their children played together, especially when house maids took their children with them to work or if they lived on the same premises although under separate roofs. A house maid is called *yaya* in Kiswahili.

Sometimes, good relations between Africans and whites went beyond accepted norms. There were those who even ate and drank together, although usually in

private. Whites who did that would normally avoid doing
so in front of other whites. They did not want to be seen
getting too friendly with Africans who were by definition
no more than servants of whites. And they did not want to
be alienated from the white settler community of which
they were an integral part simply because they wanted to
be friends of Africans and people of other races.

Yet, there were those who defied convention. They
were not the majority but they did exist, although no one
cannot be sure how many in terms of numbers or
percentage. For example, I remember my mother telling
me in the late fifties and early sixties that there was a
British couple who wanted to take me with them to Britain
as a child to provide me with education and told my father
that they would bring me back to Tanganyika every year
on holidays. I would have the benefit of excellent
education in the UK beginning at a very early age. She
said my father seriously considered doing that, but she was
strenuously opposed to the idea saying I was too young to
go so far away.

They knew my father very well. They also knew my
mother but they dealt with my father more than they did
with my mother. Language was also a barrier on my
mother's part. She did not know English like my father
did. He spoke English fluently. He even taught me the
language at home when I first started learning it in 1961 at
the age of 11 when I was in Standard Five at Mpuguso
Middle School. And that gave me an advantage over other
pupils.

I don't remember exactly where or when this took place
– I never thought about asking my mother about that. But I
know it was in the early fifties, either in Morogoro in the
Coast Province or in Mbeya in the Southern Highlands
when my parents and the British couple discussed the
possibility of my going to school in Britain at a very early
age under their guardianship.

And there was something about this British couple

which stayed in my mind through the years, especially when I was growing up in Kyimbila in Rungwe District in the Southern Highlands about four miles south of the town of Tukuyu, the district capital.

Their interest in my education showed that there were ordinary whites in Tanganyika, who were not colonial administrators but simply ordinary people who lived and worked there, who were concerned about the wellbeing of Africans yet couldn't do anything to improve the situation because they did not have the power or the means to do so. It was probably only a small minority of them but there were such people.

In fact, some of them never left Africa. They stayed in Tanganyika even after independence because it was their home even if they were not born there, although some of them were.

Some of them moved to other parts of Africa, including South Africa, after Tanganyika became independent; in fact, I even got in touch with some of them in South Africa when I was writing my book about life in Tanganyika in the fifties.

Some of them also moved to what was then Southern Rhodesia and a few to Kenya.

Their heart was, and still is, in Africa.

When I first wrote all this while living in the United States, I got in touch with some ex-Tanganyikan Britons and other whites living in other parts of the world – besides Africa – including Britain, Australia and the United States who still had relatives or friends living in Tanzania involved in various activities including philanthropic work, together with black Africans. They told me their relatives and friends never left Tanganyika after the country won independence.

Even some of those who left Tanganyika after independence *still* maintained strong ties with the country and were involved in various activities helping the people in different parts of what is Tanzania today. As Marion

Gough stated in her email to me from England on 17 January 2006:

"Tanganyika was my home and is still very much in my blood. I try to get back as much as I can and am in the process of fund raising to help the building of an Orphanage.

I have sent two shipments of text books, papers and pens to two different schools, together with several computers (used). I had such a happy, if not, lonely, childhood that I feel I must return the privilege."

And as she stated in another email on 21 January 2006:

"Jambo Godfrey,

I am raising funds for the building of an Orphanage in Mufindi and going to get all the info ready to contact big companies to see if they would be willing to help, after a little research of course. If you know of any that are sympathetic to Africa please give me a nod. The Charity in USA is called Mufindi Orphans.

It is going to be built by the Foxes. Geoff Fox (father) lives in Mufindi and has done so for 40 years. He has four sons and each helps run the company and safari camps in Ruaha, Mikumi and Katavi, also a Highland lodge in Mufindi. They look after several villages by employing a lot of staff and they grow their own food for the camps, use local craftsmen and materials for the camps.

Bruce lives in Gloucester which is 1/2 hour away from me and we keep in close touch. Great family so enthusiastic for Africa. Bruce has stopped a lot of poaching and is also fighting to keep the Ruaha River flowing as a lot of water has been taken off for the rice fields! Therefore a lot of the wetlands has been destroyed which makes the land flood instead of sinking into the water table.

Sorry could go on for ever, will close here before I get carried away.

Hope the pics don't come out too big.

Take care,

Marion"

In 2018, I came across this report about her and her work in Tanzania:

"Marion lived in Tanzania from 1949 until 1963.

In 2006, Marion returned to show family where she grew up and during that trip visited Mufindi where she met Geoff Fox MBE, founder of Foxes Community & Wildlife Conservation Trust.

Geoff highlighted the needs of the area due to an increasing HIV epidemic which was causing numerous orphans and destitution for the population. Marion and family were shown around two projects Geoff had undertaken to help support the local area.

At this point, September 2006, foundations of the first orphan houses were underway and the local Mdabulo Hospital, which was in dire straights and barely functional, was targeted for improvement. It was clear that to make any impact funding and equipment was needed, then, now and in the future.

When Orphans in the Wild was founded in the UK by Geoff Fox's son, Bruce and daughter-in-law Jane, Marion became one of the four trustees.

Since day one of its inception Marion has continued to enthusiastically and tirelessly volunteer to raise money and send hundreds of items, via containers, for the many projects involved in the ongoing holistic support of the Mufindi community, regularly visiting Mufindi herself.

Marion was honoured in the 2014 Diplomatic Service and Overseas List." – ("Patricia Marion Gough MBE: Orphans in the Wild: Mrs (Patricia) Marion GOUGH.

Trustee, Orphans in the Wild. For services to the victims of AIDS, particularly children, in Tanzania).

She was also honoured in Britain with the title, MBE (Member of the Most Excellent Order of the British Empire), for her charitable work in Tanzania, a country she had known since birth and to which she returned on a trip which was none other than "returning home."

When she left Tanganyika for Britain in 1963, she never forgot her childhood home, which is also where she grew up, in the same region I came from, the Southern Highlands Province, in a country that was renamed Tanzania in 1964 after she left.

I, of course, almost left Tanganyika even before independence when I was still a child.

Had I left with the British couple and gone to school in Britain at so early an age when I was under 10 years old, my life would probably have taken a different turn. I don't know where I would have ended up. But it was not meant to be. Instead, I remained and grew up in Tanganyika although I did not stay there. As fate would have it, I ended up in the United States after spending the first 23 years of my life in Tanganyika, later Tanzania. But that is another story.

Yet, when I look back at all those years since my childhood in Kigoma and Ujiji in western Tanganyika, I know – and I am glad – that I was exposed to other people and other cultures when I was growing up and in such a way that I ended up being what I am today as an open-minded person tolerant of other people's views and values as well as beliefs as long as they don't interfere with my wellbeing. As the saying goes, the right to swing your arm ends where my nose begins.

But it was with the innocence of a child that I looked at the world, and it was with that kind of innocence that I left Kigoma with my parents when my father was transferred to Morogoro in the Coast Province in the early fifties.

27

Although I hardly remember Kigoma to enable me to compare life there with life in Morogoro, I know that Morogoro was different. It was in the Coast Province with strong Islamic influence and only about 115 miles from the nation's capital, Dar es Salaam, where almost everything new started before spreading to other parts of the country.

By remarkable contrast, Kigoma was far away in the hinterland. And being a port on Lake Tanganyika, it was linked to what was then the Belgian Congo just across the lake. And it played a major role as a hub of activity in the cross-cultural interaction between Congo and Tanganyika as much as it still does today.

It was also in the town of Kigoma where Che Guevara had a supply base during his mission to Congo in the mid-sixties. That is also where he sought sanctuary after his mission failed before returning to Dar es Salaam to stay at the Cuban embassy for about four months.. He wrote his famous diaries when he was staying at the embassy.

Although it was far away from the coast, Kigoma was linked to Dar es Salaam by a railway which ran across the country from east to west forming the main artery of the railway network in what was then Tanganyika and which is now Tanzania.

Sparsely populated, Tanzania is a large country, bigger than Nigeria in terms of area, and Kigoma is 766 miles from Dar es Salaam.

While my memories of Kigoma are virtually none since I was only a baby under three years old when I was there, my recollections of some of the events in Morogoro are vivid mainly because of the "traumatic" experiences I had as a child in that "coastal" town.

It was also in Morogoro where my brother Lawrence was born on 29 September 1952. He was the third-born. Tragically, he died on 21 August 2005 in the town of Mbeya. I was told he died on a couch in the arms of my youngest sister Nitwele who is also the last-born.

Coincidentally, it was also in Mbeya where my sister Gwangu was born on 29 July 1954 when we lived there after leaving Morogoro. She was the fourth-born. But her life also ended in tragedy. She died in Rungwe District on 11 July 2004.

My mother died at home in our village of Mpumbuli, Kyimbila, Rungwe District, on 18 November 2006 ten days after her 77th birthday. She was born on 8 November 1929.

My sister Rehema who was born in Tukuyu on 27 September 1962 died in Mbeya on 12 June 2007. She was eighth-born.

My father died on 2 July 2015 a few months before reaching his 91st birthday. He was born on 25 October 1924.

All these tragedies were compounded by the fact that they occurred when I was far away in the United States.

And whenever I think about my siblings who passed away, I also remember them in terms of the fifties, except my sister Rehema who was born on 27 September 1962 after our country won independence. She died in Mbeya on 12 June 2007.

We all – besides Rehema among those who died – had our beginning in the early fifties, although I was born two months before the beginning of the decade in which Lawrence and Gwangu were born.

But it was in the early fifties that I really became aware of my existence in this world and when my personality started to be formed.

And it was in Morogoro where my memories of the fifties started to crystallise and reflect some of the most vivid images of my life which I clearly remember even today.

# Chapter Two

# My Early Years:
# Growing up in
# Colonial Tanganyika

LIFE in Tanganyika in the fifties meant different things to different people – African, European, Arab, and Asian (mostly Indian and Pakistani), the four main racial categories in the country. But it had one thing in common. Life was simpler, and the people friendlier. There was less crime in those days, far less than what you see today.

But it was also colonial life, although sometimes barely perceptible. To children like me under 10 years old, it meant very little in terms of racial domination. Life went on as usual as if all the people got along just fine. And they did on many occasions but not all.

Even for those who got along just fine, it was still colonial rule. We all lived in a tiered society, racially stratified, with whites on top, Asians and Arabs in the middle constituting some kind of a buffer zone, and blacks at the bottom.

It was a heap of vast black masses at the bottom. And they are the ones who propped up this lopsided structure with their cheap labour made even more abundant because of their numerical preponderance in a country that was overwhelmingly black.

Yet, in spite of all the interdependence, with Europeans and Asians – and sometimes Arabs – providing goods and services needed by a significant number of Africans especially those living in towns, and the cheap labour and raw materials provided by Africans to sustain the colonial system, there was little interaction among or between the races. The most that you could see was between Africans and Asians. And that was only during business transactions when Africans went to Indian shops in towns to buy the items they needed.

## Race relations

In the case of Tanganyika, the distance between the races, especially between Africans and Europeans, seemed to be even greater than in neighbouring Kenya because of the smaller number of white settlers in the country. The distance was magnified even in terms of perception.

Whites were not only fewer in Tanganyika than in Kenya but were also less visible because of their smaller number, yet no less dominant as colonial rulers. But, the fewer they were, the farther they also were from Africans in terms of interaction, although that was not true in all cases. Still, it was extremely rare for Europeans and Asians to socialise with Africans. The races were in most cases far apart and preferred things to be that way.

However, there was one fundamental difference. The difference in this relationship was between Europeans on the one hand and Africans as well as Asians and Arabs on the other. And it had to do with power.

It was the Europeans who instituted the social hierarchy based on race and who sanctioned the asymmetrical relationship between the races to their advantage as the rulers of Tanganyika in order justify colonial rule. In that sense, the Asians and the Arabs were equally victims of racial domination by whites even if some of them did not think that they were being victimised like blacks.

But although there is no question that Europeans were the rulers of a country that was overwhelmingly black African (there are also white Africans and Africans of Asian and Arab origin as well as others on the African continent), for many blacks, life went on as it did before the coming of the white man.

That was especially the case in the rural areas, including villages near towns, not only those far away from the urban centres, where the most visible alien intrusion in traditional life since the advent of colonial rule was the tax collector and sometimes, although rarely, a black policeman in khaki uniform and black boots coming on foot to make an arrest.

However, there was fundamental change in institutions of authority in the sense that an alien power had been imposed on us. All of us including traditional rulers became colonial subjects. African chiefs and other traditional rulers lost their power. They no longer had the same power they had before as the ultimate authority in their traditional societies.

Therefore the biggest change which took place when colonial rule was introduced was political. Africans lost power and independence. Attitudes towards life in general, and even towards traditional authority, also changed, although gradually, because of the dominant role European rulers played in the political arena. So it was a dramatic change when power shifted from Africans to Europeans.

Less perceptible were the changes which took place in other areas of life. One was the cultural arena.

Most of the people in the rural areas did not see themselves as victims of cultural imperialism in the same way the few educated Africans did. Their traditional way of life and values remained virtually intact unlike that of their brethren who lived in towns or those who acquired some education especially at the secondary school level and beyond.

The more education one had, the more one became aware of the racial disparities and imposition of alien values – by Europeans – on Africans.

But in many cases it was also far less of an imposition than a willingness by many Africans who had some education to accept European ways of life as some kind of achievement in life. In fact, a significant number of them saw it as a badge of honour to be Europeanised, live and act like Europeans.

It showed that they were now "civilized," or more "civilized" than their brethren – those who continued to live the traditional way of life in the villages and even in towns and also those who had less education.

Yet nationalist sentiments were strong especially among some politically conscious members of the African elite, although even they were not dismissive of all aspects of alien cultures including British in spite of their uncompromising stand in defence of the African traditional way of life. As Julius Nyerere said:

"A country which lacks its own culture is no more than a collection of people without the spirit which makes them a nation. Of all the crimes of colonialism there is none worse than the attempt to make us believe we had no indigenous culture of our own; or that what we did have was worthless...

A nation which refuses to learn from foreign cultures is nothing but a nation of idiots and lunatics... But to learn from other cultures does not mean we should abandon our own."

Nyerere was quoted by Dr. Graham L. Mytton, former head of the BBC's International Broadcasting Audience Research (IBAR), in his book *Mass Communications in Africa*, and by Don Moore in his article, "Reaching the Villages: Radio in Tanzania," published in *The Journal of the North American Shortwave Association.*

One British official in Tanganyika even admitted in 1955:

"We ignore their tribal dances and try to give them cricket. It's awful."

He was quoted by American journalist John Gunther in his book *Inside Africa.*

Gunther visited Tanganyika in 1954. Among the places he visited was the newly established radio station in Dar es Salaam.

The station was founded in 1951 in response to a proposal by a BBC official who felt that there was a need for such a station which should produce programmes for a native audience in Kiswahili. It was named the Dar es Salaam Broadcasting Station (DBS) and was later renamed the Tanganyika Broadcasting Service (TBS) and then the Tanganyika Broadcasting Corporation (TBC). As Sala Elise Patterson stated in a dissertation for a master's degree submitted to the School for Oriental and African Studies (SOAS) at the University of London entitled, "State Control, Broadcasting and National Development," focusing on Tanzania as a case study :

"Radio broadcasting began in Tanganyika in July 1951 in an unused attic of a house in Dar es Salaam. Aimed at city residents, the unit was called the Dar es Salaam Broadcasting Station (DBS).

One year later the colonial government invested 10,000 GBP to upgrade the radio service realizing the importance of broadcasting in the territory to further the colonial process. Another 55,000 GBP was invested from the colonial fund in 1954.

Then on May 8, 1956, the colonial authorities inaugurated the new and improved Tanganyika Broadcasting Service (TBS) with a 20-kilowatt transmitter that increased broadcasting capability to reach as far as Johannesburg.

In July of the same year, the government consolidated their national broadcasting and established the Tanganyika Broadcasting Corporation (TBC) officially as an independent broadcasting body that took over the functions of the TBS.

The colonial government closely monitored programming and the Governor had absolute power to prohibit the broadcast of any programme deemed inappropriate."

When Gunther visited the station in 1954, he was highly impressed by the staff's performance. It was a professional operation totally staffed by native Africans, in spite of the fact that the station had started, as Gunther wrote, "with little more equipment than a microphone and a blanket hung over a wall."

It became so successful that it served as a model for broadcasting services in many other British colonies in Africa and elsewhere.

I remember listening to TBC when I was growing up in Rungwe District in the Southern Highlands in the 1950s and early sixties. And I still remember the names of some of the radio announcers, mainly David Wakati and Eli Mboto. Although the reception was poor most of the time, we still were able to listen to the news and to a variety of music, mostly Swahili and Congolese, broadcast from Dar es Salaam more than 500 miles away.

Located in the Great Rift Valley in southwestern Tanzania and ringed by blue mountains, Rungwe District is strategically located to get radio broadcasts from neighbouring Malawi (Malawi Broadcasting Corporation, Blantyre) and even from South Africa. I remember the broadcasts: "This is Radio South Africa (RSA), Johannesburg." We also heard broadcasts in Swahili from Elisabethville, Katanga Province, Congo Leopoldville.

Elisabethville, renamed Lubumbashi, is about 640 miles west of Rungwe District.

I also remember the South African apartheid regime used to jam our radio broadcasts after our country became independent. It was very difficult in Rungwe District to hear news broadcasts from TBC, Dar es Salaam. As soon as the news broadcasts were over, the transmission became clear. But we had no problems listening to broadcasts from Nyasaland and Northern Rhodesia, just across the border, and even from faraway Elisabethville, Katanga.

At first, there was not much interest in establishing a radio station in Tanganyika because of the relatively small European population in the country, unlike neighbouring Kenya where there was a significant number of white settlers.

The British government did not encourage its citizens to emigrate and settle in Tanganyika mainly because the territory was not a typical British colony like Kenya but a UN trusteeship territory under British tutelage only for a limited, though not specified, period of time after which the country would become independent.

There were, however, some parts of Tanganyika which attracted a significant number of white settlers. For example, even before the British took over Tanganyika from the Germans after World War I, Lushoto in the Usambara mountains in the northeastern part of the country was a kind of "winter capital" for the Germans.

But, in spite of the relatively small number of whites in Tanganyika, there was an obvious need for a radio station for the indigenous population, although the broadcasts had a short radius – very limited range – and were initially confined to Dar es Salaam, the capital, which itself had Africans in the majority.

Even in the capital Dar es Salaam, European influence on the lives of most Africans was limited when compared to what happened in Nairobi, Kenya's capital, and elsewhere in Kenya especially in the "White Highlands" in the Central Province which had the largest number of white settlers in the country.

There were also Boers from South Africa who settled in Kenya. They founded one of Kenya's most well-known towns, Eldoret, in the former Rift Valley Province in the western part of the country.

In the case of Tanganyika, British cultural influence was very limited in terms of everyday life and only had a significant impact on the elite.

The most visible change in the African way of life was in the towns which were the administrative centres for the colonial rulers. That is where the District Commissioner, whom we simply called DC, and his white staff, worked and lived if the town was the district headquarters. If the town was the capital of a province, you had the provincial commissioner, known as PC, as the head.

That is where you would see the colonial rulers and other whites, working and living there, although in some parts of the rural areas, there were also whites who owned farms and hired black labourers to work on coffee and tea plantations and other large farms.

In Tanganyika, white settlers could be found in places such as Lushoto in the Usambara mountains in the northeastern part of the country where they owned coffee farms and also a school exclusively for white children known as Lushoto Prep School; in Arusha in northerneastern Tanganyika where they also had large farms and a school for white children called Arusha School; in Moshi near the slopes of Mount Kilimanjaro of majestic splendour where they also had a primary school exclusively for white children; and in the Southern Highlands Province where they also built the most prestigious school for white students in the whole country called St. Michael's and St. George's School in Iringa District near the town of Iringa, and another one in the town of Mbeya known as Mbeya School in the same province.

Mbeya School, which is in my home region, was established in 1942 in buildings which were once a German School. It was closed in 1963 as an exclusively European school and became a secondary school for students of all races after Tanganyika won independence. But it also became almost exclusively black after students of other races sought education elsewhere.

Besides the German School which became Mbeya School, another European school which was founded in Tanganyika to educate pupils of the same national origin was the Greek School in Moshi where there was a number of Greek farmers and other Greeks engaged in different pursuits.

The school also served Greek children from Arusha which also had a significant number of Greek settlers. As Gregory Emmanuel whose family settled in Tanganyika stated in his article "Grandfather Gregory Emmanuel 'Nisiotis' (1875 – 1977)":

"A large number of Greeks, many from Tenedos, came to Tanganyika, where Greeks became the second largest expatriate European community (Germans being the largest group).

In both Moshi and Arusha there were thriving Greek communities and the need arose for a Greek school.

As the house at Lambo was vacant, Grandfather leased it to the Greek community and it became the first Greek school in East Africa. It was a boarding school and was the first school attended by my father, Costas. (He told me that a student who sleepwalked was taken during the night by a leopard.)."

Coincidentally, another school, Kongwa School, which was open to white children of all nationalities started as a primary school on 4 October 1948, exactly one year before I was born on 4 October 1949.

It evolved from the abortive groundnut scheme funded

by the British Overseas Food Corporation at Kongwa.

After the groundnut scheme failed and was abandoned in 1954, its buildings were converted into a secondary school, upgraded from a primary school. Then in 1958, the students at Kongwa School were transferred to a new school in Iringa, St. Michael's and St. George's.

All the European schools in Tanganyika were co-educational, attended by white children and students of all ages depending on the kind of school they went to. For example, St. Michael's and St. George's was a secondary school. And it was highly competitive with a reputation for academic excellence.

Many of its former students became very successful in life in different parts of the world, including Tanganyika itself, which became Tanzania, and have been holding reunions now and then to renew ties and reminisce on life in Tanganyika in those days.

In many ways, they were good old days. Life was also much safer and simpler, and the people a lot friendlier than they are nowadays when everybody is busy fending for himself/herself, with a large number of individuals preying on others in different ways besides robbery.

Although I did not attend St. Michael's and St. George's School after independence, there are many things which the former students and I agree on in terms of how life was in school and in Tanganyika in general in those days.

And we have another thing in common. They went to school in the same province where I come from: the Southern Highlands.

Even after independence, St. Michael's and St. George's stood out among all the schools in Tanzania. It had students up to Form VI (Standard 14) and was renamed Mkwawa High School and admitted students of all races, which was not the case before Tanganyika became independent in 1961.

It was in the area of education where the colonial

authorities instituted some of the most rigid structures of racial separation in the country.

They sanctioned inequality in the allocation of funds and provision of facilities including teachers which ensured that the children of the white settlers would get the best education and enjoy a privileged life style at the expense of Africans and, to a smaller degree, Asians whose status was no better than that of the Africans as colonial subjects; although they were treated better than Africans in many cases.

Arabs had their own Koranic schools and were not really an integral part of the mainstream in terms of formal education in the Western intellectual tradition.

But the bottom line was that even if Asians – as well as Arabs – were treated better than Africans, they were still colonial subjects, therefore not equal to whites. And provision of separate educational facilities and funds affected their lives as well, although even in this case they were favoured by the colonial government when compared with Africans. As David Nettelbeck states in "Educational Separatism and the 1950s" in his book, *A History of Arusha School*:

"Because of the Government's lack of resources and unwillingness to take a strong initiative in educational provision, and in pursuance of the G.I.A. policy, there grew up three racially distinct systems of African, Asian and European education with each of the three subdivided into state controlled, state aided, and wholly private schools.

In the African sector for example in 1937, there were 9,500 pupils in Government schools, 19,500 in aided schools and 100,000 in private schools. These latter were often sub-standard bush schools, and catechetical centres or Koranic schools along the coast. It was not until 1955 that the Government required these kinds of schools to be registered.

41

In the same year, there were 985 places in Government schools for Indian children and another 3,318 in grant aided schools. The Indian community were quick to take advantage of the G.I.A. system and fulfil the requirements thus only 320 of their children were that year in private schools.

For the European community in the 1930s, the Government made direct provision in three ways. Arusha School, primarily for boarders, opened in 1934; a correspondence course was based in Dar es Salaam; and there was also a junior primary school in Dar es Salaam. The enrolment figures in 1937 show 59 children in the latter two, and 60 pupils at Arusha School.

There were in addition 704 grant-aided places for European children, a significant proportion of these being in national community schools for the Dutch, German and Greek children. Another 15 places were in a private school. The above figures are taken from the enrolment statistics 1931 – 1948 in Appendix G.

There is another way of looking at these statistics and that is to see the percentage of children being educated from each community. Listowell states that in 1933, 51% of the European children, 49% of the Asian and 2% of the African were at school.

By 1945 7.5%, of the African children attended school though few got beyond the fourth primary grade and none could attempt the entrance exam for tertiary study at Makerere in Uganda. By 1959, 40% of African children attended at least the first four years of primary education, and in 1961, 55% of the age group entered the first primary grade.

The present Government of Nyerere aims at universal primary education by 1980. (The comparative cost per head of population has been referred to above and is detailed in Appendix J.)

In 1930 an Education Tax was introduced with the primary object of affording security to the Government for the repayment of loans made to non-African communities. In 1932 the Indian and European communities were taxed for their education on a poll Tax basis and, in addition, fees were charged at their schools. Nevertheless the Government was making a far more generous per capita provision for European and Indian children than it was for African children.

The table in Appendix J shows the total expenditure for each community and the per capita cost from 1931 - 1937. Also the table in Appendix K shows that in 1955/56, 33.7% of the money spent by the Government on European education was collected in fees, 15.4% came from the European Education Tax and 49.1% from Central Revenue. In 1959 the central revenue provided for European Education an amount equivalent to 1% of the total territorial expenditure.

In 1956, £3,618,555 held by the Custodian of Enemy Property from funds collected from confiscated properties during the Second World War was distributed equally between the Tanganyika Higher Education Trust Fund for establishing tertiary education facilities, St Michael's and St George's School, a lavish secondary school for European children at Iringa, Indian education, and African education.

This 4 way split seem superficially fair but as President Nyerere has pointed out, the allocation on a per capita basis was equivalent to shs- 720/- to each European, shs. 200/- to each Asian and shs. 2/- to each African.

In 1948 and 1949, the three existing education systems described above were formalized by two ordinances, the Non-Native Education Ordinance and the Non-Native Education Tax Ordinance. This legislation brought into being an Indian Education Authority and a European Education Authority, each composed of representatives of the communities they were to serve.

They were responsible for the development and general over-sight of the systems, and for managing the education funds according to the budget approved by the Legislative Council.

There was also an Advisory Committee for Other (non-native) Education, which included Goan, Mauritian, Seychellois, Anglo-Indian, and Ceylonese children.

What began in 1948 as a very minor offshoot of basic Government responsibility for the development of the country with only 8,000 Asian and 300 European children, had become by 1961 a major concern catering for 28,000 Asian and 2,500 European children."

The three educational systems established along racial lines for Europeans, Indians and Africans – in descending order in terms of quality – were formalised in the 1940s and 1950s. And they mirrored the racial hierarchy in colonial Tanganyika instituted by the British colonial rulers. They were abolished in January 1962, soon after the country won independence on 9 December 1961, and all schools in Tanganyika were opened to students of all races.

Although the British constituted the largest group of whites during colonial rule, the white settler community in Tanganyika was a constellation of nationalities. It included many other whites such as Greeks, Germans, Italians, Afrikaners, Jews, Poles, Swedes, Danes, Russians, and Lithuanians. And that is not an exhaustive list. The white settler community was in some ways a microcosm of Europe.

There were even a few Americans in Tanganyika; for example, the first owner of the New Arusha Hotel, Kenyon Painter, a millionaire banker from Ohio. He went to Tanganyika for the first time in 1907 and started building the New Arusha Hotel in 1927. It was completed in the same year.

The hotel was formally opened in January 1928 and the opening ball – in December 1927 – was attended by the Prince of Wales, Edward VIII.

Painter continued to live in the United States but he made several hunting trips to Tanganyika, especially Arusha. He died in 1940.

Before he arrived, there was only one tiny hotel in Arusha owned by a Jewish couple, Jane and Goodall Bloom, and they named the hotel, Bloom's. It was the first Arusha Hotel. That's why when Kenyon Painter built his hotel, he called it the New Arusha Hotel.

Kenyon Painter bought 11,000 acres of land near the town of Arusha and played a major role in establishing coffee farms in the region. He also built the first post office in Arusha, a church, a hospital, and a coffee research centre at Tengeru, 16 miles from Arusha.

The New Arusha Hotel became a historic landmark and a centre of social activity for many people including Hollywood stars such as John Wayne whose famous movie, *Hatari*, which means "danger" in Kiswahili, was filmed in Arusha and released in in 1962; it was shot earlier. There was also a sign in front of the New Arusha Hotel with this message:

**THIS SPOT IS EXACTLY HALF WAY BETWEEN THE CAPE AND CAIRO AND THE EXACT CENTRE OF KENYA, UGANDA, AND TANGANYIKA.**

Arusha also was, and still is, one of the famous towns on what is known as The Great North Road from C to C, that is, from Cape (Cape Town) to Cairo. And as someone described the two main hotels in the town of Arusha and the town itself in 1957:

"Also in the main street were Arusha's two famous hotels.

The New Arusha displayed a board announcing that it was exactly midway between Cape Town and Cairo, and the Safari Hotel boasted an unusual copper topped bar to which a baby elephant had been led in for a drink in a

45

recent Hollywood film Hatari (Danger).

Mount Meru overlooked the pretty garden town beyond the golf course and the main road to Nairobi to the north.

The streets in the residential areas were lined with purple jacarandas and the well kept gardens displayed a profusion of tropical zinnias, petunias and marigolds mixed with the roses, hollyhocks, ferns and carnations of England.

At 5000 feet above sea level, the climate was perfect after the sultry heat of the coast and the early mornings were a delight with dew-dappled lawns, mists and a nip in the air, mingled with the fragrant scent of cedar hedges."

It was the kind of climate which attracted many whites to the region.

Today Arusha is the headquarters of the East African Community (EAC) comprising Kenya, Uganda, Tanzania, Rwanda, Burundi, and South Sudan, and is virtually the capital of East Africa and of the proposed East African federation which was supposed to be formed by 2013 but was not.

It has been an elusive goal since the sixties. In June 1963, the leaders of the three East African countries of Kenya, Uganda and Tanganyika – Jomo Kenyatta, Milton Obote and Julius Nyerere – met in Nairobi, Kenya, and issued a statement stating that they would form a federation before the end of the year. They never did.

Years later, Nyerere gave one of the reasons why they failed to form a federation. As he stated in interview with Ikaweba Bunting of the *New Internationalist* in January-February 1999 a few months before he died:

"I respected Jomo immensely. It has probably never happened in history. Two heads of state, Milton Obote and I, went to Jomo and said to him: 'Let's unite our countries and you be our head of state.' He said no. I think he said

46

no because it would have put him out of his element as a Kikuyu Elder." – (Julius K. Nyerere, interviewed by Ikaweba Bunting, "The Heart of Africa: Interview with Julius Nyerere on Anti-Colonialism," *New Internationalist*, Issue 309, January-February 1999).

Had the British formed a federation of Kenya, Uganda and Tanganyika when they ruled those countries, it is possible the federation could have survived if the nationalist leaders in those countries agreed to have their countries win independence on the same day as a single political entity under one government. In fact, Nyerere offered to delay Tanganyika's independence if the leaders of Kenya and Uganda would agree to have their countries emerge from colonial rule on the same with Tanganyika and form a federation; they did not.

The three countries came close to being one political entity only when they were under the same colonial power, Britain, and were members of the East African Common Services Organisation formed by the British who presided over the organisation. Its capital was Nairobi.

After independence, the three countries chose Arusha in Tanganyika to be the headquarters of the East African Community (EAC) which succeeded the East African Common Services Organisation.

Other whites who lived in Arusha during the British colonial era included Germans, Greeks, South Africans, Italians, and the British themselves. They had farms around Arusha. Some of them had small businesses in town.

Some of the crops grown in this fertile region included cereals, cherries, apples, citrus, coffee, cocoa, vanilla, and rubber. They were grown mostly by the Germans but other Europeans participated as well.

At the beginning of World War II, there were about 3,000 Germans and Italians living in Tanganyika. That was out of a total population of about 8,000 whites in the country. During the war itself, there were about 3,000 Italians including those who were held as prisoners of war in camps in Tanganyika; 9,000 Poles, 500 Greeks, and 180 Cypriot Jews, among many others.

According to the British Foreign and Commonwealth Office, the total number of Italians who were interned in Tanganyika, mainly in Arusha and Tabora, and in Uganda and Southern Rhodesia during World War II was almost 15,000. The number given in May 1945 was 14,900.

Many whites came to live in Tanganyika after the Second World War. Also after Germany was defeated in World War I, she lost her colony of Deutsch-Ostafrika – German East Africa – which became Tanganyika, taken over by the British, and Ruanda-Urundi, by the Belgians. After the British took over the colony, they also used it for detaining prisoners of war (POWs) who included Germans and their allies.

Many of them ended up staying in Tanganyika. The Italians, for example, did not have any historical connection to Tanganyika like the Germans did, but they still settled in the country in significant numbers. Most of them had been preceded earlier by a group of Italian missionaries as far back as the 1920s.

The Italians who were interned in Tanganyika during World War II were sent back to Italy after the war but many of them returned because they liked living there. They also felt that Tanganyika had better prospects for them than Italy did.

Many of them were craftsmen and worked in technical fields and in construction and knew that their skills were in great in demand in an underdeveloped colonial territory like Tanganyika. In fact, some of them had done the same kind of work when they in internment camps in Tanganyika.

The situation got even much better for them and other prisoners of war or detainees in Tanganyika after 1947 when the property which had been confiscated from

48

foreigners including some Italians by the "Custodian of the Enemy Properties," in essence the British colonial government itself, was returned to them.

Therefore the 1950s was a period when Tanganyika witnessed the arrival of a significant number of Italians who came to settle in the country in addition to those who were already there.

Some of them were employed on farms, for example on sisal plantations in Morogoro in the Coast Province, on tobacco farms in Iringa in the Southern Highlands, and in the cultivation of coffee and pyrethrum in Arusha and Moshi in the Nothern Province.

Other Italians went to work in the mines, mostly gold. They went to Geita in the Lake Province where they worked for the Gold Mining Company; in Musoma where they were employed by Tangold Company; and in the diamond mines of Mwadui in Shinyanga where they worked for the Williamson Diamonds Ltd. of Mwadui. There were, of course, people of other nationalities working in these mines, including the British and Afrikaners.

It was also during the same period that another development took place which improved prospects for a number of Italians seeking employment in Tanganyika in the 1950s.

Two projects were launched under the direction of the M. Gonella Company based in Nairobi. These were the construction of some oil depots at Kurasini in Dar es Salaam and of the first sewerage system also in Dar es Salaam, the country's capital in the Coast Province.

An average of about 200 Italians came to Tanganyika every year in the fifties to live or seek employment. The number may have been small but when looked at in the larger context of all the immigrants who came to Tanganyika in those years, the figure was not really that small and Italy was one of the main countries of origin of the immigrants who settled in Tanganyika in the 1950s.

49

In 1952, a census was done and showed that there were 17,885 Europeans living in Tanganyika. A total of 12,395, or 69.3 percent of the white population in the country, were British. Greeks were the second-largest group, 1,292; followed by the Italians, 1,071; the Dutch, 515; the Germans, 499; the Swiss, 496; and the Americans, 331.

Other sources arrive at pretty much the same figure showing that the population of white settlers in Tanganyika in the fifties was much closer to 20,000. That was about a third of those in Kenya.

Some cited a higher figure. For example, *Time* magazine, in one of its 1965 editions stated:

"Tanzania, which as Tanganyika once had 22,700 whites, now has 17,000."

But all these settlers had one thing in common. They were white and therefore members of the white settler community. Although they settled in significant numbers in only a few parts of Tanganyika, the areas where they settled were mostly in the fertile and cooler regions at high altitudes with temperatures most whites were comfortable with. There were, however, also significant numbers of whites in Dar es Salaam in the Coast Province because it was the capital and commercial centre of colonial Tanganyika.

Other whites were spread throughout the country living in different places such as Lindi, Nachingwea, Masasi and Mtwara in the Southern Province and other parts of the region; Kilosa in the Coast Province; Dodoma in the Central Province; Tabora in the Western Province; Mwanza and Bukoba in the Lake Province and other parts of Tanganyika.

Yet, even in areas with significant numbers of whites such as the Southern Highlands which were "extensively" occupied by the British, there was little interaction with Africans besides servants, farm labourers and house boys and maids, whose relationship with whites was defined by their subordinate status. There was also some interaction of the master-servant type in towns as well where whites lived and worked.

And the relationship couldn't be anything but that in a colony and racially stratified society dominated by Europeans even if most Africans in Tanganyika rarely saw a white person in their lives or at least during the period of colonial rule. Most of them lived in villages and spent their entire lives without going into towns where whites were.

Even when they went into towns to buy and sell things, they did not always see white people, although many of them did on a number of occasions now and then in their lives.

I remember when I was growing up in Rungwe District in Mpumbuli village, Kyimbila, about four miles south of the town of Tukuyu which was the district headquarters, I rarely saw whites whenever I went into town. That was in the late fifties when I was under 10 years old and quite often ventured into town, walking or sometimes catching the bus.

The only time we saw quite a few whites was when they played golf and tennis in the town of Tukuyu. I remember when we passed by as children, they now and then gave us tennis balls which we used to play with as soccer, popularly known as football. And it was the right size of "football", or "soccer ball," for us as little boys between 6 and 9 years old.

To us the whites, who were mostly British, were friendly and we saw them simply as white people who were in town playing golf and tennis. Politics was the last thing on our minds – it did not even enter our minds as children. We did not have the slightest idea of what was going on. We didn't even know why they came to Tanganyika all the way from Europe.

Even our knowledge of geography was very limited at

that age. To us, our home district was the entire world. We couldn't envision anything beyond the misty blue mountains which surround Rungwe District in the Great Rift Valley. Next to that, as our world, after we grew a little older and learned more about geography, was our province, the Southern Highlands, and then Tanganyika, our country.

We hardly knew about the rest of East Africa when we were six and seven years old and did not even know much about the neighbouring countries of Nyasaland and Northern Rhodesia which border our region.

We did not learn that in Standard One and Standard Two in primary school until later when we were in Standard Three and Standard Four, which in my case in 1958 and 1959. And why whites were in Tanganyika, and when they came to Tanganyika and to Africa in general, was in the realm of history and politics far beyond our knowledge at that age.

The whites who came to Tukuyu to play golf came from Mbeya, then 45 miles away before the road was improved. Some even came from Northern Rhodesia, which is Zambia today. And there were, of course, those who lived in Tukuyu, although not many. From what I remember, it was only a few of them who lived in the town of Tukuyu.

The town was first built by the Germans, the first colonial rulers, and was named Neu Langenburg. They are the ones who first made it the headquarters of Rungwe District. The town was destroyed twice by earthquakes, first in 1910, and again in 1919, but was rebuilt by the British after they took control of Tanganyika following the end of World War I. And it is still the headquarters of Rungwe District.

Among the whites whom I remember when I was growing up in Rungwe District in the late fifties were the District Commissioner (DC), the most powerful man in the town of Tukuyu and in the whole district of no fewer than

300,000 people during that period; the manager of Shell BP petrol station who was British like the DC, also in the town of Tukuyu where my father once worked under him as an assistant manager in the late fifties and about whom I have more to say later; and the manager of Kyimbila Tea Estate and his wife, both British, about a mile-and-a-half from our house whom I also address later.

The tea estate manager and his wife lived on the premises at Kyimbila next to Kyimbila Moravian Church of which my family and I were members and whose pastor, Asegelile Mwankemwa, was my mother's uncle, younger brother of her mother Tungapesyaga, hence my maternal grand uncle. He was the first African pastor of the church built by German missionaries in 1912.

He was also the one who helped to take care of my mother and her brothers and sisters after their parents died. My maternal grandmother died in 1943 when my mother was almost 14 years old. She died and was buried on her brother's family compound. She went to live with him after her husband Mwambapa died in 1929.

That was also the year in which my mother was born. She was born in her uncle's household, Asegelile Mwankemwa's, in the village of Katusyo about six miles southeast of the town of Tukuyu.

She was brought up on the same family compound with her first cousins, the chlldren of Asegelile Mwankemwa. She later went to live with one of her elder brothers, Johan Chonde Mwambapa, a primary school teacher, who was 13 years older than she was. He took care of her.

She lived with him until she got married. She said she could have been married sooner, before 1948, probably in 1946 or 1947, but her brother Chonde, as he was popularly known, refused to allow her to do so. He said she was too young to get married.

With regard to the whites I mentioned, I don't remember the names of any of them except one, although when we were in primary school – I went to Kyimbila Primary School from 1956 to 1959 about two miles south of Tukuyu and two miles north of our home – we knew the name of the District Commissioner (DC) of Rungwe District.

But I do remember the name of one Provincial Commissioner (PC), Mr. J.T.A. Pearce. He was PC in the late 1950s and lived in Mbeya which was then the capital of the Southern Highlands Province. The former capital was Iringa but it was moved to Mbeya, although I don't remember exactly when; it was sometime in the late fifties, I believe.

The most visible symbol of colonial authority I remember when I was eight and nine years old in the late fifties was a wooden sign on the outskirts of the town of Tukuyu with the words, "Native Authority," written on it. I remember it very well, many decades later, and even exactly where it was. It was a white sign with black capital letters.

It was on the right-hand side of the road at the foot of a small hill on the outskirts of Tukuyu on my way into town, and on the left on my way home; on the same road that went all the way to Kyela, a town near the border with Nyasaland. It was very close to a junction where there was an Anglican Church. The other road led to a place called Makandana which was only about a mile southwest of Tukuyu and where the new Tukuyu Hospital was built.

I did not know what kind of sign it was – for direction, warning, whatever – and it meant absolutely nothing to me. I had not even started learning English during that time until later when I went to Mpuguso Middle School. It was a boarding school. I first went there in 1961, the same year I started learning English. I was 11 years and three months old when I started learning the language in January.

I was a day student – going to school from my home and then back every day – from 1961 to 1962 before I was enrolled as a boarding student (boarder) in January 1963.

It was an all-boys school with a reputation for rigorous intellectual discipline and was one of the best middle schools in the Southern Highlands Province and in the whole country. It was also one of the oldest.

Among its alumni was David Mwakyusa who was once a professor of medicine at Muhimbili College of Medicine, a constituent college of the University of Dar es Salaam, and who later served as President Nyerere's personal physician. He also served as minister of health and social welfare under President Jakaya Kikwete, Tanzania's fourth president since independence.

Other alumni through the years included doctors, lawyers and academics; and a brigadier-general in the Tanzania People's Defence Forces (TPDF), my first cousin, Owen Rhodfrey Mwambapa, son of my maternal uncle Johan Chonde Mwambapa.

He later became head of the Tanzania Military Academy, an officers' training school in Monduli, Arusha Region, northern Tanzania, whose students came from many parts of Africa. He went to Sandhurst, a royal military academy in the United Kingdom, when he joined the Tanzania People's Defence Forces (TPDF) in the sixties and graduated as a lieutenant.

Another cousin of mine, Oscar Mwamwaja, who became one of Tanzania's first airline pilots, was also a product of Mpuguso Middle School.

It was not until a few years later after I was at Mpuguso Middle School that I understood what that (Native Authority) sign meant when I learned some English, and even much later before I understood its political significance as a demarcation line between the coloniser and colonised.

It symbolised colonial power enforced by indirect rule, a system of administration first introduced by Lord Lugard in Northern Nigeria under which the colonial government ruled vast expanses of territory through native rulers including chiefs in my home district of Rungwe.

The town of Tukuyu was under direct rule by the British district commissioner (DC), and the rest of the district under indirect rule through native authority; hence the sign, "Native Authority," showing where direct rule ended and indirect rule began.

Africans and Indian shopkeepers who lived in the town of Tukuyu were under direct rule of the white colonial administrators who also lived there.

But if the colonial authorities felt that direct intervention was warranted, they did not hesitate to exercise their power in the rural areas and other parts of the district.

I remember one tragic incident in the late fifties when two Nyakyusa chiefs and their people in Kyela were involved in a bloody conflict, the exact nature of which I never understood; some said the conflict had to do with disputes over land, which seemed to be a plausible explanation, given the scarcity of land in Rungwe District of which Kyela was then an integral part. Today Kyela is a separate district and has been one for years.

When the conflict erupted, an urgent message was sent to Mbeya, the provincial capital, and within the same day, the colonial authorities dispatched a contingent of Field Force Units (FFU) to stop the fighting. The FFUs, which still exist in Tanzania today, specialise in riot control and in stopping other violent conflicts and have a reputation for being tough and ruthless, using guns when necessary.

It was one of those instances during my life time when the British invoked – and I witnessed – *Pax Britannica* in the quest for peace under the Union Jack in their colony of Tanganyika. The FFU riot policemen were black but their officers white.

There were other whites I remember in Rungwe District including missionaries; for example, Catholic priests at Kisa Catholic Mission about five miles southwest from our home. They used to walk most of the

56

time all the way from Kisa to Tukuyu and back. I remember they wore black robes.

There was also another white man whom I remember very well. He used to drive down the road near our house on his way to Ilima coal mine and back to Tukuyu and Mbeya. They said he was the owner of the coal mine which was about 15 miles from my home in Mpumbuli village, Kyimbila. The Nyakyusa called him Tojilwe, obviously a corruption of his name, whatever it was; today, it sounds like Trujillo or Torrijos to me.

There is no "r" in the Nyakyusa language; it is replaced by "l," "v" is replaced by "f," "z" by "s," and "w" by "b" or "bw" depending on the word and on the context in which it is used.

The "owner" – or "manager" – of the Ilima cola mine could have been Spanish, I don't know; if his name was indeed Trujillo or Torrijos, what my fellow Nyakyusas called Tojilwe.

The mine was almost mid-way between Tukuyu and Kyela, a town near the Tanzanian-Malawian border. And the road goes all the way to Malawi which was Nyasaland in those days.

Although Tojiliwe was in charge of the Ilima coal mine, and the people who did all the hard work were Africans, to him they were just that, coal miners.

His relationship with the coal miners was basically no different from the relationship other whites had with Africans in general. Few whites interacted with Africans on personal basis. Africans were no more than colonial subjects under the imperial flag fluttering under the tropical sun.

The interaction was minimal for racial and cultural reasons, as well as for reasons of personal taste probably on both sides.

Africans who may have wanted to associate with whites – usually for social status more than anything else as members of "civilized" society which by colonial

57

definition meant white – were inhibited in their desire by their well-founded fear and suspicion that they would not be accepted, let alone treated as equals, by a people who were their masters. As members of the ruling race, many whites considered Africans to be their subjects, hence superior to them in social status. And there were whites – including the functionally illiterate – who did not want to mingle with blacks because they did not consider them to be their equal in any conceivable way including mental capacity regardless of how much education they had.

Africans dealt mostly with Indians who owned shops where African customers bought a variety of items such as clothes, soap, cooking oil, salt and sugar. And they communicated very well. I remember many Indians in Tukuyu who spoke our tribal language Kinyakyusa. They communicated with their customers without problems. Some of them knew the language very well.

Although many Africans probably did not notice or feel the colonial presence, and white domination did not have a direct impact on their lives, there were those who were acutely aware of the disparities in life among the races purely along racial lines. They knew the disparities or inequities were not merely accidental but a product of deliberate decisions by the colonial rulers who instituted a system of racial hierarchy to maintain colonial rule and dominate Africans.

What set them apart from the other Africans besides their political consciousness was education. They were mostly educated, with secondary school education or higher and sometimes even less, and they worked directly under the supervision of whites especially in towns. And they are the ones who led the struggle for independence, not only in Tanganyika but in other African countries as well.

There was another politically conscious group of Africans who constituted a critical mass during the struggle for independence. These were the workers in towns. They formed trade unions demanding better wages and beter working conditions which eventually led to demands for political equality and representation at the local and national levels.

Most of them were not educated in the traditional sense. They never got the chance to go to school, although a significant number of them did and had at least primary school education enabling them to read and write as well as count.

But because they worked directly under whites, they became very much aware of the differences in living conditions among the races and were among some of the most politically conscious people in Tanganyika and in all the other colonies across the continent; for example, in the Belgian Congo where Patrice Lumumba, a postal worker, led the independence struggle and became prime minister when the country won independence in June 1960; and in Guinea where Sekou Toure, a trade union leader, also led the nationalist movement and became president after the country won independence from France in October 1958, the first among Francophone countries on the continent to emerge from colonial rule.

And both, Lumumba and Sekou Toure, did not have high formal education yet were extremely successful in mobilising the masses in the struggle for independence.

The consciousness of the workers, especially in towns and cities, was best demonstrated on a number of occasions when they went on strike to force the colonial authorities to listen to their demands and make concessions, a strategy which helped to galvanise the independence struggle in Tanganyika and elsewhere including neighbouring Kenya.

In fact, labour union leaders became some of the most prominent and radical leaders in the independence struggle and assumed power in East Africa after the end of colonial rule. For example, Rashidi Mfaume Kawawa, a prominent labour union leader in Tanganyika, became prime minister and later vice president of Tanganyika and later of Tanzania. And in Kenya, Tom Mboya, another highly influential labour union leader, became the most prominent national figure after President Jomo Kenyatta and was his heir apparent. He also held senior cabinet posts including the ministry of economic planning and development until his assassination in July 1969 at the age of 39.

I remember there were even songs by Kenyan musicians played on the radio, Tanganyika Broadcasting Corporation, which in those days we simply called TBC, in the late fifties about Tom Mboya when he was one of the brightest stars on the Kenyan political scene before independence. One popular song was "Tom Mboya gerezani..." demanding his release from jail where he was confined for his political activities.

In the case of Tanganyika, the late fifties were a turning point in the independence struggle, as much as they were for neighbouring Kenya, and witnessed among other things the departure of one of the last two governors of this vast country, the largest among the East African British colonies.

I witnessed some of those events, although I was only 8 and 9 years old.

I remember when Sir Edward Francis Twining, one of the last two governors of Tanganyika, came to Tukuyu in 1958. It was a farewell visit.

He was governor from 18 June 1949 (about four months before I was born) to June 1958. He was succeeded by Sir Richard Gordon Turnbull who was the last governor of Tanganyika from 15 July 1958 until independence day on 9 December 1961. Twining died in June 1967, and Turnbull in December 1998.

I remember the day Governor Twining came to Tukuyu in 1958 to say good-bye. I was about eight-and-a-half years old. It was a bright, sunny day, in the afternoon. I was then a pupil in Standard Three at Kyimbila Primary

60

School and our head teacher made arrangements for us to go and see the governor. So we were in school only half of the day and walked the two miles to the town of Tukuyu to see the governor for the last time; it was also the first time most of us saw him on that day.

I even remember his attire. He was dressed in white. He also had on a white hat – white pith helmet typical of colonial rulers – and white gloves. And Nyakyusa dancers performed the traditional dance called *mang'oma* in farewell to him.

There were also many whites on the scene. Some had accompanied him from Dar es Salaam and Mbeya and others simply came to see him. Also on the scene was the Provincial Commissioner (PC) of the Southern Highlands Province from Mbeya, the provincial capital, and the District Commissioner (DC) of Rungwe District who lived right there in Tukuyu, the district headquarters.

I remember it was a festive occasion. People were in jovial mood. Politics seemed to be the last thing on their minds, as the dancers swayed and swivelled to the rhythm and drumbeat of *mang'oma*, the most popular Nyakyusa traditional dance.

Others who were there joyously clapped their hands for the governor when he climbed up the steps of the Barclays Bank building from where he waved to the crowd, smiling.

I remember the area well. The Clock Tower and the golf and tennis course were only a few yards away on the right hand-side when you faced the Barclays Bank Building going up on the road.

Although I was too young to know what was going on in the country in terms of politics and the campaign for independence under the leadership of the Tanganyika African National Union (TANU) whose charismatic leader, Julius Nyerere, electrified his audiences with his mere presence even before he spoke whenever he campaigned in different parts of Tanganyika, I was still

61

able to tell that there was no hostility of any kind towards the governor and other whites on the part of the Africans who were there on that day.

And that seemed to be the case even during the campaign for independence itself. There were no attacks on the British and other whites, and the people of all races seemed to get along just fine even if they did not mingle. The campaign for independence was peaceful and was waged along constitutional lines.

When reflecting on the transition from colonial rule to independence, Nyerere himself said that Tanganyika won independence by peaceful means, and there was no hostility towards whites even after the country attained sovereign status. As he stated in parliament during a debate on the citizenship bill when a few members wanted only black Africans to be citizens after Tanganyika became independent, as reported in the *Tanganyika National Assembly Debates* (Hansard), in October 1961 less than two months before the country won independence from Britain:

"If we in Tanganyika are going to divorce citizenship from loyalty and marry it to colour, it won't stop there...until you break up the country....They are preaching discrimination as a religion to us. And they stand like Hitlers and begin to glorify race. We glorify human beings, not colour."

Nyerere was furious when he heard a few members of the National Assembly speaking against citizenship for whites, Indians, Arabs and others. He was known to be very calm, tolerant and kind but lost his temper during the course of the debate and accused them of being racist and talking rubbish and behaving like Nazis.

Earlier as a little boy, before Nyerere gave that speech in the National Assembly in October 1961, I witnessed an event which embodied his vision of a multiracial society.

The reception the governor, Sir Edward Twining, was given by Africans and other people on that day in Tukuyu in 1958 during his last visit there was in many ways highly indicative of how things were going to be after Tanganyika won independence: people of different races and ethnic groups living and working together in harmony without hate and fear of each other or one another in the best interest of the country and for the sake of peace and stability enjoyed by all.

Governor Edward Twining's farewell visit marked the beginning of the end of British colonial rule in Tanganyika.

But, at that tender age, little did I or any of the other children – including many adults – know that independence was only three-and-a-half years away after 42 years of British colonial rule.

# Chapter Three

# Tanganyika before and after independence

WHAT IS Tanzania today did not come into existence until Tanganyika united with Zanzibar in 1964 to form one country.

I was born and brought up in Tanganyika. And it is Tanganyika that I focus on as the land of my birth where my personality and identity was shaped during British colonial rule in the fifties and in the first decade of independence in the sixties.

## Formation of Tanganyika

Tanganyika itself did not exist as a territorial entity until 1885 when it was annexed by Germany. It was created as a colony by the Germans whose claim to the territory was given formal recognition at the Berlin conference during the partition of Africa.

The German Colonization Society led by Dr. Karl Peters claimed the territory in 1884. He was supported by his home government under Bismarck and went on to establish the German East Africa Company to rule the territory.

In 1886 and 1890, the British and the Germans signed

agreements which defined their spheres of influence in the interior of East Africa and along the coast previously claimed by the sultan of Oman who had moved his capital from Muscat, Oman, to Zanzibar.

In 1891, the German government took over direct administration of the territory from the German East Africa Company and appointed a governor with headquarters in Dar es Salaam, a port city founded by the Arabs and whose name means Haven of Peace in Arabic.

European powers drew territorial boundaries to define their spheres of influence, creating the countries we have in Africa today.

In East Africa, the British had Kenya, Uganda, and Zanzibar; and the Germans, Tanganyika, and Ruanda-Urundi – what is now Rwanda and Burundi – which together formed one colony called Deutsch-Ostafrika (German East Africa) which existed from 1885 to 1919.

After that, the British took over what became Tanganyika following Germany's defeat in World War I. The Belgians acquired Ruanda-Urundi which became two separate colonies but administered together with Belgian Congo.

British formal presence on Tanganyikan soil began in 1914 at the beginning of World War I when the Royal Navy occupied Mafia island in the Indian ocean a few miles southeast of Dar es Salaam, the capital.

During World War I, German East Africa was occupied by the Allied forces including troops from South Africa led by General Smuts. It was – minus Ruanda-Urundi – renamed Tanganyika Territory in 1920 and placed under the League of Nations mandate administered by Britain after American President Woodrow Wilson refused to assume responsibility for the former German colony as proposed by British Prime Minister Lloyd George of the Liberal Party.

In 1921, the Belgians transferred Kigoma District in western Tanganyika to British administration, making it a part of Tanganyika. They had administered the district – together with Ruanda-Urundi – since the Allied occupation of the former German colony in 1916.

And in 1924, Britain and Belgium signed an agreement defining the border between Tanganyika and Ruanda-Urundi.

Until 1925, Tanganyika was administered in an improvised way and followed German administrative practices, after which the system of indirect rule was introduced.

Indirect rule was first practised by Lord Lugard in Northern Nigeria where he used traditional rulers including emirs to administer a vast expanse of territory.

In 1946, Tanganyika became a UN trusteeship territory.

## Colonial federations

Coincidentally, it was in the same year, 1946, that the Nigerian federation was formed out of three massive regions created by the British: Northern Nigeria dominated by the Hausa-Fulani, Eastern Nigeria by the Igbo, and Western Nigeria by the Yoruba.

Nigeria itself was created in 1914 with the amalgamation of the North and the South which had been administered separately as if they were two distinct colonies but under the same colonial power.

When Europeans came to Africa and established colonies, they thought they could transform at least some of them into permanent homes for white settlers as the British did in Australia and New Zealand as well as South Africa, Southern Rhodesia – what is now Zimbabwe – and Kenya. In fact, Kenya was declared a "White Man's Country" from the beginning of formal British occupation of the territory under Lord Delamere.

Neighbouring Tanganyika would have met the same fate had the British colonialists succeeded in establishing a giant federation stretching from Kenya all the way down to South Africa.

The governors and other leaders of all the colonies in the region – Kenya, Uganda, Tanganyika, Nyasaland (now Malawi), Northern Rhodesia (Zambia today), and Southern Rhodesia – met in Tukuyu, southern Tanganyika, in October 1925 to work on a plan to form such a federation.

But, years later as political awakening among Africans began to take place, the proposed federation was strongly opposed by African nationalists who feared that the establishment of such a giant political entity would consolidate and perpetuate white domination over Africans who constituted the vast majority of the population throughout the region as much as they did in the rest of the continent.

Yet, in spite of such opposition, it is interesting to note that years later Ugandan leader Milton Obote took a firm stand against the dissolution of one federation, the Central African Federation (of Northern Rhodesia, Southern Rhodesia and Nyasaland), an imperial creation, arguing that it would not be in the best interest of Africa if the federation was dissolved.

He argued that it would be beneficial to Africa if the federation remained intact and became a supra-nation upon attainment of independence.

He was virtually alone among African leaders in his support of the continued existence of the Central African Federation – also known as the Federation of Rhodesia and Nyasaland – which was formed in August 1953. It was dissolved 10 years later in December 1963.

## Racial cooperation

There were always whites in all these territories who supported Africans in their quest for justice and racial equality across the spectrum, including the former governor of Northern Rhodesia, Sir Roy Welensky, who also once served as federal prime minister of the Federation of Rhodesia and Nyasaland, although his espousal of the doctrine of racial equality did not go far enough.

But he at least acknowledged the genuine aspirations of Africans even if he may not have believed that black Africans really deserved the same rights whites did.

Another example of genuine commitment to racial equality was Derek Bryceson, a British, who emigrated from Kenya to Tanganyika in 1952 and became a cabinet member soon after the country won independence.

There was also Dr. Leader Sterling, another British, who first came to Tanganyika in the 1930s. He also became a nominated member of parliament and served in the cabinet as minister of health under President Julius Nyerere.

Bryceson was also an elected member of parliament representing a predominantly black district, Kilosa, and never lost an election against black political candidates contesting for the same seat; nor did Amir H. Jamal, of Indian origin, representing Morogoro, who was also, like Bryceson, a cabinet member under Nyerere for more than two decades since independence. They won elections in overwhelmingly black districts.

There were other whites – not only in Tanganyika but in other colonies as well, across the continent – who felt the same way, including those who privately expressed their interest in building multiracial societies on the basis of equality but did not express their feelings publicly for fear of offending and alienating other whites who were not as liberal or open-minded as they were. As Harry Hodson stated in his autobiography:

"A new constitution for Southern Rhodesia, which would have kept the white majority in parliament but extended the black franchise, and which had the nucleus of a common electoral roll, had been proposed from London and was being hotly debated. (It was to avert this far from radical constitution that Mr Ian Smith declared UDI two years later.)

Over his customary tankard of beer Sir Edgar Whitehead, the colony's Prime Minister, a taciturn, introspective character, gave me his opinion that if all went according to plan the reforms would give rise to a genuine multiracial government with a multiracial parliament.

Sir Roy Welensky, Prime Minister of the moribund Central African Federation, amid a great deal of bluster, agreed with Whitehead at least on the point that time and opportunity had to be used to break down race barriers.

Sir Robert Tredgold, who later became fainéant head of state under UDI, deplored the lack of communication between Africans and the great majority of Europeans: 'the trouble with most of our people here is that they live in a deaf world.'

Lord Malvern, who as Sir Godfrey Huggins had been Prime Minister of Southern Rhodesia for 10 years, and at 77 was as amusing, vigorous and earthy as ever, gave a luncheon party for me.

I reminded him that several years earlier, dining with the Round Table Moot, he had likened the mass of Africans in Rhodesia to the London East-Enders among whom he had worked as a young doctor – poor and ignorant, and like children, but as capable as they of education and advance. Did he hold to that? 'Yes – and they will grow up just as quickly.'"

Yet these white Rhodesian leaders were not the most liberal kind. They were racist. For example, Godfrey Huggins, who was acclaimed as a great British liberal, said at a press conference in London in 1952:

"There will be no Africans in a federal government (of Rhodesia – Northern and Southern – and Nyasaland formed in 1953).

They are quite incapable of playing a full part....They may have a university degree, but their background is all wrong.

It is time for the people in England to realize that the white man in Africa is not prepared, and never will be prepared, to accept the African as an equal either socially or politically."

His racist remarks were published in British papers and elsewhere. He was also quoted by Colin M. Turnbull in his book *The Lonely African*. I have also quoted him in my book *Africa and the West*.

But the mere fact that even such racist liberals at one time or another acknowledged the imperative need for change and knew that such change was inevitable; and the more enlightened amongst them articulated genuinely liberal sentiments – that Africans were entitled to racial equality – shows that there were whites who were interested in achieving racial harmony and equality; and a number of them were far more committed to achieving this goal than most of their leaders were.

They could be found in all African countries, including apartheid South Africa. Tanganyika was no exception.

Therefore the struggle in all these African countries was essentially democratic and not racial – black versus white – best exemplified by the new dispensation in post-apartheid South Africa where common aspirations shared by blacks, whites, Indians, Coloureds and others led to the adoption of one of the most liberal constitutions in the world guaranteeing equality for all South Africans. As one black South African cabinet member said in his emphatic declaration that non-black South Africans were also Africans just like black Africans: Indians are in India, and Europeans in Europe.

71

It's very interesting to know how the European settlers felt about their new life in the colonies they had established under the tropical sun far away from Europe.

In spite of the difficulties they faced living in underdeveloped regions of the world, they were still very much satisfied with their new life. That is why they did not want to leave or return to Europe except in some cases after independence when conditions became intolerable even for many black Africans who were born in those countries.

## Dream shattered

Political repression and worsening economic conditions became a way of life in many African countries after the end of colonial rule. And through the years, tens of thousands of Africans have left the continent in search of greener pastures especially in the West.

By the end of 2005, there were more than 5 million Africans living outside Africa, tens of thousands of them highly educated and trained professionals. And tens of thousands of African students who go to school in Europe, North America and other parts of the world every year don't return to their home countries or to any other part of Africa after they finish their studies.

In 2006, there were more than 30,000 Nigerian doctors living and working in the United States alone. In New York City, there were more than 600 Ghanaian doctors. In Chicago, there were more doctors from Sierra Leone than there were in Sierra Leone.

And that's just the tip of the iceberg.

About 50,000 Kenyan professionals lived and worked in the United States in 2006. That's without even counting those in the United Kingdom where, for historical reasons because of former colonial ties, they have gone in the past in larger numbers than they have anywhere else.

Add Nigerians, Ghanaians, Tanzanians, Zimbabweans, Zambians, Sierra Leoneans and others who live in Britain, North America and other parts of the world including Australia. Also think about how many Africans from Senegal, the Ivory Coast, Guinea, Mali and other former French African colonies live and work in France alone. And why.

Then you can see why our continent is in such a mess. It is a continental crisis, a massive brain drain, and it is killing Africa because of rotten leadership – more than anything else – in most parts of the continent since the end of colonial rule.

And we have to be brutally frank about it. Glossing over the problem is not going to solve it.

Those are grim statistics. They tell a sad story about the conditions in our countries which force tens of thousands of highly educated people including professionals such as doctors, engineers, scientists and many others in different critical fields to flee the continent every year in search of better life in Western countries and elsewhere in the industrialized world. They constitute the critical mass without which Africa cannot develop. They keep on fleeing the continent. And it has been that way since independence.

In fact many Africans, especially the older ones, remember with nostalgia how life was in "the good ol' days" before independence when there was law and order and no shortages of essential items. They also remember that they could get jobs, even if the jobs weren't paying much; and that in spite of difficulties, roads and railways were well-maintained and the people could travel to different parts of the country without fear of being robbed or killed.

And they did not have to pay bribes in those days to get a job, buy a bus ticket or even a simple bar of soap or some toothpaste as happened in many countries across the continent after independence.

Those are some of the reasons why many people remember the fifties with nostalgia; a nostalgic feeling which may seem to justify or defend colonial rule although that is not the case. It is simply a desire by many people to live better, even if simpler, lives. And the deplorable condition in which tens of millions of Africans live more than 50 years after independence is a searing indictment against Africa's post-colonial leadership.

It is no wonder that millions of Africans who are old enough to have lived under colonial rule remember those days with nostalgia.

## Good life for the colonial rulers and settlers

For whites, life was even better for them when compared with the way Africans lived. In fact, life couldn't have been better for some of them since many colonial administrators would not have been able to get in their own countries – in Britain and elsewhere in Europe – the kind of jobs they had in colonial Africa.

Since I focus on Tanganyika, the examples I cite come from East Africa to illustrate my point. As Erika Johnson, writing about the 1950s in colonial Tanganyika, stated in *The Other Side of Kilimanjaro*:

"Robin [Robin Johnson was a District Commissioner, simply known as D.C. throughout British colonial Africa] maintains that there was no better life for a man in those days than that of a District Commissioner. It was a marvellous combination of an active open air life, coupled with a wide, varied and interesting amount of office work.

You did long walking safaris through your area and slept under canvas, and in this way you got to know your parishioners and their problems.

Responsible for a vast area, you were father, mentor and disciplinarian to everyone, sorting out family and tribal disputes. You had to do anything and everything:

74

build roads, dams and bridges, dig wells and be a magistrate and administrator of law and order.

Your problems could vary from shooting a rogue elephant despoiling villagers' crops to trying a stock thief in court.

In later years, [Julius] Nyerere once said to a silent Robin that the D.C's had made little contribution other than collecting taxes!" – (Erika Johnson, *The Other Side of Kilimanjaro*, London: Johnson Publications Ltd., 1971, p. 16. See also, Donald Cameroon, *My Tanganyika Service and some in Nigeria*, London: Allen and Unwin, 1939; Lanham, Maryland: The University Press of America, second edition, 1982).

Many projects started by the colonial rulers provided employment for a number of Africans. And it was Africans who played a major role in building roads, dams and bridges, making bricks, digging wells and doing many other things, providing cheap labour.

## My childhood
## in the Southern Highlands Province

I personally remember seeing African men doing hard work, building roads, in the town and on the outskirts of Mbeya and also working on the road from Mbeya to Chunya, a district north of Mbeya; and in Rungwe District working on the road from Tukuyu to Kyela, 30 miles south of Tukuyu close to the Tanganyika-Nyasaland (now Malawi) border, when I was a little boy under 10 in the 1950s.

They worked for the colonial Public Works Department, which was simply known as PWD, and rode in the back of Bedford lorries; they were British lorries imported from Britain. The lorries also were simply called PWD. I even remember their colour. They were painted

75

green on the sides and white on top.

The African labourers worked hard, all day long, often in scorching sun.

The buses which used those roads, besides other vehicles, were the East African Railways & Harbours Corporation (EAR&H) buses. I remember they were Leyland buses.

The wages for Africans working on those roads and elsewhere were low but better than nothing if you needed some money to buy a few things now and then – and pay taxes, of course.

Many other Africans earned some money by selling agricultural products, and sometimes handicrafts, at open markets in villages and sometimes in town. In our case it was in the town of Tukuyu, built on small hills with a majestic view below all the way to Lake Nyasa clearly visible about 34 miles away on the Malawian-Tanzanian border.

Some of the people at the market whom I remember vividly were Kikuyu women. They were originally from Kenya and had, like many other Kenyans, come to Tanganyika to take advantage of the opportunities available to make money in a country where the indigenous people, including my fellow Nyakyusa in Rungwe District, were supposedly not as aggressive as the Kenyans were.

The Kenyans were seen as "more enterprising," "more adventurous" and "more of risk takers" than Tanganyikans although all those are relative terms.

Even today, many Tanzanians are apprehensive about their future in the proposed East African federation. They say the federation will be dominated by Kenyans and Ugandans who are more "aggressive" and better educated.

They also say problems of tribalism, so common in Kenya, Uganda, Rwanda, Burundi and South Sudan will spread to Tanzania and the country will lose the peace and stability it has enjoyed since – and even before –

76

independence.

When I recall the fifties and early sixties, I can understand why many of my fellow countrymen feel the way they do in terms of competition between Tanzanians and Kenyans as well as Ugandans in the economic arena, besides their fear of tribalism becoming a major problem in Tanzania – which won't exist anymore as a sovereign entity – if the countries do indeed unite to form a supranation.

I remember what my mother said more than once in the late fifties and early sixties after she saw Kikuyu women at the market in Tukuyu when she now and then went into town to buy a variety of items. She described them as very aggressive and determined to make money. They were the first to arrive at the market early in the morning before dawn to make sure that they had the best spot where they could attract the largest number of customers.

I went to the market myself a few times and I remember seeing them selling beans, rice and other items.

And what was so good about all this is that there was no hostility towards the Kikuyu on the part of the Nyakyusa. I don't remember hearing anyone saying these Kikuyus have come all the way from Kenya to Rungwe District, down here, near the border with Nyasaland and Northern Rhodesia to take over our market and steal our customers! It was business as usual, although many Nyakyusas were outmaneuvred on their own turf, at their own market, in their own town and home district, by these "strangers" from Kenya.

But some of them may have learned a thing or two from the Kikuyu women who had mastered the art of salesmanship and tricks of the trade. However, most of the Nyakyusa women at the market were equally competent and were a perfect match for the Kikuyu and may even have welcomed the challenge from them to demonstrate their own marketing skills. The challenge itself was a source of inspiration to others to excel and was therefore a positive thing.

Besides the women and some men selling food and other items at the market in Tukuyu, there were other Africans, although not many, who worked in that town. My father was one of them. He was assistant manager at a Shell BP petrol station under a British manager. I remember the manager had a son who was around my age. Whenever I went to see my father now and then when I was in town for a walk or to buy a few things, I would see the boy there with his father.

It has been more than 50 years since I last bought some items from the Indian shops in the town of Tukuyu – they were the only ones, except one Somali shop owned by Rajab who knew my father well – but I still remember some of the owners and the names of those shops, Hirji, Merali, and Makanji which were also said to be the biggest in town. There were no African shops in Tukuyu in those days.

I remember that some Indian shop owners even spoke Kinyakyusa, the native language of the Nyakyusa in Rungwe District, and had very good relations with their customers. I also remember seeing and listening to many Nyakyusa women negotiating with the shop owners over prices when they were buying clothes, sugar, cooking oil, kerosene for their lamps in the villages and other items.

One of the popular items bought by some women was a cotton cloth called *mwasungo* in Kinyakyusa. It was black and cheap and the people who bought that were usually very poor. If you bought *mwasungo*, people would assume you had nothin'. Some people even made fun of the material. It's sad but it happened.

Hardly any African women worked in the town of Tukuyu except may be a *yaya* (house maid) here and there.

There were, however, a few men who worked as watchmen staying awake all night outside Indian shops with their *pangas*, in spite of the fact that we never heard of anybody trying to break into the shops – which were also Indian family residences – even when there were no night watchmen at all at some of the shops.

My father was one of the few men who had a regular job in Tukuyu when he worked as an assistant manager at the Shell BP petrol station.

I also remember one very small African restaurant near the football field in the town of Tukuyu. The soccer field was also used by politicians to address mass rallies.

I remember my father took me to that restaurant quite often when we were in town and he knew the owners, husband and wife, well.

But it was Africans working on road projects, building or repairing roads, who were probably the most visible people in the labour market of the formal sector besides teachers and other employees.

I saw them working on roads many times in the fifties. And I remember many of them liked to sing or shout a lot when they worked, repairing or building roads. They worked hard until late in the evening, sometimes until dusk.

I also once got into trouble with some of them when we lived in Mbeya. That was between 1954 and 1955 when I was around four and five years old.

I was not yet in school then, although that was not an excuse for what I did. I remember I used to play a lot near the road going from Mbeya to Chunya. Our house was very close to the road just on the outskirts of Mbeya. The town was within walking distance from our house.

Almost everyday I would collect small stones, big enough for my size, and pile them up under a shrub near the road as I waited for the Bedford PWD lorries to come by. Because I was small, it was easy for me to hide. The lorries always carried African workers on their way to and from work. As soon as the lorries were getting ready to pass by, I would throw stones at them, targeting the labourers riding in the back of the lorries. And quite often

I scored direct hits.

As soon as I did that, I would duck under the bush. They sometimes saw me but I would dash back home and the driver never stopped. But one day he did! I remember that very well. The PWD lorry was headed towards Chunya, without necessarily going that far. It was simply the direction the lorry went.

About two or three of the labourers jumped out of the lorry and came after me. I couldn't outrun them and they caught me. One of them grabbed my hand. I was so terrified that I thought they were going to do something bad to me. But my age and size saved me. Sometimes weakness is the best defence.

I was crying when they grabbed me. They ordered me to take them to my parents. I did, crying all the way. My mother was there and she gave me a severe tongue lashing in front of them and they let me go.

I expected the worst and would probably have been rewarded with that had my father been there during that time. He was a very strict disciplinarian who regularly administered corporal punishment when we were growing up, especially in my case and my younger brother Lawrence. But he was at work in town and didn't come back home until evening everyday. I remember he worked for Brooke Bond, a British tea company and the largest in the world, in the town of Mbeya during those days.

That was the end of my adventure. I never tossed stones at PWD lorries again for a long time, although the thrill was not gone.

I think I did it again a couple of times or so much later after that incident. But basically, I stopped doing it.

That is one of my most memorable experiences when we lived in Mbeya in the fifties besides the circus I attended in town, elephants being the most prominent animals in the show.

But something tragic happened during the circus. My father hoisted me on his shoulders so that I could have a clear view of the performance.

Besides the elephants and other animals, I saw one white man who had a snake around his neck. He got my attention and probably the attention of many other people who were there. It was quite a spectacle.

While still at the circus, we heard that he was bitten by the snake and taken to the hospital.

After the circus, may be after a day or two, I heard from my parents that he died from the snake bite. The snake was said to be a cobra. That was in 1954 when I was about five years old.

And on another day, my father took me to the hospital in the town of Mbeya to visit one of his friends who was an inpatient there.

When we entered the hospital, I saw some people had their legs tied up and hoisted on to something – it looked like a ceiling to me or the straps on their legs were tied to or hooked on to something hanging down from the ceiling. One of them was my father's friend. I also heard some groaning from some of the patients.

Not knowing what was going on, and being so young, I panicked and ran out of the hospital until my father came to get me and take me to see his friend.

I thought the people were dying or being killed – for whatever reason – especially after I heard some of them groaning.

It was also when we lived in Mbeya that I saw a tortoise for the first time. There was a chap who used to go around showing the tortoise to earn some money. He would somehow coax the tortoise to stick its head out of the shell and the people would give him a few coins for performing the "trick." He actually did nothing; the tortoise did, and I believe only when it was ready to do so.

One day he came to our house. It was in the afternoon, on a sunny day, and I was playing outside. He showed the tortoise to my mother and to my sister Maria and we all, together with my brother Lawrence, looked at it.

I remember thinking how slow it moved when he put it on the ground. And to me, it looked sad because of the way it moved. I was simply too young to know that was simply its nature and that's the way it looked and moved.

It was quite an experience and I learned something from that, especially since that was the first time that I saw that kind of animal. I had never seen anything like it before. And I remember the day well, in fact very well.

But my favourite pastime even after I started school in Rungwe District was catching grasshoppers and butterflies. That was after my parents returned to their home district – hence ours as well – in 1955 and I went there with them for the first time together with my brother Lawrence and my two sisters, Maria and Gwangu.

None of us was born in Rungwe District, and none of us had been there before. But the rest of my sisters and my only other brother David were all born in Rungwe District after my parents returned there.

I used to play outside a lot and loved catching and feeding grasshoppers, giving them blades of grass. I treated them as if they were my "cows," and I in fact called them that.

After living in urban areas during the first five years of my life, it was quite a dramatic change when we finally went to live in the rural areas. And twice, I came perilously close to getting killed because of my adventures.

Before we settled in Kyimbila which is in the highlands of the northern part of Rungwe District, we lived in Kyela in the southern part of the district. That was in 1955. Kyela is now a separate district but it was then a part of Rungwe District. It is mostly lowland, hot and humid and borders Malawi, what was then Nyasaland.

I had not started school when we lived in Kyela and did not enroll in primary school, Kyimbila Primary School, until we moved to the highlands of Rungwe District, what the Nyakyusa in Kyela call Mwamba; the

Nyakyusa in the highlands are also sometimes called *Bamwamba* by those in Kyela.

*Bamwamba* in Nyakyusa means "those of the highlands" or "highlanders." And Nyakyusa highlanders call the Kyela area Ntebela, or lowland, and the people who live down there *"Bantebela,"* meaning, "of the lowlands" or "lowlanders."

It was when we lived in Kyela that I almost got killed when I was playing outside. We lived in a rural area, Kandete, a few miles north of the town of Kyela.

I remember there was a mango tree on our land only a few yards from our house. I used to go to that tree almost everyday to play. And that is where I came face to face with two cobras. I think they were king cobras.

I was 5 years old and did not really know what they were. But I do know and remember very well that I did not take them seriously.

I also remember that I saw the snakes more than once around that tree, on the ground, and whenever I saw one or both, I used to throw stones and sticks at them, playing, and they would slither away fast.

One day, I remember one of the snakes stuck its head out of the grass facing me after I threw stones and sticks at it. That's when I ran back to the house and told my mother what happened; my father was not there during that time.

And that was when I realised how I came perilously close to getting killed by one of those snakes.

My mother told me I was playing with snakes, extremely dangerous snakes, and would have been killed had I confronted the one which stuck its head out, no longer afraid of me, if it ever was.

It had its head puffed out while facing me, yet I did not have the slightest idea of what that meant because whenever I threw stones and sticks at the snakes around that mango tree, they ran away.

From then on, I was forbidden from going to that tree, although I think I went there again just out of curiosity.

But I was more "cautious" than before. Obviously the word "caution" meant something different to me at that age.

But, thank God, I managed to get out of there alive and my parents and I, together with my brother Lawrence and my two sisters Maria and Gwangu, moved to Kyimbila in the mountainous part of Rungwe District where my parents originally came from.

We settled in Mpumbuli village surrounded by relatives including my paternal grandmother, aunts, uncles and cousins and felt really at home. All these relatives lived in the area of Kyimbila not far from our house.

Some of them lived right there in Mpumbuli. And it was when we lived there that I started going to school. I was six years old when I enrolled in standard one at Kyimbila Primary School in January 1956, not long after we moved from Kyela the previous year.

It was also when we lived in Mpumbuli village that I once again came close to losing my life. Our house was only a few yards – not more than 20 or 30 yards – away from a small river called Lubalisi.

The river goes around our property of a few acres, probably not more than five, since land is so scarce in densely populated Rungwe District, and serves as a demarcation line separating our land from the property of some of our neighbours.

I used to go to the river everyday, bathing and playing with crabs. It was also an area which was known to have pythons and other snakes. I never saw a python but I saw many small green snakes on tree branches and guava trees which grow in abundance in our area.

The guava trees were just wild plants and people in the area cut them down if they had to clear the land for farming. We ate guavas now and then but never valued them as food or as a staple item of our diet. They were simply wild fruit and we plucked them from the trees now and then just for fun and throwing them away.

Birds and monkeys valued them more than we did since we had plenty of food including bananas, maize, sweet potatoes, beans, cabbage and other vegetables in this highly fertile district where we also grow coffee and tea. Pine trees, suited to cool climate, also grow in Rungwe District including our area.

I helped harvest coffee on our farm when I was growing up and I remember seeing small green snakes on coffee tree branches as well. But they were harmless and not aggressive.

I did, however, have a close encounter with one river snake when I was washing my legs in River Lubalisi one evening. I was standing on a big stone where I stood all the time whenever I went to the river, and was washing my legs when something just told me instinctively to look in the water behind the stone. And sure enough, there was something there, a snake, its head straight up moving slowly towards my heel trying to sneak up on me.

As soon as the snake saw me looking at it, it ducked back into the water and disappeared under the stone. I did not even finish washing my legs and ran back to the house where I did the rest. We had plenty of water stored in buckets for bathing, after heating it up, using firewood, but it was still a thrill for us, especially boys, to go to the river and bathe even if we could avoid that and bathe at home.

I don't know what would have happened had I been bitten by that snake. I don't know what kind of snake it was and whether or not it was poisonous. I just remember that it was a small black snake. If it was highly poisonous, I would have been in trouble and could even have died.

Tukuyu Government Hospital was about four miles away. And we had no car. It was not until about five years later that my father bought a used Land Rover from an African businessman known as Mr. Katule. He also bought a car from an Indian family in Tukuyu at a different time.

Even if we had a car during that time, there was no guarantee that the hospital would have been able to save my life had I been bitten by a highly poisonous snake. I'm not sure it was well-equipped with the necessary staff and medicine including antivenom for snake bites. What I know is that such antivenom was rare in African hospitals during those days; and it still is.

But the worst never happened and so I lived to tell the story. Yet that was not the end of it.

I had another encounter, right on our property, and close to the same river during which I was severely tested and forced to "mature overnight." I was still under 10 years old, sometime in 1958 or 1959.

There was a small shrub on our land right on the bank of the river we passed by whenever we went to draw some water for various activities around the house.

We never drank the water from River Lubalisi and never used it for cooking. It was not clean. And since we were downstream, the people upstream polluted it even more for us everyday.

Fortunately, we had fresh, spring water coming straight out of a small high bank of a small stream – which was itself spring water – only about 50 yards away from our house and next to River Lubalisi on the other side of the river bank. Also our paternal grandmother did not live far from there; may be about 150 yards or so.

My sisters Maria and Gwangu and my brother Lawrence and I used to go there almost every day to get some drinking water in different containers.

Although the water was supposed to be clean, our father did not want to take chances and bought a water filter to make sure that we all drank clean water in the house.

We even went there at night, sometimes, with a torch (what Americans call flashlight), taking chances with creatures of the night we could run into anytime. But nothing ever happened to us.

But something happened to me at that shrub on the river bank close to our house.

When I was playing there one day, I noticed that there was a big hole under the shrub and was fully convinced right away that there was a big snake in there; my belief reinforced by what we had heard before that there were pythons in the area; in fact only a few yards from our house since we lived very close to the river. Or it could have been some other creature. I was not sure but was still convinced that if anything lived in there, it had to be a large snake.

It was during daytime, in the afternoon, with the sun blazing. And I had plenty of time to investigate or do whatever I wanted to do. I came up with an idea that if there was indeed a big snake or some other creature in there, I would be able to flush it out and see what it was, and fire would do the trick.

So, I collected some dry grass and banana leaves, and a few dry sticks, and piled them up on the hole. I struck a match and up went the flames. But within seconds, whatever was in that hole put out the fire. I heard some noise, like loud hissing or a small wind, and saw the ashes and sparks scattering around the shrub as the fire immediately went out.

Until this day, I don't know what it was or how the fire was put out so quickly within seconds right in front of me. I assumed it was a python in that hole and it put out the fire with a jet of saliva. But I could be wrong.

It could have been a different creature, although I doubt that seriously.

I leave that to experts to determine or conclude whether or not the fire was, most likely, extinguished by saliva from a python or some other kind of large snake.

I believe it was a python because right next to the shrub and the hole, where we walked to and from the river, now and then we used to see a wide mark or path on the soil and dust which we assumed had been left by a large snake slithering.

But that was not the end of my close encounter with

nature in Mpumbuli village in the fifties when I was growing up.

On another day, my father and I were returning home from my grandmother's – his mother's – house on the other side of River Lubalisi. It was night time and as we got to the bank getting ready to cross, I saw an animal sitting on the left-hand side very close to where we used to get spring water.

My father also glanced at the animal but didn't say anything. I didn't either. After we crossed the river and had climbed up a small hill leading to our house and were only only a few yards away, may be 50 yards or so before we reached home, my father said the animal we just saw was a leopard!

And he made the right decision not to tell me that when we were crossing the river. I probably would have panicked. I don't know if the leopard would have attacked us or not had I screamed or made some other kind of noise. But it's possible any commotion could have been misinterpreted by the leopard as an attack on it, triggering a retaliatory response, hence an attack on us.

A few years later, my maternal uncle Chonde Mwambapa shot and killed a leopard in our village one evening. It had, some days or weeks before, attacked someone in the village. The person who was attacked fought the leopard and miraculously survived the attack. My uncle was one of only two individuals in the area who had shot guns.

It was also at the same crossing of River Lubalisi on another night when I was returning home that I heard some noise in the bushes on the opposite bank. It was loud as if something big was slithering towards the river. And it was indeed. I was sure it was a python! Nothing slithers like that unless it is a snake. And if it's snake, it's a big one. And if it's a big one, it's a python, especially in that area. The conclusion was obvious to me, since there were pythons in the area.

As I was getting ready to cross the river, I heard some loud splashing and as if something big was wiggling in the water like as huge snake. And I was right. After it crossed the river, I heard it slithering and going into the bushes on the same side of the bank where I was standing when I was getting ready to cross. I still remember the noise. The creature slithered like a huge snake. It could not have been but that. And I believe it was a python. It went straight to the area where we used to get spring water.

Miraculously, in all the years I lived in Mpumbuli village, eight years altogether before I went to boarding school in January 1963 at the age of 13, I never heard of anyone or any animal being eaten by a python. We had two cows and I took them grazing a few times but nothing happened.

And my uncle Chonde once gave me a small white pig as a gift when I went to visit him and his family. I was about seven or eight years old.

It was in the evening when he gave me the pig at his house. I had to take it home with me about a mile-and-a-half away, going down a hill, crossing a stream, climbing up another hill, crossing the Tukuyu-Kyela road, then going down another hill and finally crossing River Lubalisi and climbing yet another hill to get to our house.

I also had to go through some bushes on the way home from my uncle's house. Yet nothing happened, although the pig made a lot of noise all the way.

That's in an area where there were some pythons. None of them may have been hungry but if there were any in that area during that time, they would have heard the pig squealing. Pythons are known to have a keen sense of hearing. Some experts say they can detect the slightest movement, of a mouse, a hundred yards away.

The worst incident I knew about involved our dog, Jack, a German shepherd, who was almost killed near the bank of the same river at the south-end of our property.

Our father went to look for the dog along the river

bank on our land and when he found him he noticed that the dog couldn't walk well.

We never found out what happened to Jack but our father suspected that a python might have tried to kill the dog. But that was only speculation and it probably wasn't the case since it takes only a few seconds for a python to wrap around its prey and squeeze it to death once it gets hold of it.

Those are some of the most memorable events in my life when I was growing up in Mpumbuli village in Kyimbila and which were in sharp contrast with what I experienced during the first five years of my life in Kigoma, Ujiji, Morogoro, and Mbeya where we lived in urban areas.

I had other experiences, of course, in the mid- and late fifties; for example, when our head teacher at Kyimbila Primary School, Samuel Mwaijande, who was married to one of my mother's first cousins, Miriam, sent us – all boys – down the valley near our school to hunt. His wife was one of the daughters of my mother's maternal uncle Asegelile Mwankemwa.

The Nyakyusa don't do that to boys, what our head teacher did to us, send us to hunt. Working on the farm is manly enough but in his own peculiar way, what he did to us was probably a form of initiation into manhood he felt, rightly or wrongly, that we needed!

Whatever the case, he opened another window for us into the world when he sent us down into the valley near our school, to hunt, since he was the one who taught us geography.

I also remember well that it was when I was in Standard Four at Kyimbila Primary School in 1959 that our head teacher taught us some things about African countries, including the names of some leaders such as Kwame Nkrumah, Nnamdi Azikiwe, Jomo Kenyatta and Ahmed Sekou Toure besides Julius Nyerere. And I still remember the map he used in class, although I don't have vivid memory of everything he taught us in that class.

But I remember that the map he used, and obviously the one that was most current in those days, had only few huge patches, some red, some green and I think others beige, orange or yellow.

I remember two distinctly. One large patch was green and covered most of West Africa and was labelled French West Africa. The other large patch on the same map was red and was labelled British, although I'm not sure it said British East Africa.

But I remember that all the colonial territories had names – Kenya Colony, Uganda Protectorate, Tanganyika Trust or Trusteeship Territory or simply Tanganyika Territory, Zanzibar Protectorate in our East African region – and some of them were identified by their colonial rulers; for example, British and French Somaliland, Portuguese Guinea, and so forth.

So, while I lived in a village, my school attendance at Kyimbila Primary School and later at Mpuguso Middle School opened my eyes to the rest of the world, not just Africa, I had never known before. As expected, it was formal education at those schools, complemented by my firsthand knowledge of rural life in Rungwe District after we left Mbeya in 1955.

It was a dramatic change in my life starting with a transition from urban to rural life and it left an indelible mark on my mind.

All this dramatic transition and transformation in my life took place in what was then the Southern Highlands Province when I finally went to live a typical African way of life in a village where I also learned Kinyakyusa, my "tribal" language, for the first time.

I had learned some Nyakyusa earlier, listening to my parents and other relatives we had in Mbeya including my aunt, my mother's eldest sister Mbage Mwakanema and her children, speak the language. But that was not enough for me to learn it well.

Up until then, I spoke Kiswahili. And my playmates in Morogoro, who were not Nyakyusa, also spoke Kiswahili. But all that changed when we moved from Morogoro to Mbeya in the Southern Hilghlands Province in 1954. And it is a province that I will always remember, and will always cherish, the way it was back then.

The province was under a British provincial commissioner (PC). The town of Mbeya was the provincial capital. My parents and I together with my siblings lived on its outskirts before we moved to Rungwe district.

During those days of colonial rule, Tanganyika was divided into seven provinces: The Southern Highlands Province, the Southern Province, the Central Province, the Western Province, the Lake Province, the Coast Province, and the Northern Province.

After independence, the Southern Highlands was divided into Mbeya Region and Iringa Region; so were the rest, also broken down into smaller regional administrative units called regions.

## From Tanganyika to South Africa: Working in the mines

I remember that the fifties were also a period when many people from Tanganyika went to work in the mines in South Africa. Some of them came from my area of Kyimbila which has several villages including Mpumbuli, Nkuju, Ndola, Mabonde, Katusyo and others; my home village of Mpumbuli being four miles south of the town of Tukuyu.

One of the people who went to work in the mines in South Africa was my cousin Daudi who lived in a different part of Rungwe District several miles away from Kyimbila.

Coincidentally, Daudi's father William, my father's

elder brother, migrated to Northern Rhodesia (now Zambia) in 1943 never to be heard from again, except once or twice when he wrote my father back then not long after he settled there. He got married again and had another family in Zambia. He also died there.

Although I was under 10 years old in the fifties, I remember the people who went to work in the mines were flown from Mbeya to South Africa. I remember talking to some of those who came back, including my cousin Daudi, and asking them about South Africa.

They had plenty of stories to tell about the City of Gold, Johannesburg, and how big it was. The Nyakyusa called it Joni.

They also told us stories about the fights they had in the mines with some people of other ethnic groups. The Nyakyusa had a reputation on the mine compounds as fierce fighters. I heard the same story about twenty years later in the early seventies when I came to the United States.

One of the people who stayed with me and other African students in Detroit, Michigan, in the United States during that time was Ndiko, a South African; I don't know if he spelt his name as Ndiko or Ndhiko.

He was with us for only a few weeks at the house where we lived. The house was owned by the Pan-African Congress-USA, an African American organisation which sponsored us.

I remember that when I told him that I was a Nyakyusa, he got excited and started telling me how tough the Nyakyusa were as fighters in South Africa; a spirit which, I believe, can partly be attributed to ethnocentric tendencies common among many groups whose members think, wrongly, that they are better than others as fighters and probably in many other ways, although not everybody believes that. I am one of those who don't.

Anyway, Ndiko (or Ndhiko), also had a relative, Lindiwe Pettiford Mabuzo, who taught at Ohio University in Athens, Ohio. When he and I went to visit her in 1974, she said the same thing about the reputation of the Nyakyusa as fierce fighters on the mine compounds in South Africa. I also remember she tried to help me get a scholarship from Ohio University but I returned to Detroit where I graduated from Wayne State University.

She later became South Africa's high commissioner (ambassador) to the United Kingdom, appointed by President Nelson Mandela, after the end of apartheid.

I was then relatively new in the United States and moved from New York to Detroit towards the end of December 1972.

I stayed in New York for about two months with a relative-in-law, Weidi Ngwilulupi Mwasakafyuka, who worked at the Tanzania Mission to the UN. He later served as Tanzania's ambassador to France in the 1980s and high commissioner to Nigeria in the 1990s.

He was the only person I knew when I first landed on American soil.

I left Dar es Salaam on November 3rd and arrived in New York the next day. I went straight to Greensboro, North Carolina, before going back to New York. I stayed in Greensboro for only a few days.

But that is another story. I have written about that in another book, *Relations Between Africans and African Americans: Misconceptions, Myths and Realities.*

Coincidentally, Weidi Mwasakafyuka also came from Mpumbuli village, my home, and was the second person from our village to go to school in the United States. He graduated from the University of California-Los Angeles (UCLA) and from Carleton University in Canada in the sixties. He did his postgraduate studies in international relations at Carleton.

I was the third from our village to go to school in the United States. The first one was Henry Mwakyoma, a cousin on my mother's side, who graduated from the University of Virginia where he first went in the late

94

fifties.

I remember when he came back to Tanganyika, he used to come to our house and tell us stories about life in the United States. He was one of the first people who inspired me to go to school in America. And he remains one of the people whom I remember the most from the fifties.

Unfortunately, Henry died many years ago in the 1970s, a victim of a brutal attack by thugs in the town of Mbeya who literally beat him to death, according to reports I got from my relatives – James Mwakisyala and others – when I was in the United States. He happened to be in the wrong place at the wrong time in that town.

Times had really changed through the years. Those kinds of attacks and crimes were unheard of in Tanganyika in the fifties.

The fifties were without question some of the most important years of my life. They were my formative years as much as the sixties were. I remember listening to many inspiring stories which helped to enlarge my mental horizon at such an early age. And they have remained a source of inspiration to me throughout my life.

My father was one of the people who liked to tell stories about hard work and success in life and played a critical role in shaping my personality when I was growing up.

I also remember hearing stories of valour about the Nyakyusa during my time and in the past including their successful campaigns against the Ngoni in the 1830s, '40s and '50s when the Ngoni tried to invade and penetrate Nyakyusaland. The Nyakyusa also successfully repelled the Sangu who invaded Rungwe District in the 1870s and 1880s from neighbouring Usangu in Mbeya District. Like the Nyakyusa and the Ngoni, the Sangu also had a reputation as fierce fighters. But they were no match for the Nyakyusa who stopped their incursions into Nyakyusaland as much as they did the Ngoni attacks.

The few white missionaries who settled in Rungwe

District also tried to intervene and act as mediators in conflicts not only between the Nyakyusa and the Sangu but also between the Nyakyusa and the Safwa, then the largest ethnic group in Mbeya District until they were outnumbered by the Nyakyusa years later.

The missionaries also played a mediating role in other conflicts including intra-tribal (or intra-ethnic) disputes but not always successfully.

But, besides the Nyakyusa, it was the Ngoni whom I remember the most for their reputation as fierce fighters mainly because I interacted with them in the sixties. Their legendary reputation as fearless fighters sent a chill down the spine and many of their neighbours were afraid of them except a few like the Nyakyusa, and the Hehe who, under their leader Chief Mkwawa, once defeated the Germans.

Originally from Natal Province in South Africa, the Ngoni settled in Songea District in southern Tanganyika, as well as Sumbawanga in the western part of the country. They had a reputation as fierce fighters even in South Africa itself before they left during the *imfecane* in the 1820s and '30s headed north, finally settling in what is now Malawi, Mozambique and Tanzania. Some of them even went to Congo and settled there after passing through Tanganyika and Burundi.

I went to Songea Secondary School which was a boarding school in Songea District in southern Tanzania. It was – and still is – the home of the Ngoni. I talked to many of them including some who were old enough to be my parents. I was a teenager back then.

Almost without exception, they recalled the stories they were told by their elders when they were growing up on how the Nyakyusa and the Ngoni fought when the Ngoni tried to invade Nyakyusaland.

They told me the Nyakyusa *ni watani wetu*, a Swahili expression meaning they are our friends and we tell jokes about each other.

Many of those "jokes" have to do with how hard the Nyakyusa fought to repel the Ngoni invaders after the Ngoni failed to steal Nyakyusa cows and women!

Some of the Ngoni also went to work in the mines in South Africa – where they originally came from – but not in significant numbers as the Nyakyusa and other people from the Southern Highlands did, especially from Rungwe and Mbeya districts in a region bordering what was then Northern Rhodesia, now Zambia.

Northern Rhodesia itself attracted many mine workers from my region. Many of them settled in that country. Even today, you will find many Nyakyusas who settled in Kitwe and other parts of the Copperbelt many years ago after they went to work there in the mines. For example, in 1954 the Nyakyusa in Kitwe formed an organisation to preserve, protect and promote their interests as an ethnic group.

The Lozi, members of another ethnic group from Baraotseland or Barotse Province in the western part of the country and one of the largest in Zambia, also formed their own organisation around the same time, as did the Nyakyusa and other groups; some of them, including the Ngoni, even before then. And they were all cited as examples of ethnic solidarity among the mine workers in Kitwe and other parts of the Copperbelt in Northern Rhodesia. The Nyakyusa presence in what is now Zambia is still strong even today.

In fact, one of my mother's first cousins, Isaac, who was older than my mother emigrated from Tanganyika to Northern Rhodesia as a young man in the early 1940s. He was the son of my mother's maternal uncle, Asegelile Mwankemwa, the pastor of Kyimbila Moravian Church.

He returned to Tanzania in the 1990s to spend his last days in the land of his birth. Tragically, he had forgotten Kinyakyusa and did not know Kiswahili after so many years of absence from Tanganyika, later Tanzania, and could communicate only in English and Bemba, one of the major languages in Zambia. All his children were also born and brought up in Northern Rhodesia.

He was just one of the many people from my district who migrated to Northern Rhodesia. Some of them even settled in South Africa. Jobs in the mines in both countries was the biggest attraction, encouraging many Tanganyikans to go there in those days.

The town of Mbeya was their main departure point and the largest town in the region.

The people who had been recruited to work in the mines in South Africa boarded planes called WENELA. I remember the name very well because I heard it all the time when I was growing up in the fifties. The people would say so-and-so has gone to Wenela, meaning to work in the mines in South Africa. The term became an integral part of our vocabulary in the 1950s probably as much as it was even before then among the Nyakyusa and others.

The name WENELA was an acronym for the Witwatersrand Native Labour Association which was responsible for the recruitment of cheap labour from Africans in neighbouring countries including Tanganyika to work in the mines in South Africa during the apartheid era and before my home country won independence. They were sometimes recruited to work in other sectors of the economy but primarily in the mines.

Many of the people who were recruited in Tanganyika were flown down there unlike, for example, those from Basutoland (now Lesotho) or Bechuanaland (now Botswana) who, because of their proximity to South Africa, were transported by buses.

But many people from Tanganyika were also transported by road from Mbeya to Broken Hill in Northern Rhodesia. And from there they were taken to Mungu in Barotseland, the western province of Northern Rhodesia, and then flown to Francistown in Bechuanaland; and finally transported by railway to Johannesburg.

Working in the mines was hard labour, with little pay. But it was still something for people who virtually had nothing in terms of money. That's why they were drawn down there.

I remember my cousin Daudi worked for three years in the mines in Johannesburg. But when he came back to Tanganyika, he hardly had anything besides a wooden box he used as a "suitcase" – and which was the only popular and common "suitcase" among many Africans in those days – and may be a couple of shirts, two pairs of trousers, and a simple pair of shoes he wore when he returned home. In fact, he came straight to our village, from Johannesburg, to live with us.

My father was also his father, and the only one had, since his own biological father migrated to Northern Rhodesia in the early forties. He left behind two children, Daudi himself, and his only sister, Esther, who was also younger than Daudi. Tragically, she died only a few years after Daudi returned from South Africa.

He went to South Africa to earn some money, yet returned hardly with any. It was hard life not only for him but for most Africans who went to work in the mines and even for those who remained in the villages.

The people were not starving in Tanganyika in the fifties. There was plenty of food, especially in fertile regions such as the Southern Highlands. And my home district, Rungwe, is one of the most fertile in the entire East Africa and on the whole continent.

Almost anything, any kind of food, grows there: from bananas to sweet potatoes, groundnuts to beans, and all kinds of fruits and vegetables, besides cash crops such as coffee and tea.

But the people were poor in terms of financial resources. They had very little money. And that is why some of them went all the way to South Africa and to neighbouring Northern Rhodesia to work in the mines.

Some of them also ended up in Katanga Province, in

Congo, which is about 300 miles west from my home region of Mbeya. With all its minerals as the treasure trove of Congo, Katanga Province was another magnet and prime destination for job seekers from neighbouring countries who were seeking employment in the mines.

The Nyakyusa from my home district were some of the people who ended up there. For example, I vividly remember a photograph of a Nyakyusa family published in the *Daily News*, Dar es Salaam, in 1972 when I worked there as a news reporter.

They had lived in Congo for more than 40 years but were expelled by President Mobutu's government and forced to return to Tanzania in what seemed to be a xenophobic campaign fuelled by anti-foreign sentiments in spite of the fact that members of this family, as well as many others, had lived in Congo for decades and their children were born and brought up there.

Therefore there was quite a contrast in terms of living standards between Africans and Europeans as well as Asians; also between Africans and Arabs. Africans were the poorest.

But there was no hostility, at least not overt, on the part of Africans towards whites and members of other races in spite of such disparity in living standards; certainly not to the extent that the social order was disrupted or threatened in a way that could have led to chaos in the country.

For me as a child growing up, life was good as much as it was for many other youngsters. Our parents took care of us. I was never hungry. I always had clothes, although not shoes all the time. My father even gave me pocket money to buy sweets, soft drinks such as Fanta, Sprite and Coca Cola; cake and other delicacies as well as other things I wanted, including marbles we boys used to play a game called *goroli* (marbles) in Kiswahili. It was one of my favourite games.

# Whites I saw in the fifties:
## My perception

For the colonial rulers and other whites, life was even much better than ours in many respects. They usually had a lot more money than we did; and they had many things we didn't have.

There are also some things I remember about the kind of relationship some of us had with them as children.

There is one thing in particular that always comes to mind when I recall those days as a young boy in Rungwe District in the 1950s and how I saw whites.

I remember British men and women playing golf and tennis in Tukuyu. Many of them were friendly and used to give us tennis balls now and then when we passed through the golf course.

I was, of course, too young then to know what was going on in terms of colonial domination, or what it meant to be ruled by the British or Europeans in general. But I do remember that whenever we saw them, they seemed to be very happy and satisfied with their lives, which were made much easier by African servants in almost every European household. It was unthinkable not to have one, since they all could afford it. African servants provided cheap labour.

But I never associated their status with racism; nor did the other children. We did not know whites had privileged status and more money because they favoured themselves as whites who had the power to rule us. All we knew was that they had what we did not have.

Africans also needed income and they were glad to have jobs as house maids and as house boys or as farm workers working for Europeans. They also, the men especially, had to have a way to earn some money in order to pay taxes. Otherwise they would be in serious trouble with the colonial authorities. And like in every other country, there were those who simply did not want to pay taxes even if you told them, and could prove to them, that the money would be used to help them as well, even if not as much as whites.

Europeans were in full control and the colonial authorities had no interest in sharing power with Africans, Asians or Arabs on equal basis as equal citizens of the same country. Yet there were whites who worked with Africans and other non-whites for the benefit of all. Therefore, it would be a mistake to say that there were no whites in Tanganyika or in other parts of Africa who were interested in the well-being of Africans. But even they benefited from the colonial system whose policies were intended to benefit whites even if they were opposed to such policies.

In fact, many whites were Africans themselves as citizens of African countries. Or they considered themselves to be African because they were born and brought up in Africa even if they retained British citizenship or that of any other European country. And when some of them had to leave for different reasons, they were sad they had to go, leaving the only country or countries they knew as their home.

In spite of all that, many whites stayed in Africa.

There are still millions of white Africans, mostly in South Africa, about five million of them. And there are tens of thousands of others elsewhere in different countries on the continent. Their identity as Africans and allegiance to Africa inspired coinage of the term "white tribes" of Africa.

But there were some who were die-hard colonialists and had no intention of sharing power or identifying with non-whites – black Africans, Asians and Arabs – as fellow Africans. They were the ones who were opposed to independence in spite of the fact that there were whites who supported the nationalist aspirations of Africans in their quest for freedom or simply acknowledged the fact that independence would come some day whether they liked it or not.

## Quest for independence
## on multiracial basis

Some British settlers in Tanganyika formed the United
Tanganyika Party, known as UTP, to stem the nationalist
tide that started to sweep across the country. But in spite of
the differences they had with those who felt that
Tanganyika should be a truly multiracial society ruled on
democratic basis, there was no bitterness or hostility
between the two sides which characterised race relations
in some parts of Africa such as Kenya, Southern Rhodesia
and the citadel of white supremacy on the continent,
apartheid South Africa.

Leaders such as Julius Nyerere, Derek Bryceson who
was British, Dr. Leader Sterling also British, Amir H.
Jamal who was Indian, and their colleagues argued that the
future of Tanganyika as a nation and as a united country
could not be guaranteed without racial equality.

When some African members of TANU – Christopher
Kasanga Tumbo, John Mwakangale and others – argued
that people of other races should not be allowed to join the
party, be cabinet members, hold other high government
positions or become citizens of Tanganyika after the
country won independence, Nyerere made it clear that he
would not tolerate that and would resign as a leader; a
threat which brought others back in line to conform to the
wishes of the majority of the TANU members who were
committed to the creation of a truly non-racial society in
which no one would be denied equal rights as explained
by Nyerere and others during the campaign for
independence. As he stated in parliament in October 1961
about two months before independence:

"A day will come when we will say all people were

103

created equal except the Masai, except the Wagogo, except the Waha, except the polygamists, except the Muslims, etc...

You know what happens when people begin to get drunk with power and glorify their race, the Hitlers, that is what they do. You know where they lead the human race, the Verwoerds of South Africa, that is what they do...

I am going to repeat, and repeat very firmly, that this Government has rejected, and rejected completely any ideas that citizenship with the duties and rights of citizenship of this country, are going to based on anything except loyalty to this country." n – (Julius Nyerere, quoted by Paul Bjerk, *Building a Peaceful Nation: Julius Nyerere and the Establishment of Sovereignty in Tanzania, 1960 – 1964*, Rochester, New York: University of Rochester Press, 2015, pp. 72 – 73).

Unlike West Africa, East Africa attracted a large number of white settlers for different reasons. One of the main reasons was climate. Another one was the fact that the largest number of British colonies in Africa were in East, Central and Southern Africa; which partly explains why a significant number of British settlers ended up in that part of the continent.

The largest number of the white settlers in Tanganyika and other parts of East Africa were not colonial administrators or rulers but ordinary citizens who simply wanted to live in Africa. Others went there because they had been offered jobs. Yet others felt that there was great potential for employment and economic development in different fields in those countries.

One of the areas in which British settlers in East Africa became deeply involved was commercial farming. East Africa is endowed with an abundance of fertile land, much of it at high altitude with a cool climate, although still tropical. But it somewhat reminded the Europeans of the temperate climate back home in Europe, at temperatures they were comfortable with, and many of them came to settle in the region for this reason.

Much of East Africa is, of course, also hot, in fact very hot: along the coast, in the lowlands and other parts of the region. But it also has more arable land, at higher altitudes, than West Africa does. For example, in an area where I come from, Kyimbila, there is a large tea estate, Kyimbila Tea Estate stretching for miles. We also grow a lot of coffee in Rungwe District.

The area of Kyimbila, including my home village of Mpumbuli, also has many pine trees. We even have some on our family property. These are the kind of trees which grow in temperate zones or in a cool climate.

Kyimbila Tea Estate is one of the largest in Tanzania and in the whole of East Africa and was originally established by the Germans.

There was also a German settlement at Kyimbila, about a mile and a half from our house, when the Germans ruled Tanganyika as *Deutsch Ostafrika* (German East Africa). Also German missionaries built a large church there: Kyimbila Moravian Church.

There is also a large graveyard at Kyimbila where Germans are buried. I remember reading the headstones showing the deceased were born in the 1800s; they were born in Germany. After the Germans lost World War I, the British took over the tea estate.

## More than a dog bite:
## Reflections

When the British ran the tea estate when I was growing up, they always had a British manager who lived on the premises. I also vividly remember one tragic incident that happened in 1956 when I was in Standard One, what Americans call the First Grade.

I was six years old then, and my schoolmates and I

used to take a shortcut, walking past the manager's residence, going to Kyimbila Primary School about two miles from our house. I was the youngest in the group.

The manager was married.

Everyday we went by their house, their dogs, a German shepherd and another one that looked like a Dalmatian with patches of brown and black hair, used to bark at us.

They were not always tied – most of the time they weren't – so quite often they used to chase us before being called back by their master or by his African servant who washed clothes and cooked for the British couple and cleaned up the house and the premises.

One morning on our way to school, both dogs were loose and they started chasing us. Although I was a fast runner, in fact a sprinter even at my tender age, my friends outran me on that day. One of them was James Mwakisyala, the closest neighbour I had in Mpumbuli village. His parents' house was only about 40 or 50 yards from our house.

He was a relative by marriage. His uncle, Brown Ngwilulupi who was his mother's younger brother, was married to my mother's first cousin, Lugano, one of the daughters of Asegelile Mwankemwa. Brown was the elder brother of Weidi Ngwilulupi Mwasakafyuka I mentioned earlier.

James and I were very close when we were growing up.

Years later in the seventies, he went to Carleton University in Ottawa, Canada, around the same time I went to Wayne State University in Detroit in the United States and we used to talk on the telephone quite often.

He later became bureau chief of *The East African* in Dar es Salaam, Tanzania. *The East African*, a weekly paper, is based in Nairobi, Kenya, and is a sister publication of the *Daily Nation*, Nairobi. He died in Dar es Salaam in July 2012. He was 64.

106

Among all the pupils from Mpumbuli village and elsewhere who went to Kyimbila Primary School, he was also closest to me in age; only a year older than I was. We were also the same size in terms of physical stature. And both of us were small and slim. But he also outran me on that day which I vividly remember as if it was only yesterday because of what happened to me.

As the dogs kept on chasing us, I turned and looked back and knew I was not going to outrun them. So I dove under the tea shrubs, on my right-hand side, to hide. The German shepherd went past me and kept on chasing the other children. But the "Dalmatian" saw me where I was hiding and came right under the bush and bit me on my right knee. I still have a highly visible scar on my knee, as I write this more than sixty years later, and obviously will for the rest of my life.

I almost lost my leg, and my life, on that day and came perilously closing to meeting the same fate on other occasions when we were being chased by the same dogs. But something good came out of that. We all learned to run faster, and longer.

Quite often we took a detour on our way to school and back home to avoid the dogs, taking us longer to get home and to school simply because the white couple would not restrain or tie their dogs.

They knew we went by their house and saw us on our way to and from school everyday – and still did not tie the dogs or keep them on leashes.

After I was bitten by the dog, I went on to school where I attended class without getting any help – there was no medical assistance at our primary school, not even a First Aid kit – until I returned home in the evening when my mother put some iodine on my wound. I continued to go to school in the following days, limping. My knee was swollen for a long time.

And nothing could be done to the dog owners during those days. It was  colonial rule. We did not have the same rights whites had. And we knew our place in society as colonial subjects not as equal citizens. We were not even citizens in terms of social status. We were just there.

It was a racially divided society vertically structured not only to keep whites on top of us and members of other races, especially blacks; it was designed to keep them virtually above the law.

There is no question that justice was colour-conscious during colonial rule. That was one of the tragedies of being colonialised; our status defined by the colour of our skin.

Colour is immaterial but it carries a lot of weight.

After I was bitten by the dog, the attack was seared in my memory, leaving an indelible mark. But as a six-year-old child, I did not see it in terms of racism until years later when I was in my teens.

I have thought about that incident numerous times in my life. There is no doubt in my mind that had we been white children, the white couple would probably not have allowed their dogs to roam freely knowing they could attack us and may be even kill us. But we were black and therefore worthless.

The white couple did not care about our safety as children – or the safety of any other blacks – passing by their house even though we walked on a public road. And they knew it was a public road. They also knew we were not on their private property, trespassing.

Whenever I recall that incident, I remember my student days at Kyimbila Primary School in the late fifties which were some of the most important years of my life.

I also vividly remember that it was later in the same year when I was bitten by the dog that Princess Margaret came to Mbeya. She also visited Sao Hill, which was also in the Southern Highlands Province, and other parts of Tanganyika. That was in October 1956.

I had just reached the age of 7 in that month which also symbolically marked the beginning of the end of colonial rule in Tanganyika.

Princess Margaret's visit symbolised British imperial power over Tanganyika. But it also took place at a time when African leaders were busy waging a campaign for independence from our colonial masters.

More than ten years before I became a pupil at Kyimbila Primary School, my mother also had been a student at Kyimbila. That was in the early forties. She went to Kyimbila Girls' School while the school I attended more than ten years later was for both – boys and girls.

Her maiden name was Syabumi Mwambapa.

My father went to a different school, Tukuyu Primary School, in the town of Tukuyu, capital of Rungwe District. He enrolled there in 1936.

My parents were married at 10 AM, on Saturday, 7 August 1948.

Kyimbila was one of the leading girls' schools in Tanganyika when my mother was a student there. It was also one of the very few girls' schools in the entire country. Machame near Mount Kilimanjaro in what was then the Northern Province was one of them:

"Both Kyimbila and Machame Government girls' schools have had girls in Standard IX this year and about twelve girls are, in spite of difficulties, continuing to Standard X in 1950. Kyimbila School has become in many ways a centre of social life for the District....

At Kyimbila, the Government girls' school in the Southern Highlands Province, a successful performance was given of the *Merchant of Venice* adapted to the circumstances of a production in Swahili." – (Tanganyika Department of Education, *Tanganyika Territory, Annual Report of the Education Department 1944*, Dar es Salaam, Tanganyika, pp. 22, 18).

The headmistress of Kyimbila Girls' School was the renowned – at least in Tanganyika – British feminist educator Mary Hancock. She was the founder of the school and was also a friend of Julius Nyerere and his family since the 1950s before Nyerere became prime minister and then president of Tanganyika:

"Maureen Cowan and March Hancock have told me about Tabora Girls' School, of which both have been headmistresses. Miss Hancock is a devoted friend of the Nyerere family; while Julius and Maria Nyerere were struggling with financial difficulties, two of their children lived with her." – (Judith Listowel, *The Making of Tanganyika*, London: Chatto & Windus, 1965, p. 428).

And as William Edgett Smith stated in his book, *We Must Run While Others Walk: A Portrait of Africa's Julius Nyerere*:

"Miss Mary Hancock, a peppery little Englishwoman who had come to Tanganyika in 1940 'to help the black people, as we called them then, has recalled, 'Oh, that man, how he thinks! The civil servants in Musoma couldn't see. why I remained his friend after he declared for Uhuru. We civil servants had to be careful, you know --- we couldn't attend political meetings. I would say, 'He's my friend. If you can'r differentiate, I can. Well! You should have seen the civil servants change when it became clear that he was winning." – (William Edgett Smith, *We Must Run While Others Walk: A Portrait of Africa's Julius Nyerere*, New York: Random House, 1972, p. 84; W. E. Smith, *Nyerere of Tanzania*, Faraday Close, Worthing, UK: Littlehampton Book Services, 1973, p. 65; The New Yorker, Volume 47, Issues 27 - 35, 1971, p. 84).

Mary Hancock was the district education officer (DEO) of Musoma in the 1950s when she first met Nyerere and his family. Musoma was Nyerere's home district. – (Pat Holden, *Women Administrative Officers in*

110

*Colonial Africa 1944 – 1960,* Oxford Development Records Project, 1985, p. 194).

She later, in the late fifties, became a provincial education officer (PEO) for the Lake Province and was based in Mwanza, the provincial capital.

Mary Hancock played a major role in the education of girls in colonial Tanganyika and after independence.

She was born in 1910 in England and went to Tanganyika in 1940 to work as a volunteer teacher focusing on education for girls. She became headmistress of Tabora Girls' School in the Western Province not long after she arrived in Tanganyika.

She later taught at Kyimbila Girls' School, three miles south of the town of Tukuyu in Rungwe District in the Southern Highlands Province in the 1940s. She also founded Loleza Girls' School in the town of Mbeya in the same province during the same period.

She became a citizen of Tanzania and a senior education inspector. She was elected member of parliament in 1970 representing women. Fondly known as Mama Hancock, she died in October 1977:

"In 1970, she was nominated to Parliament by the women's organisation, Umoja wa Wanawake wa Tanzania (UWT) and elected by the National Assembly (Parliament). Mama Hancock was a much loved and respected figure. A requiem mass was celebrated by the Cardinal Archbishop in Dar es Salaam Cathedral on 28th October." – ("Obituary: Mary Hancock," *Tanzanian Affairs*, August 1977 – January 1978).

I remember my mother talking about Mary Hancock as a devoted teacher and very strict disciplinarian during her student days at Kyimbila Girls' School.

The school was in the same area where my mother's uncle – and my grand uncle – Asegelile Mwankemwa

111

served as pastor of the Moravian Church.

## Kyimbila Moravian Church

The church was first ministered by German missionaries before my grand uncle Asegelile Mwankemwa became the pastor. Although records show it was established in 1912, some reports state that it was built in 1907.

There are historical records showing that 1907 was an important year in the history of Moravians at Kyimbila. That was the year when a missionary was sent to work there. It does not necessarily mean the church also was built in the same year simply because a missionary was assigned to the area. According to a historical work, *The Moravian Church in Tanzania Southern Province: A Short History*:

"Kyimbila Station: This station is just seven kilometres from Lutengano. The distance from Kyimbila to Rungwe is about 20 kilometres....The decision was reached to send a missionary in 1907, who was to perform all pastoral duties (at Kyimbila)." – (Angetile Yesaya Musomba, *The Moravian Church in Tanzania Southern Province: A Short History*, Nairobi, Kenya: Institut Francais de recherche en Afrique (IFRA), 2005, p. 36).

Historical works also show the role the Germans played in establishing Kyimbila not only as a mission but as a plantation:

"There were some attempts to establish rubber plantations in the southern highlands region. The missionaries of the Hermhuter Mission at Kyimbila in Langenburg District successfully established a plantation of *Landolphia stolzii busse*. In 1907 they had planted four

112

hectares with 4,000 vine plants and 2,000 support trees." – (*African Economic History*, African Studies Center, Boston University, 1993, p. 126).

The church at Kyimbila was built in an area where the Germans also established a tea estate in 1904 which did not become fully operational on commercial basis until 1926.

The first Moravian Church in Rungwe District was established near Mount Rungwe in 1891. According to the history of Moravian missions:

"The Berlin Missionary Society was already at work in German East Africa; with that Society the Moravian Church did not want to compete and, therefore, to prevent friction or overlapping,...the two Societies, working side by side, will found stations north of Lake Nyassa....

In 1891 the campaign began. For twenty-three years the chief leader and superintendent of the work in German Nyassaland was Theodore Meyer, son of Henry Meyer, the pioneer in Hlubiland. One of his colleagues was a Swiss, Theophilus Richard, and these two, pushing north from Lake Nyassa, discovered, at the foot of Mt. Rungwe, a spur of the Livingstone Hills, a splendid sight for the first station. The date was August 21st.

The two men had never beheld a more gorgeous scene. On the north-west rose Mt. Rungwe; on the west lay a dense forest; on the south-east lay the teeming dales of Kondeland; and gazing southwards towards Lake Nyassa....

Rungwe seemed an ideal site for a mission-station. The land was high, the water pure, and the air clear and bracing." – (Joseph E. Hutton, "A History of Moravian Missions," Internet Archive).

The founding of the Moravian Church near Mount Rungwe was followed by the establishment of two

113

missions at Lutengano and Ipyana in 1894.

Lutengano Moravian Church is four miles southwest of Kyimbila and about three miles west of my home village of Mpumbuli. I had my second baptism at age 14 at Lutengano Moravian Church under Reverend Mwatonoka in June 1964 when I was on holidays for one month from boarding school at Mpuguso Middle School. I was in Standard Eight and in my last year at Mpuguso.

Other mission stations were established by the Moravians in Rungwe District and beyond in about fifteen years, some of them in neighbouring Mbeya District:

""In 1903 they opened a Training College for Evangelists, and in 1910 they opened a Normal School, and thus Rungwe (mission near at the foot of Rungwe Mountain) became the centre of widespread evangelistic and educational activity.

For twenty years the Brethren were engaged, not merely in building a model Christian village at Rungwe, but in attempting to christianize the whole surrounding neighbourhood. In this work they employed twenty missionaries, fifty-three native helpers, thirty-seven native evangelists, and twenty-seven volunteer assistants. And in each of the five districts mentioned, strong stations, surrounded by many preaching places, were founded.

In Kondeland, besides Rungwe, they founded Rutenganiot (1894), Ipiana (1894), Mueia (1907), and Kyimbila (1912); in Bundah, Isoko (1900); in Nyika, Mbozi (1900); in Usafwa, Utengulet (1895); and in Mawanda, Ileya (1906).

In addition, however, to these head stations, the Brethren had also thirty-five out-stations and one thousand and eighty-one preaching places. The number of converts rose to 1,955; the number of schools was 144; and the number of scholars attending them, 4,949....

The missionaries..., in some cases,...introduced entirely new forms of industry. At Rungwe there was a carpenters' shop and wood-working establishment; there sixteen large saws could be seen working at once; and the natives learned to manufacture beams, joists, boards, doors, cupboards and chairs, and other articles of domestic furniture. At Utengule there was a large boot factory. At Kyimbila there was a rubber plantation.

Some of the missionaries introduced Muscat donkeys, said to be able, unlike horses, to resist the attacks of the tsetse fly; others planted rice in the lowlands and potatoes in the hilly districts; others introduced sheep and a new and hardier breed of cattle; others cultivated coffee and tea; and others, with varying success, introduced strawberries, gooseberries, plums, peaches, apricots, oranges, lemons, grapes, and other fruits previously unknown to the natives...

Formerly the natives had few implements; now they became experts in the use of hoes, knives and axes. At the head stations the Church as such generally owned a large tract of land...and the natives preferred to live near a station...partly because they felt sure that their children would be well educated." – (Ibid.).

About a quarter of mile north of Kyimbila Moravian Church, which was in the midst of a large tea estate, was Kyimbila Primary School.

There was also a land dispute between Kyimbila Tea Estate and the congregation of Kyimbila Moravian Church which had a sad ending:

"In 1951, the African congregation of Kyimbila Mission turned to the UN, desperate for help. They felt betrayed by their own missionaries who had apparently sold the church lands to a tea estate without informing the congregation. They were told that all the buildings would have to be torn down within a year. The mission owned the land freehold, and it had the legal title to sell it." – (Ullrich Lohrmann, *Voices from Tanganyika: Great*

*Britain, the United Nations and the Decolonization of a Trust Territory, 1946 – 1961*, Munster, Germany: LIT Verlag, 2008, p. 311).

The authorities of the tea estate won the case and the church was demolished in the sixties.

The congregation found another site farther north, away from the estate, and rebuilt the church but with a different architectural design.

When the original church building went down, so did its history. People of the younger generation, and those who were born after it was torn down, have no memory of it. It was a historical building and would have served as a reminder of the area's history and the coming of German missionaries to the region had it been left intact. It is as if it had never even existed.

After the spot where it stood was taken over by the tea estate, the memory was also erased, except in the minds of those who knew where the church was during the old days when Asegelile Mwankemwa became the first African pastor and continued to serve the congregation in the following years.

The area of Kyimbila became a major centre of activities in the area because of three institutions which were inextricably linked by history and geography: Kyimbila Tea Estate established in 1904; Kyimbila Moravian Church built in 1912; and Kyimbila Primary School founded in the early 1940s – by the colonial government – under the stewardship of Mary Hancock.

One of my teachers at Kyimbila Primary School was Eslie Mwakyambiki. His first name was Africanised and became Esili in the Nyakyusa language spoken by the people of Rungwe District.

Years later, Esili Mwakyambiki, as he was locally known, was elected member of parliament representing Rungwe District. He was also appointed by President Nyerere to serve in the cabinet as deputy minister of defence and national service.

National service was mandatory for all those who had completed secondary school, high school and college or university studies. I underwent training, which included basic military training, at Ruvu National Service camp when it was headed by my former primary school teacher Eslie Mwakyambiki before he became a member of parliament and deputy minister of defence and national service.

I also vividly remember Eslie Mwakyambiki was my teacher at Kyimbila Primary School when I was bitten by the dog, an incident I will never forget; the scar on my right knee being a constant reminder of what happened to me on that day.

## My father:
## victim of racism

Another incident I vividly remember had to do with my father when he worked as an assistant manager at a Shell BP station in the town of Tukuyu about four miles north of our home in Mpumbuli village. He often took lunch to work prepared by my mother, mostly *chapati*.

One day he was told by the British manager of the petrol station that he could not put his lunch on the table used by the manager or eat in the office he shared with him; it was *chapati* my mother had cooked for him on that day. I remember that very well.

My father was very bitter about the incident and told us what happened when he came back home that evening. That was in 1958 or 1959.

Having secondary school education, my father was one of the few people in the area who knew English. And that was one of the reasons he was hired as the assistant manager at the petrol station.

In fact, secondary school education in those days and

even during the first years of independence was considered to be high education not only in Tanganyika but in other African countries as well.

## Racial incidents and injustices

The dog incident, when I was bitten by the Dalmatian-looking dog, and what my father went through at the hands of the white manager at the petrol station in the town of Tukuyu, were very important when looked at in the context of the times. We were not equal to whites in our own country. They were our rulers and we were at their mercy.

Yet there was no bitterness towards them amongst us as children. Even when I became a teenager and recalled those days, I still did not hate whites. But I was offended by the racial injustices we suffered, yet without having feelings of hatred towards white people.

Change was also on the way. The 1950s were also a defining decade in terms of race relations even in my case as a child. I spent my first twelve years under British colonial rule in a decade when agitation for independence was at its peak, finally leading to independence for Tanganyika, the first country in East Africa to emerge from colonial rule.

But in spite of its reputation as a peaceful country, Tanganyika was not an ideal example of a racially harmonious society during colonial rule. It was structured along racial lines and upheld racial injustices as a racially stratified society. I lived under this system of racial segregation and discrimination when I was growing up in Tanganyika in the fifties; injustices which continued even after independence perpetrated by diehard racists, although fewer than before.

During colonial rule, we were subjected to indignities of colour bar similar to those under apartheid in South

Africa, humiliated and insulted in our own country. There were signs designating racial categories. Lavatories were labelled "Europeans," "Asians" and "Africans." Some hotels and bars were labelled "Europeans." There were separate schools for Europeans, Asians and Africans.

Our facilities, as blacks, were the worst.

African leaders, including including Julius Nyerere campaigning for independence, were subjected to the same racial indignities and humiliation which continued even after the end of colonial rule, especially during the early years, but drew a swift response from the new government which was predominantly black and multi-racial. As I stated in my book *Nyerere and Africa: End of an Era*:

"Mwalimu himself had experienced racial discrimination, what we in East Africa – and elsewhere including southern Africa – also call colour bar. As Colin Legum states in a book he edited with Tanzanian professor, Geoffrey Mmari, *Mwalimu: The Influence of Nyerere*:

'I was privileged to meet Nyerere while he was still a young teacher in short trousers at the very beginning of his political career, and to engage in private conversations with him since the early 1950s.

My very first encounter in 1953 taught me something about his calm authority in the face of racism in colonial Tanganyika. I had arranged a meeting with four leaders of the nascent nationalist movement at the Old Africa Hotel in Dar es Salaam. We sat at a table on the pavement and ordered five beers, but before we could lift our glasses an African waiter rushed up and whipped away all the glasses except mine.

I rose to protest to the white manager, but Nyerere restrained me. 'I am glad it happened,' he said, 'now you can go and tell your friend Sir Edward Twining [the governor at the time] how things are in this country.'

His manner was light and amusing, with no hint of anger.'

Simple, yet profound. For, beneath the surface lay a steely character with a deep passion for justice across the colour line and an uncompromising commitment to the egalitarian ideals he espoused and implemented throughout his political career, favouring none.

Years later his son, Andrew Nyerere, told me about an incident that also took place in the capital Dar es Salaam shortly after Tanganyika won independence in 1961 near the school he and I attended and where we also stayed from 1969 – 1970. Like the incident earlier when Julius Nyerere was humiliated at the Old Africa Hotel back in 1953, this one also involved race. As Andrew stated in a letter to me in 2002 when I was writing this book:

'As you remember, Sheikh Amri Abeid was the first mayor of Dar es Salaam. Soon after independence, the mayor went to Palm Beach Hotel (near our high school, Tambaza, on United Nations Road in Upanga). There was a sign at the hotel which clearly stated: 'No Africans and dogs allowed inside.' He was blocked from entering the hotel, and said in protest, 'But I am the Mayor.' Still he was told, 'You will not get in.' Shortly thereafter, the owner of the hotel was given 48 hours to leave the country. When the nationalization exercise began, that hotel was the first to be nationalized.'

Such insults were the last thing that could be tolerated in newly independent Tanganyika. And President Nyerere, probably more than any other African leader, would not have tolerated, and did not tolerate, seeing even the humblest of peasants being insulted and humiliated by anyone including fellow countrymen." – (Godfrey Mwakikagile, *Nyerere and Africa: End of an Era*, New Africa Press, 2010, pp. 501 – 502. See also Andrew

Nyerere in his letter to the author, 2002, in *Nyerere and Africa: End of an Era*; also in Godfrey Mwakikagile, *Tanzania under Mwalimu Nyerere: Reflections on an African Statesman*, p. 18; G. Mwakikagile, *Post-colonial Africa: A General Survey*, p. 264; G. Mwakikagile, *My Life as an African: Autobiographical Writings*, p. 92).

There was also residential segregation in urban areas reminiscent of apartheid South Africa and the United States during and even after the era of segregation. Members of different races lived in their own areas. Dar es Salaam was a typical example. As Trevor Grundy, a British journalist who worked in Tanzania at the same newspaper where I also worked as a news reporter during the same period, stated in his review of Professor Thomas Molony's book, *Nyerere: The Early Years*:

"The British turned Tanganyika into an undeclared apartheid state that was socially divided between divided Africans, Europeans and Asians....It was British-style apartheid – their secret was never to give racial segregation a name."

The years I spent under segregation when I was growing up in different parts of Tanganyika shaped my thinking and perspective on race relations and on the impact of colonial rule on the colonised when I became a writer of non-fiction books about colonial and post-colonial Africa.

There was also racial discrimination in employment during colonial rule when I was growing up in the fifties. Europeans, Asians and members of other races earned more money than Africans did even if they had the same skills and level of education. My father was a victim of such discrimination when he worked for the colonial government.

The struggle for independence in Tanganyika in the

1950s, my formative years, was partly fuelled by such racial injustices which, years later, became the focus of some of my writings.

The colonial rulers and many white settlers had total disregard for the wellbeing of Africans as I myself experienced when I was growing up in colonial Tanganyika and almost lost my life when I was attacked by a large dog owned by a white couple who did not care about the safety of African children, or any other blacks, passing by their house even though we walked on a public road.

Such disregard for the wellbeing of Africans was a continental phenomenon even if the parallels were not exact; it was the same experience, and humiliation, nonetheless, be it in Tanganyika, Kenya, Guinea or Mali. As I stated in my book *Africa and The West*:

"In all the African colonies, exploitation went hand in hand with degradation and brutality. In the Congo under the Belgian King Leopold II, Belgians chopped off the hands and arms of Africans who did not collect enough rubber from the forest. In Tanganyika, when it was German East Africa, Germans introduced forced labor and corporal punishment, virtually enslaving Africans, a practice which triggered the Maji Maji war of resistance from 1905 – 07 and covered almost half of the country. The uprising almost ended German rule which was saved only after reinforcements were rushed from Germany.

The French in West Africa also introduced forced labor. Some of the leaders of independent Africa toiled in those labor camps. Madeira Keita, a native of Mali who was active in the politics of Guinea before it won independence in 1958 and collaborated closely with Sekou Toure in founding the Democratic Party of Guinea, was one of them. In April 1959, he became Interior Minister of Mali, and in August 1960, he also became Minister of National Defense, holding two ministerial posts under

President Modibo Keita. He related his experience as a conscripted laborer:

'Before 1945, there was a colonial regime with government by decree, the regime of the *indignat*. The *indignat* form of government permitted the colonial administration to put Africans in prison without any trial. Sometimes you were put in prison for two weeks because you did not greet the administrator or the commander. You were happy enough if they did not throw stones at you or send you to a work camp, because there was also forced labor at that time. In 1947, I met French journalists who were very surprised to learn that forced labor was nonvoluntary and not paid for. Transportation was not even covered; nor were food and lodging. The only thing that was covered was work.'

The conquest of Africa inexorably led to such brutality because its purpose was exploitation which has no room for compassion. It was an invasion we could very well have done without. The baneful foreign influence Africa is still subjected to is a result of that invasion. And we are now inextricably linked with our former conquerors, for better or for worse, in an international system which accentuates inequalities and from which no part of humanity can extricate itself.

But the materialism of the West, which has found its way into Africa with devastating impact, must be counterbalanced with the spirituality and sense of sharing of the African which animates his culture, indeed his very being." – Godfrey Mwakikagile, *Africa and The West*, Huntington, New York: Nova Science Publishers, Inc., 2000, pp. 14 – 15; Madeira Keita, "Le Parti Unique en Afrique," in *Presence Africaine*, No. 30, February – March 1960; and Madeira Keita, "The Single Party in Africa," in Paul E. Sigmund, ed., *The Ideologies of the Developing Nations*, New York: Praeger, 1963, p. 170. On the African uprising and war of resistance against German colonial rule in Tanganyika, see, among other works, G. C. K. Gwassa and John Iliffe, eds., *Records of the Maji-Maji Rising*, Dar es Salaam: Tanzania Publishing House, 1968).

I also stated in the same book:

"The argument that we blacks are genetically inferior to members of other races is nothing new. It is a stereotype rooted in Western intellectual tradition and has even been given "credibility" by some of the most eminent thinkers of the Western world including Immanuel Kant, Georg Hegel, David Hume, and Baron de Montesquieu. Some of them did not even consider blacks to be full human beings. As Montesquieu stated in *The Spirit of the Laws*:

'These creatures are all over black, and with such a flat nose, that they can scarcely be pitied. It is hardly to be believed that God, who is a wise Being, should place a soul, especially a good soul, in such a black, ugly body. The Negroes prefer a glass necklace to that gold which polite nations so highly value: can there be a greater proof of their wanting common sense? It is impossible for us to suppose these creatures to be men.'

The other philosophers were no less racist. According to Kant:

'The Negroes of Africa have received from nature no intelligence that rises above the foolish. The difference between the two races (black and white) is thus a substantial one: it appears to be just as great in respect of the faculties of the mind as in color.'

Hume:

'I am apt to suspect the Negroes...to be naturally

inferior to the whites. There never was any civilized nation of any other complexion than white, nor even any individual eminent in action or speculation. No ingenious manufactures among them, no arts, no sciences...Such a uniform and constant difference could not happen, in so many countries and ages, if nature had not made an original distinction betwixt these breeds of men.'

And according to Hegel:

'Africa...is no historical part of the world; it has no movement or development to exhibit.'

It is a sentiment echoed more than 100 years later in contemporary times by many people including British historian Arnold Toynbee who died in 1975. As he put it:

'The black races alone have not contributed positively to any civilization.'

And in the words of that great humanitarian Dr. Albert Schweitzer:

'The Negro is a child, and with children nothing can be done without the use of authority. We must, therefore, so arrange the circumstances of daily life that my natural authority can find expression. With regard to the Negroes, then, I have coined the formula: 'I am your brother, it is true, but your elder brother"...

The conquest of Africa led not only to oppression and exploitation, but also to denigration of her culture and indigenous institutions. Africans, at least a vary large number of them, were brainwashed into believing that they had no history they could be proud of; that all their customs and traditions were bad, and that even their languages were bad....

When Africa was conquered by the imperial powers, she was also conquered by ideas...as a very effective weapon for conquering other people by conquering their minds....

There is no other continent which is endowed with so much in terms of natural resources. But there is also no other continent where it has been so easy for foreigners to take what does not belong to them....

Because of the pervasive nature of Western influence, its negative impact has reached all parts of the world, including Africa where the devastation wrought is difficult to contain because of the underdeveloped nature of our economies, and also because of our inability to resist such penetration. The sheer scope of such influence, as well as its negative attraction especially among the youth who are mesmerized by the glitter of the West, is mind-boggling and far beyond our capacity to resist it. That is especially the case in the cities which continue to attract millions of people in search of better – read, Western – life. It is a burden Africa cannot bear.

The West may have harnessed the forces of nature and pushed the frontiers of knowledge in many areas, from which Africa has indeed benefited as has the rest of the world. But Africa's contribution – material and spiritual as well as intellectual – to the growth of Western civilization has never been fully acknowledged. Nor has the destruction of African civilization by the West through imperial conquest. That is undoubtedly one of the saddest chapters in the history of relations between Africa and the West. As Immanuel Kant, although a racist, conceded in one of his works *Eternal Peace and Other Essays*:

'If we compare the barbarian instances of inhospitality...with the inhuman behavior of the civilized, and especially the commercial, states of our continent, the injustice practiced by them even in their first contact with foreign lands and peoples fills us with horror; the mere visiting of such peoples being regarded by them as equivalent to a conquest...The Negro lands,...The Cape of Good Hope, etc., on being discovered, were treated as countries that belonged to nobody; for the aboriginal inhabitants were reckoned as nothing...And all this has been done by nations who make a great ado about their piety, and who, while drinking up iniquity like water, would have themselves regarded as the very elect of orthodox faith.'

Africa has yet to recover from the multiple wounds inflicted on her by this Western invasion. But there is a glimmer of hope. And that is traditional Africa. In spite of all the devastating blows our continent has sustained from the West, traditional Africa continues to be the continent's spiritual anchor and bedrock of our values without which we are no more than a dilapidated house shifting on quick sand. It is to traditional society that we must turn to save Africa from the West, and also save ourselves – from ourselves." – (G. Mwakikagile, *Africa and The West*, ibid., pp. vii – ix, 208, 218).

East Africans who were born and brought up during colonial rule had more direct experience with racism than West Africans did. That was because of the larger white population in East Africa. The region had significant settler communities, especially in Kenya, although smaller and fewer in Tanganyika.

Many Africans had bitter experience with the colonial rulers and the white settlers. The racial injustices perpetrated against them spanned the spectrum, covering all areas of life. Many whites even expressed doubts about the intelligence – and even common sense – of black people. As I stated in *Africa and The West*:

"Colonialism, as a system of oppression and exploitation, not only continued to plunder Africa but sought to instill in the minds of Africans feelings of inferiority to justify such domination...This is just one example – what Colonel Ewart Grogan, the doyen of the white settlers in colonial Kenya and leader of the Kenya British Empire Party, said about Africans attending the renowned Makerere University College in Uganda:

'Just teaching a lot of stupid monkeys to dress up like Europeans. Won't do any good. Just cause a lot of discontent. They can never be like us, so better for them not to try.'

Another (Kenyan) settler in the 'Dark Continent' had this:

'I've actually got a farm hand who wears a tie – but the stupid bastard doesn't realize you don't wear a tie without a shirt!'

The implication is obvious. It is a sweeping indictment against all "native Africans" as a bunch of idiots.

Yet another one, Sir Godfrey Huggins, Prime Minister of Southern Rhodesia, acclaimed as a British liberal, shot point-blank at a press conference in London:

"It is time for the people in England to realize that the white man in Africa is not prepared and never will be prepared to accept the African as an equal, either socially or politically. Is there something in their chromosomes which makes them more backward and different from peoples living in the East and West?" – (Godfrey Mwakikagile, ibid., pp. 9 - 10, 69; Colin M. Turnbull, *The Lonely African*, New York: Simon and Schuster, 1962, pp. 89, 21, 90, 97).

The total disregard for the rights and wellbeing of Africans – utter contempt for an entire people – was earlier demonstrated by the arrogance of the imperial powers when they met at the Berlin Conference in 1885. The conference led to the partition of Africa and was one of the most tragic events in the history of imperial conquest of non-Europeans round the globe.

Africans were not consulted about their fate. They were not even represented at the conference. Yet it was their fate, and the fate of their continent, that was being discussed and determined by Europeans who decided to divide Africa among themselves as if Africans did not even exist.

This kind of arrogance and utter contempt for Africans was also demonstrated and expressed in its crudest form in many ways including verbal abuse, torture and even inflicting humiliating punishment on full-grown black men in front of their wives and children as well as other people, some of whom even looked up to them as role models in society. They were subjected to corporal punishment at the hands of the white settlers some of whom were young enough to be their sons and even grandsons.

Shooting blacks was equated with shooting wild animals, as some white settlers in Kenya conceded, including those who had moved there from apartheid South Africa. It was equivalent to game hunting for sport but was also, symbolically, a way of getting rid of the black scourge, cleansing the land of members of the lesser breed, black natives, if they could.

What is known as land grab nowadays – taking or grabbing the land away from African peasants and giving it to foreign investors and corporations in this era of globalisation – was practised before, during colonial rule, in the interest of white settlers.

Such arbitrary seizure of land, depriving Africans of their only means of livelihood which was also equivalent to life insurance, was simply seen as a white man's right exercised at will in what had become the white man's possession under the tropical sun.

129

In my book *Nyerere and Africa: End of an Era*, I have given one example of this kind of imperial arrogance demonstrated by what happened to Tom Mboya who, together with Oginga Odinga, was one of the leaders of the Kenyan delegation to the constitutional talks in London in 1960 – Jomo Kenyatta was still in prison – when Kenya was approaching independence and the country had to have a new constitution to validate its sovereign status.

One of the luminaries of the African independence movement who also became Kenyatta's heir apparent after Kenya emerged from colonial rule, Mboya stated in his book *Freedom and After* that he was walking on a street in London one day during the constitutional talks when he was stopped by an old English lady who asked him:

"From which one of our possessions do you come from?"

It was the height of imperial arrogance.

Many white settlers in Africa felt the same way; so did a significant number of their fellow countrymen back home in Europe. They really believed they owned our countries and we owned nothing or only what they allowed us to have. Some of them may even have believed they owned us because we were at their mercy.

This kind of arrogance and domination was based on some mysterious logic that, for some inexplicable reason, they were superior to us as human beings.

As I stated earlier, the British settlers in East Africa, especially in Kenya, even wanted to form a giant federation comprising the British-ruled territories in the region stretching from Kenya to Southern Rhodesia. It would have been turned into a bastion of white supremacy like apartheid South Africa and as Southern Rhodesia attempted to do.

The white settlers in Kenya even declared the colony to be a "white man's country" as if black people did not even exist there. It was a sentiment articulated by many white settlers. Ewart Grogan, the most outspoken leader of the white settlers in Kenya, was known for such imperial arrogance and raw-naked racism. As I stated in my book *Africa and The West*:

"A man with a flair for controversy and an outspoken racist, Grogan described himself as 'the baddest and boldest of a bold bad gang.' He also gained notoriety for publicly flogging Africans in Nairobi. The settlers from South Africa also came 'with the racial prejudices of that country. Frederick Jackson, Sir Charles Eliot's Deputy Commissioner, told the Foreign Office that the Protectorate was becoming a country of 'nigger-' and game-shooters....

Colonel Ewart Grogan, a leader of the white settlers, bluntly stated: 'We Europeans have to go on ruling this country and rule it with iron discipline...If the whole of the Kikuyu land unit is reverted to the Crown, then every Kikuyu would know that our little queen was a great Bwana.'" – (G. Mwakikagile, ibid., pp. 97, 113; E. S. Grogan, in the *East African Standard*, Nairobi, Kenya, 12 November 1910; Elspeth Huxley, *White Man's Country*, Vol. I, London and New York: Macmillan, 1935, pp. 222 – 223, 261 – 262; George Padmore, *Pan-Africanism or Communism?: The Coming Struggle for Africa*, London: Denis Dobson, 1956, pp. 255, 256).

The humanity of Africans and their lives meant absolutely nothing to many whites, even if not all. Such callousness was demonstrated by the injustices and indignities black people suffered under colonial rule whose legitimacy was derived from the "inferiority" of Africans; hence the right of Europeans to rule them which some whites even claimed had divine mandate. Therefore, the "inferiority" of black people was "permanent."

They would never catch up with or be equal to their

masters who were "superior" to them. Dominating and humiliating them was simply an accepted way of life.

Even African children sometimes witnessed their parents and other adults being insulted and humiliated by their colonial masters. It happened in Kenya; it also happened in my home country, Tanganyika, even when the countries were on the verge of independence; the fifties, when I was growing up, being one of the most critical periods in the history of colonial rule in Africa.

Those of us who grew up the fifties as school children also suffered injustices because of racial inequalities. The problem was compounded by inequities in the provision of funds and facilities for education. Only meagre resources were allocated to education for African children.

That was in sharp contrast with the amount of money spent on schools for European and Asian children. The school I attended was no exception in terms of resource allocation. It was also the dawn of a new era in the history of Tanganyika, the largest colonial territory in East Africa.

The fifties which was a decade that preceded independence was a transitional period. It symbolised the identity and partly shaped the thinking of those who grew up during that period as a product of both eras, colonial and post-colonial. They also served as a bridge between the two.

As I stated earlier, it was in the same year I was bitten by the white couple's dog on my way to Kyimbila Primary School that Princess Margaret visited Mbeya and Sao Hill in my home region, the Southern Highlands Province, as well as other parts of the country, in October 1956; a visit that symbolised British imperial rule over Tanganyika but also at a time when the nationalist movement was gaining momentum in the struggle for independence.

The party that led the country to independence, Tanganyika African National Union (TANU), which was actually a national movement and not just a political party, had been formed just two years before, in July 1954, and within months succeeded in mobilising massive support in all parts of the country in its quest to end colonial rule. Independence was inevitable. It was only a matter of when.

Colonial rulers and the white settlers in Tanganyika basked in imperial glory when Princess Margaret visited the country. It was imperial pride at its best. Little did they – and probably even she – know that independence for Tanganyika was only five years away.

The freedom torch had been lit and it was shining in all parts of the continent. A few months after Princess Margaret visited Tanganyika, the Gold Coast became the first black African country to emerge from colonial rule as the new nation of Ghana in March 1957. It blazed the trail for the African independence movement, while Tanganyika did so in East Africa four years later.

I have written about the fifties – the political climate, race relations, incidents of racial injustice and other subjects – to show how life was in colonial Tanganyika during that period from the perspective of colonial subjects who hardly had any rights in their own country ruled and dominated by whites. Africans were lowest in the racial hierarchy, with Asians and Arabs ranked next to whites. Race was the prime determinant.

It has also been the nature imperialism to place Africans deliberately in the sub-human category not only in terms of intellect but also in every other conceivable way; a characterisation that had a profound impact on the lives of many Africans even in terms of self-esteem.

There were Africans who really believed we were inferior to whites, socially and intellectually and may be even genetically, and that we deserved to be brought up under colonial tutelage.

That mentality persists even today among some of them, including those of the younger generation, because of our history as a conquered people which is used to justify our "inferior" status.

That was also the attitude of some white settlers even in Tanganyika, placing Africans in the same category with dogs or other animals, especially monkeys, when I was growing up in the fifties.

That was the case even after independence in the early sixties.

The case of a white manager of a hotel in Dar es Salaam is a typical example when he put up a sign at the entrance of his hotel clearly stating, "No Africans and dogs allowed inside," and even refused to let in the mayor of the nation's capital simply because the mayor was black.

Even members of other races, not just whites, have been equally condescending and outright racist towards blacks.

Many people of Asian origin – mostly Indian and Pakistani – and Arabs in Tanganyika, later Tanzania, also harboured racist views about black people. But they did not express them openly in a country where they were far outnumbered by blacks and whose destiny lay in the hands of the black majority.

## My early political awakening

My earliest political awakening can be attributed to my great interest in reading newspapers. That was in the late 1950s.

When I was growing up in Rungwe District, my father listened to BBC in English and Kiswahili everyday. And he had profound influence on me.

I also started listening to BBC at a very young age when I was under ten years old. I did not know English then; so I listened to the Swahili Service on BBC and on TBC (Tanganyika Broadcasting Corporation) broadcast from Dar es Salaam more than 500 miles away from where we lived in Rungwe District.

And to make sure that I was paying attention, my father would sometimes walk away from the radio and then ask me later to give him a summary of the news. I already had a good memory and this exercise only helped improve it further.

I also remember the kind of shortwave radio we had. It was Philips with an external antennae stretched out and attached to a dry bamboo tree outside our house.

All this reminds of the simpler life many people lived in Tanganyika in the fifties. It had its inconveniences, and quite a few of them for Africans because of poverty, but still exciting.

The papers I read were published in Kiswahili. They were Kenyan and Tanganyikan newspapers. The stories they published included coverage of the Mau Mau uprising in Kenya. I remember seeing pictures of the Mau Mau freedom fighters, with their dreadlocks, in the papers.

I also wanted to read newspapers published in English but could not because I did not know the language.

Although I could not read English newspapers during that time, the Swahili papers I read – *Mwafrika* (The African), *Mambo Leo* (Current Events) and others – provided ample coverage of what was going on in Tanganyika and Kenya.

Events covered included political rallies during the campaign for independence. I even attended some of the rallies, including one held in the town of Tukuyu addressed by Julius Nyerere. That was in 1958 or 1959, when I was in Standard Three or Standard Four at Kyimbila Primary School, shortly before he led our country to independence.

Even at that age, we knew the names of some of the African leaders who led their countries in the struggle for independence. We were taught that in primary school as much as we learned about all the African countries in our geography class.

My interest in current affairs, which during that period were saturated with political news as our country approached independence, was fuelled by my father who followed political events very closely.

He not only had a habit of asking me to listen to BBC Swahili Service and TBC (Tanganyika Broadcasting Corporation) and give him a summary of the news to make sure I was paying attention; his primary motive was to instil positive values in me and teach me to pay attention not only to news broadcasts but to other important things in life including what I was being taught in school.

I lived with my parents during that time. That was before I went to boarding school.

My mother also kept up with the news. She also taught Sunday school. And during a nationwide campaign launched by the government to fight illiteracy in the early part of independence, she also – for some time – taught some people in our village how to read and write. It was volunteer work. She was not – nor were the other volunteers – paid anything.

I therefore grew up in a politically conscious family and knew some things about politics – especially the campaign for independence – at an early age.

My parents and I knew some of the leading figures in the independence struggle who came from the Southern Highlands Province and other parts of Tanganyika.

They included Austin Shaba who did not come from the Southern Highlands Province but was my father's classmate at a medical training centre at the national hospital in Dar es Salaam – years later transformed into a medical school – and became a cabinet member in the first independence cabinet serving as minister of local government. Shaba was also a member of parliament for Mtwara and later served as minister of health and housing and as deputy speaker of parliament.

My father was trained as a medical assistant in the mid-1940s. The hospital where he underwent training was known as Sewa Haji. It was later renamed Princess Margaret Hospital. It has always been the country's only national hospital and was renamed Muhimbili National Hospital after independence.

The medical training centre he attended – it was an integral part of the hospital – was transformed into the country's first medical school in 1963, less than two years after the country won independence in December 1961.

Although Austin Shaba was brought up in Tanganyika, he lost his "citizenship" and cabinet post as well as other government positions because the government found out that his parents, who moved to Tanganyika from Nyasaland, were born in Nyasaland and were not Tanganyikan citizens. Therefore he himself was not a citizen and lost something he really never had, although it had been assumed through the years that he was a citizen; he was not, according to the law. He and his parents came form Mzimba, Nyasaland. He returned to his home country and later died there.

There was also a time when Austin Shaba and my father worked together when they were medical assistants. Years later, when I became a news reporter, I once interviewed Shaba on the telephone when he was chairman of the Tanganyika Sisal Marketing Board based in the coastal town of Tanga, then the second-largest after Dar es Salaam which during that time was the only city in the country. He asked me:

"Are you Elijah Mwakikagile's son? I know your parents and knew you when you were a child."

When I was growing up, my parents told me about some of the people they knew, especially my father's classmates, schoolmates and co-workers who were involved in the nationalist movement during the struggle for independence. I knew some of them.

They came from Rungwe District. They included

137

Jeremiah Kasambala, John Mwakangale, and William Mwambenja who was the chairman of the Tanganyika African National Union (TANU) in Rungwe District, the party that led the struggle for independence. He was chairman until 1969.

Like Kasambala and Mwakangale, Mwambenja also knew my father very well.

Voluble, highly energetic and relentless as a campaigner, Mwambenja infused TANU with vigour and vitality and made it one of the most effective party branches in the whole country.

There were other people in Rungwe District, less well-known but no less important in the independence struggle, whom my parents, especially my father, knew.

My father went to Malangali Secondary School in Iringa District in the Southern Highlands Province. It was one of the best schools in colonial Tanganyika and even after independence.

He was head prefect at Malangali, responsible for disciplining other students and overseeing other prefects who, like him, were also students and were chosen by the headmaster and other teachers to be in charge of other students. The toughest and most disciplined ones were chosen for the job.

He excelled in school and was supposed to go to Tabora Government School (founded in 1924, coincidentally in the same year he was born) for further education but couldn't because of family obligations. Instead, he went to what is now Muhimbili National Hospital in Dar es Salaam for medical training for three years and qualified as a medical assistant.

Also known as Tabora Boys, Tabora Government School was, like Malangali, a highly-rated academic institution in colonial Tanganyika. Professor Julian Huxley described it as "the Eton of Africa," patterned after the British school.

My father's classmates at Malangali Secondary School

included Jeremiah Kasambala who, as the leader of one of the largest farmers' unions – Rungwe Cooperative Union – in the country which played a major role in the struggle for independence, became a cabinet member in the early years of independence under Prime Minister (later President) Julius Nyerere and represented Rungwe District in parliament; and John Mwakangale who in the 1950s became a political activist and one of the leaders of the independence movement in Tanganyika led by Nyerere. Mwakangale and my father knew each other since childhood when they were classmates in primary school.

Mwakangale also served in the cabinet as minister of labour under Nyerere in the early 1960s before Kasambala joined the cabinet during the same period and became minister of trade and cooperatives and later minister of industries, minerals and energy.

John Mwakangale was also described as the most "anti-white" or "anti-British" member of the government before and after independence. He was also very defensive of the interests of African workers.

Humphrey Taylor, a British colonial administrator who was a District Officer (D.O.) in Tanganyika from 1959 to 1962, wrote the following about John Mwakangale when Mwakangale was minister of labour under Prime Minister Nyerere:

"Soon after Tanganyika became independent, and near the end of my time as a District Officer in Njombe, I received a call from the British manager of the Commonwealth Development Corporation's wattle plantation and factory a few miles from the District Office. The factory took the bark that was stripped from the wattle trees and used it to make tannin.

The workers there were on strike for higher pay, in part because they expected to earn more now that the country was no longer a British colony.

The manager called me because he was afraid that a

large crowd of strikers near the factory might attack and damage it. He asked for police protection.

I arrived a little while later with ten or fifteen African policemen. I cannot remember if they were armed with anything other than truncheons. It is possible that they also brought rifles.

Anyway, everything passed off peacefully without a serious incident. The police and I stood for a couple of hours between the strikers and the factory. The strikers then dispersed and went away. There was no violence of any kind.

However the local union leader sent a fiery telegram to the Minister of Labour, John Mwakangale in Dar es Salaam, in which he wrote that there was a dangerous crisis with provocative action by the British colonial District Officer and the police and that there was a 'danger of the spilling of blood.'

Mwakangale was believed to be the most aggressively anti-white or anti- British member of the government. He telegrammed back to say he was coming to Njombe the next day and he sent us a very sharp message criticizing my action and asking to meet with us as soon as he arrived.

At the start of the meeting he was very aggressive and hostile, but as he listened to the manager, the police and to me, he understood what had, and had not, happened. At the end of the meeting we went off and had some beers together.

A little while later, I was in Dar es Salaam to catch the plane on my way home at the end of my brief colonial career. As I was walking on a street there I saw a small group of African cabinet ministers, including Mwakangale, walking towards me on the other side of the street.

When he saw me, he dashed across the road, welcomed me enthusiastically, took me by the hand, and brought me across to meet his cabinet colleagues. He told me how

sorry he was to hear that I was leaving Tanganyika." –
(Humphrey Taylor, "Danger of Spilling Blood,"
BritishEmpire, www.britishempire.co.uk/article/
dangerofspillingblood.htm).

Professor John Iliffe in his book, *A Modern History of Tanganyika*, described John Mwakangale as a "vehement nationalist," an assessment underscored by some of the remarks Mwakangale himself made in parliament where he was very outspoken. According to Professor Paul Bjerk in his book, *Building a Peaceful Nation: Julius Nyerere and the Establishment of Sovereignty in Tanzania, 1960 – 1964*:

"In October 1961, racialist sentiments sprang up even among his (Nyerere's) own party members when a proposal was brought forward to delay citizenship for non-Africans for five years after independence. Christopher (Kasanga) Tumbo urged for a distinction between 'native' and 'immigrant races.'

A TANU member from Mbeya, J. B. Mwakangale, went so far as to call for the resignation of non-African ministers after independence. 'We have no proof of their loyalty. They are bluffing and cheating us,' Mwakangale alleged.

In response, Nyerere threatened that he and his ministers would resign if the assembly did not support TANU's policy. Nyerere denounced the hypocrisy of a policy favoring Africans in a country that was just about to emerge from a racially prejudiced colonial state.

Visibly angry, he argued that once racial bias was introduced to Tanganyikan politics its logic would take a life of its own, leading to widespread ethnic animosity:

'A day will come when we will say all people were created equal except the Masai, except the Wagogo, except the Waha, except the polygamists, except the Muslims,

141

etc...

You know what happens when people begin to get drunk with power and glorify their race, the Hitlers, that is what they do. You know where they lead the human race, the Verwoerds of South Africa, that is what they do...

I am going to repeat, and repeat very firmly, that this Government has rejected, and rejected completely, any ideas that citizenship with the duties and rights of citizenship of this country are going to based on anything except loyalty to this country.'" – (Paul Bjerk, *Building a Peaceful Nation: Julius Nyerere and the Establishment of Sovereignty in Tanzania, 1960 – 1964*, Rochester, New York: University of Rochester Press, 2015, pp. 72 – 73).

John Mwakangale also strongly opposed the recruitment of American Peace Corps to work in Tanganyika, contending that they were in the country to cause trouble, destabilise and topple the government:

"Wherever they are we always hear of trouble, you hear of people trying to overthrow the government. These people are not here for peace, they are here for trouble. We do not want any more Peace Corps."

He was quoted in a news report, "M.P. Attacks American Peace Corps," which was the main story on the front page of the Tanganyika *Standard* published on 12 June 1964. The paper was renamed *Daily News* in 1972.

John Mwakangale was also the first leader of Tanganyika whom Nelson Mandela met in January 1962 when Mandela secretly left South Africa to seek assistance from other African countries in the struggle against apartheid in his home country.

Tanganyika was the first country in the region to win independence. It was also the first independent African country Mandela visited after he left South Africa for the first time on 11 January 1962. And in May 1963,

Tanganyika was chosen by other African leaders – heads of state and prime ministers – to be the headquarters of all the African liberation movements when they met in Addis Ababa, Ethiopia, to form the Organisation of African Unity (OAU).

Throughout the organisation's history, among all the OAU committees which collectively constituted the organisation, the OAU Liberation Committee based in Dar es Salaam, Tanzania, was the most effective and most successful. It was under the stewardship of President Nyerere who also became chairman of the Frontline States which spearheaded the liberation struggle in the countries of southern Africa.

John Mwakangale was also one of the leaders of the Pan-African Freedom Movement for East and Central Africa (PAFMECA) which was formed in Mwanza, Tanganyika, in September 1958 under the leadership of Julius Nyerere.

PAFMECA mobilised forces and coordinated the independence struggle in the East-Central African region composed of Tanganyika, Kenya, Zanzibar, Uganda, Nyasaland, Northern Rhodesia and Southern Rhodesia and played a major role in forming the Organisation of African Unity.

Nelson Mandela met John Mwakangale in Mbeya, the capital of the Southern Highlands Province which bordered Northern Rhodesia and Nyasaland. The two countries were renamed Zambia and Malawi, respectively, after they won independence.

Mwakangale was assigned to receive Mandela in Mbeya on behalf of the government of Tanganyika. Mandela flew from Bechuanaland to Tanganyika in a small plane and arrived in Mbeya on the same day. Bechuanaland was renamed Botswana after the country won independence.

After meeting Mwakangale, Mandela flew to Dar es Salaam the next day where he met Prime Minister Julius

Nyerere who became president of Tanganyika on 9 December 1962 on the first anniversary of the country's independence when it became a republic.

Nyerere was the first leader of an independent African country Mandela met.

In his autobiography, *Long Walk to Freedom*, Mandela recalled his meeting with John Mwakangale at a hotel, formerly for whites only, in the town of Mbeya and how, for the first time in his life, he felt free and proud to be in an independent African country where his skin colour was no longer a liability as it was in his home country under apartheid. As he stated:

"Early the next morning we left (Bechuanaland, now Botswana) for Mbeya, a town near the Northern Rhodesian border....We booked in a local hotel and found a crowd of blacks and whites sitting on the veranda making polite conversation.

Never before had I been in a public place or hotel where there was no color bar. We were waiting for Mr. John Mwakangale of the Tanganyika African National Union, a member of Parliament and unbeknown to us he had already called looking for us.

An African guest approached the white receptionist. 'Madam, did a Mr. Mwakangale inquire after these two gentlemen?' he asked, pointing to us. 'I am sorry, sir,' she replied. 'He did but I forgot to tell them.' 'Please be careful, madam,' he said in a polite but firm tone. 'These men are our guests and we would like them to receive proper attention.'

I then truly realized that I was in a country ruled by Africans. For the first time in my life, I was a free man. Though I was a fugitive and wanted in my own land, I felt the burden of oppression lifting from my shoulders. Everywhere I went in Tanganyika my skin color was automatically accepted rather than instantly reviled. I was being judged for the first time not by the color of my skin by the measure of my mind and character. Although I was often homesick during my travels, I nevertheless felt as though I were truly home for the first time....

We arrived in Dar es Salaam the next day and I met with Julius Nyerere, the newly independent country's first president (prime minister). We talked at his house, which was not at all grand, and I recall that he drove himself in a simple car, a little Austin. This impressed me, for it suggested that he was a man of the people. Class, Nyerere always insisted, was alien to Africa; socialism indigenous." – (Nelson Mandela, *Long Walk to Freedom: The Autobiography of Nelson Mandela*, New York: Little, Brown and Co., 1994, p. 538).

When he received Nelson Mandela, John Mwakangale was a member of parliament (MP) representing Mbeya. A few months later in the same year, he was appointed by Prime Minister Nyerere to be the regional commissioner of the Southern Highlands Province, a position equivalent to that of governor of a state in the United States. He also continued to be a member parliament.

John Mwakangale and my father came from the same area in Rungwe District in the Southern Highlands Province. Their home villages were five miles apart. They were classmates from Standard One at Tukuyu Primary School in the town of Tukuyu, the capital of Rungwe District, all the way to Malangali Secondary School in Iringa District in the same province.

Another classmate of my father and John Mwakangale from Tukuyu Primary School to Malangali Secondary School was Brown Ngwilulupi who was appointed by President Nyerere as secretary-general of the largest farmers' union in the country, the Cooperative Union of Tanganyika (CUT).

Ngwilulupi later left the ruling party and became one of the founders of the largest opposition party in Tanzania,

Chadema, and served as the party's vice chairman under Edwin Mtei, the first governor of the Bank of Tanzania and former minister of finance under President Nyerere who also left the government and became a director at the World Bank representing Africa.

Brown Ngwilulupi and my father came from the same village of Mpumbuli in Kyimbila four miles south of the town of Tukuyu. John Mwakangale's home village was five miles north of theirs near Tukuyu. Ngwilulupi and my father later became relatives-in-law when they got married. Their wives were first cousins to each other, who were also born and brought up in the same household of Asegelile Mwankemwa, and came from the same area of Kyimbila (Katusyo village) their husbands came from.

Brown Ngwilulupi's younger brother, Weidi Ngwilulupi Mwasakafyuka – their father was Ngwilulupi Mwasakafyuka – who once served as a senior diplomat at the Tanzania Mission to the UN and at the Tanzania Embassy in Ethiopia and later as Tanzania's ambassador to France and Nigeria, also left the ruling party and the government and joined one of the opposition parties where became head of its foreign affairs division.

Another classmate of my father, Brown Ngwilulupi and John Mwakangale from Tukuyu Primary School to Malangali Secondary School was W.B.K. Mwanjisi. He was trained as a doctor and became a leading figure in the nationalist movement fighting for independence.

His home was near the town of Tukuyu where he returned to work at Tukuyu Hospital after leaving government service in 1954, the same year the nationalist party, TANU, was formed. He became a prominent member of TANU.

Mwanjisi was once president of the national organisation of African government employees. Many of its members supported the struggle for independence but could not openly support it because of their position as employees of the colonial government. Some of them left

146

government service to support the nationalist movement that was formally launched when the Tanganyika African National Union (TANU) was formed in Dar es Salaam on 7 July 1954. Nyerere was elected TANU president.

Coincidentally, it was also in 1954 – the year the struggle for Tanganyika's independence started in earnest – when we moved from Morogoro in the Coast Province to Mbeya in the Southern Highlands.

We moved to Rungwe District in 1955 when I was five years years old after living in different parts of Tanganyika: Kigoma, Ujiji, Morogoro, Kilosa and Mbeya. There were five members in our family during that time: our parents and four children.

Rungwe was our home district. That is where our parents came from. That is also where most of our relatives were.

Although my parents came from Rungwe District and it is also my home, I still consider other parts of Tanganyika, especially Kigoma where I was born, to be my home as well.

After we moved to Rungwe in 1955, the place was new to me. I had no emotional attachment to Rungwe District, having lived in other parts of Tanganyika during my first five years.

But it later served as an incubator for me because that is where I grew up, besides the four years I spent in secondary school in Ruvuma Region in southern Tanzania from 1965 – 1968. By the time I went to Tambaza High School in Dar es Salaam from 1969 – 1970, I was full-grown, although still a teenager in 1969.

My pursuit of education took me to different parts of the country almost as much as my father's career as a medical assistant did for him.

When my father worked as a medical assistant, he worked as a colonial employee because the hospitals where he worked were government hospitals.

Had he wanted to engage in politics to support the

147

independence struggle as an active campaigner, he would have to make a choice: agitate for independence and suffer reprisals from the colonial authorities, forcing him to leave government service, or continue to work without engaging in politics. He chose the latter although he fully supported the nationalist cause to end colonial rule.

Even after he left government service and agitation for independence was at its peak in the later 1950s, he could have joined some of his colleagues to go into politics but decided not to. Yet that did not diminish his commitment to the liberation struggle. He just did not want to go into politics full-time as some of his colleagues such as John Mwakangale did. Among all the political leaders my father knew, it was John Mwakangale whom he knew the longest, having known each other since childhood when they were classmates at Tukuyu Primary School.

Considering my father's experience with the British colonial rulers and the indignities he suffered and was subjected to, including the incident at the Shell BP petrol station in Tukuyu in the late fifties, it was a miracle he did not go into politics right away. That was not his destiny.

Still, those are the kind of incidents, and insults, which turn people into militants and revolutionaries as would have the dog incident in my case had I been an adult when I was bitten by that Dalmatian-looking dog back in 1956. Had there been a Mau Mau in Tanganyika, I definitely would have supported it, fully, at the very least.

But my father made an important contribution in the medical field. He was one of the very few medical assistants who formed the backbone of the medical system in colonial Tanganyika; that was also the case in other British colonies across Africa.

Medical assistants in Tanganyika underwent intensive training for three years after finishing secondary school and were in fact considered to be "doctors" by their patients and other people in general. They were even called "daktari" (Swahili for "doctor") or "madaktari ("doctors").

In a country with an acute shortage of doctors, they played a critical role in the provision of vital medical services which were not available to the vast majority of the population. Well-trained and with a lot of practical experience, they were, for all practical purposes, a substitute for doctors not only during during colonial rule but also after Tanganyika won independence.

When Tanganyika won independence from Britain on 9 December 1961, it had only 12 doctors in a vast expanse of territory of about 365,000 square miles with millions of people to serve. According to Professor John Illiffe in his book, *East African Doctors: A History of the Modern Profession*, there were only about 300 medical assistants in January 1961 in the entire country, the same year Tanganyika won independence.

Tanganyika had a population of 12 million during that time. With only 12 doctors, that was one doctor for one million people, and one medical assistant for 40,000, an astonishing ratio.

Besides Tanga, Kigoma, Ujiji, Kilosa,and Morogoro, my father also worked as a medical assistant in Handeni.

Most of the places where he worked as a medical assistant were in the Coast Province: Tanga, Handeni, Kilosa, and Morogoro.

My father also worked at Amani Research Institute in Muheza District, also in the Coast Province.

During German colonial rule, Amani Research Institute was world-renowned for its research in a number of areas including tropical medicine and biological and agricultural sciences. It had highly trained scientists who were internationally recognised in their fields. It excelled in high-quality research and retained its international reputation under British rule after Germany lost its colony in World War I.

Tanganyika was then known as Deutsch-Ostafrika (German East Africa) which included Ruanda-Urundi, now Rwanda and Burundi, as one colony.

It is this land of my birth, Tanganyika, which shaped my personality because that is where I spent my formative years and my first years of adulthood until I was 23 years old.

# Chapter Four

# Campaign for independence

IT WAS during the fifties that the campaign for independence in Tanganyika began in earnest under the leadership of TANU – Tanganyika African National Union – which became one of the best-organised and most successful nationalist movements in the history of decolonisation round the globe.

As in most parts of Africa, the struggle for independence in Tanganyika was non-violent unlike in neighbouring Kenya where it became violent and bloody during Mau Mau.

Although I was very young when Mau Mau was going on, I remember seeing pictures of the Mau Mau freedom fighters in some newspapers published in Kiswahili. The most vivid image I still have of these fighters was their hair style, what they call dreadlocks nowadays.

The main Kiswahili papers during those days were *Mambo Leo* and *Mwafrika*. And I remember others: *Ngurumo* (meaning Thnuder), *Mwangaza* (Brightness) and *Baragumu* (Trumpet).

Although *Baragumu* was published in Kiswahili, it was not sympathetic to the nationalist cause articulated by TANU during the struggle for independence. It was, instead, used by the United Tanganyika Party (UTP) to promote its agenda among Africans by telling them that the country was not ready for independence and that supporting TANU would not serve their interests.

UTP was founded in February 1956 with the encouragement of Governor Sir Edward Twining as a counterweight to TANU in order to maintain the privileged status of the white minority settlers and was one of the three main political parties in Tanganyika before independence. It supported a multi-racial constitution but rejected universal suffrage without which genuine democratic representation is impossible.

The other party was the radical African National Congress (ANC) formed by Zuberi Mtemvu in 1958. Mtemvu and his supporters broke away from TANU because they were highly critical of Nyerere's moderate policies advocating equality for all Tanganyikans regardless of race.

The ANC secretary general was John Lifa Chipaka who, until his death in August 2017, continued to harshly criticise Nyerere contending that he did have the interests of the country at heart and was not a true patriot because he accepted non-blacks – people of all races – as fellow citizens.

A close relative – reportedly a cousin – of former foreign affairs minister, Oscar Kambona, Chipaka, together with his younger brother, Captain Elia Lifa Chipaka and others, was involved in a plot to overthrow Nyerere in October 1969. Kambona was the mastermind of the plot. They were convicted of treason.

I have addressed the treason trial extensively in my book, *Nyerere and Africa: End of an Era*, and had the opportunity to be in the high court in Dar es Salaam many times and listen to the proceedings.

In an interview with Elias Msuya of *Mwananchi*, a Swahili newspaper in Dar es Salaam on 20 March 2013, Chipaka – who, during the interview, said he was 83 years old – even falsely claimed that Amir H. Jamal was not a citizen of Tanzania. He implied he was a citizen of India and was even born in India because he was of Indian origin. Yet Nyerere appointed him a cabinet member; in fact, he was one since independence. Therefore, Nyerere betrayed his people, meaning black Tanganyikans.

Chipaka said the same thing about Derek Bryceson who was of British origin – he was also a cabinet member under Nyerere – and asked if anyone really believed he and Jamal had renounced their citizenship, implying citizenship of Britain and India, respectively. As he stated in the interview:

"Nyerere had no patriotism. We were demanding freedom for Tanganyikans, he was demanding freedom for everybody.

In India, there was Jawaharlal Nehru who was demanding freedom for Indians, Kwame Nkrumah demanded freedom for Ghanaians, even Britain was only for the British.

But Nyerere included even those who were not relevant to us and to the struggle; for example, in his government there was an Indian cabinet member Amir Jamal and a white man known as Noel Bryceson. Do you think they gave up their citizenship of their home countries?" – (John Lifa Chipaka, in an interview with Elias Msuya, "John Lifa Chipaka: He Started Being Critical Before Independence and He is Still Critical Today," *Mwananchi*, Dar es Salaam, Tanzania, 20 March 2013, translated from Kiswahili into English by Godfrey Mwakikagile).

Jamal was a citizen of Tanganyika, later Tanzania, and was in born Tanganyika, not in India. He was born in Dar es Salaam and, coincidentally, in the same year Nyerere was, in 1922. As I have stated about Jamal in my book, *The People of Ghana: Ethnic Diversity and National Unity*, in which I have also written about Nyerere's and Nkrumah's shared Pan-African commitment and

153

uncompromising stand against racism:

"Amir H. Jamal was the most intellectual cabinet member in the first independence cabinet besides Nyerere and the longest-serving minister of finance in the country's history. He held other high-profile ministerial posts and was one of the most respected and most knowledgeable cabinet members....He was a close friend of Nyerere.

A technocrat of high intellectual calibre, he was independent-minded and the best adviser Nyerere had. He had sharp political instincts but as a public servant never did anything for political expediency. His integrity was unimpeachable. I knew him when I was a news reporter." – (Godfrey Mwakikagile, *The People of Ghana: Ethnic Diversity and National Unity*, Dar es Salaam, Tanzania: New Africa Press, 2017, pp. 11 – 12).

The struggle for Tanganyika's independence was not based on race but on human equality – the equality of the people of all races. But according to Chipaka and his colleagues in the African National Congress (ANC), people like Jamal and Bryceson and other non-blacks did not have any rights as citizens of Tanganyika, later Tanzania. They should have been denied or stripped of their citizenship simply because they were not African – black African.

The ANC argued that the interests of Africans were paramount even if it meant sacrificing the interests and well-being of whites, Asians and Arabs. Nyerere was resolutely opposed to that and won overwhelming support from the vast majority of the people in Tanganyika for his policies of racial tolerance and equality.

One of the organs he used to articulate his views was a Kiswahili newspaper, *Sauti Ya TANU* (Voice of TANU) founded in 1957. He edited the paper himself.

The main English newspaper was the Tanganyika *Standard*, the oldest English newspaper in the country founded in 1930. And it had a lot to do with my life only a few years later.

The future was never meant for us to see, and had someone told me back then in the late 1950s that my life would somehow be influenced by that English newspaper, I would not have believed that even though I was only a child then, hence naïve.

But that is exactly what happened. About 10 years later, I joined the editorial staff of the *Standard* in Dar es Salaam. I was first hired as a new reporter in June 1969 when I was still a student at Tambaza High School, formerly H.H. The Aga Khan, in Dar es Salaam. I was 19 years old and the youngest reporter on the staff. I was hired by David Martin, the news and deputy managing editor, and Brendon Grimshaw, the managing editor.

After completing Form VI (Standard 14), I joined the National Service which was mandatory for all those who finished secondary school, high school as well as college and university studies. After National Service, I worked briefly at the Ministry of Information and Broadcasting in Dar es Salaam as an information officer before returning to the *Standard* which was renamed *Daily News*.

And in November 1972, my editor Benjamin Mkapa, whom we simply called Ben Mkapa, helped me to go to school in the United States for further education. My trip was financed by the newspaper. They bought me a plane ticket and gave me a travelling allowance.

Years later, Mkapa was elected president of Tanzania and served two five-year terms.

Had I not joined the *Standard* as a news reporter, I may not have gone to school in the United States. And you probably would not be reading this book or any of the others I have written.

Although the *Standard* was a colonial newspaper in the fifties and articulated the sentiments of the white settler community and defended colonial policies, it provided ample coverage of political events during the struggle for independence even if such coverage was not always balanced and quite often reflected official thinking of the colonial authorities.

I remember when I was a news reporter at the *Standard* as it was known then before it was nationalised in 1970 and became the *Daily News* in 1972, our rivals at the militant newspaper, *The Nationalist* which was the official organ of the ruling party TANU, used to publish stories, editorials and feature articles in which they said we worked for "an imperialist newspaper" and sometimes even called us "imperialist agents"!

We simply ignored them, and even laughed at them, whenever we came face-to-face covering the same events. There was no hostility between us. They were simply articulating the ideological position of the ruling party which owned the paper they worked for.

And although the *Standard* defended white minority interests during colonial rule, it did not ignore what was going on in those days, even if it wanted to, and the leading African nationalist during that time, Julius Nyerere, had his views published in the paper many times, although not always the way he had articulated them. There was usually a slant in favour of the colonial government, since the paper was its organ even if not officially so.

And as a moderate who was also committed to building a multiracial society, Nyerere was seen as a responsible leader who was not a threat to the interests of racial minorities in the country. He also sought to achieve his goals by constitutional means. Therefore ignoring him, or refusing to report what he said at public rallies and in interviews would have been counterproductive and not in the best interests of the white settlers themselves.

Although Nyerere was committed to non-violence to achieve independence, he could not guarantee that some of the people in Tanganyika would not resort to violence as some, especially the Kikuyu, had done in neighbouring

Kenya. As Robert A. Senser, an American journalist and editor of *Human Rights for Workers*, recalled what Nyerere told him when they met in the United States in 1957 in his article, "Remembering A Visitor from Tanganyika," published in *Human Rights for Workers: Bulletin No. IV-22*, December 1, 1999, not long after Nyerere died:

"The other day Ed Marciniak, once a Chicago colleague of mine in editing a monthly called *Work*, mailed me the obituary of Julius Nyerere, president of Tanzania from 1964 to 1985.

Stapled to the clipping was a note from Ed saying:

'I still remember your interview with him in *Work*.'

After all these years, I also remember that interview one evening 42 years ago, when Nyerere had dinner with my wife and me in our small apartment on Chicago's South Side.

Nyerere, 35, then president of a political party in a British colony in East Africa called Tanganyika, had just come from London, where the British colonial secretary had rejected his case for Britain loosening its hold on the colony.

'It's a tragic state of affairs,' Nyerere told me, 'because the British government has an attitude that in effect says, 'There's no trouble in Tanganyika--no Mau Mau there or anything of that sort. So why bother with it?"

That quotation is from a yellowed clipping in an old scrapbook of mine--a page one article in the January 1957 issue of *Work*.

Its headline, based on Nyerere's prediction, was: 'Africa: Free in 30 Years.'

As I wrote my article, Nyerere quickly added that the prediction 'sounds absurd to many, especially to the white settlers in Tanganyika.'

# History Can Outpace Human Expectations

In fact, of course, freedom came much quicker than even Nyerere expected. In 1962, only five years after we spoke, Nyerere, head of the Tanganyika African National Union, became Prime Minister of the newly independent Tanganyika and then, three years later, after his country's union with nearby Zanzibar, President of the new state of Tanzania. He retired voluntarily in 1985.

In the article I mentioned Nyerere's early career as a teacher in a Catholic secondary school in Dar es Salaam, the capital, before he started devoting full time to politics.

The obituary, from the *London Tablet*, emphasizes that throughout his adult life Nyerere 'never ceased to be a teacher by temperament, mission, and title: he was always Mwalimu.'

After citing his political successes and failures, and his many talents (he translated two Shakespeare plays into Swahili), the article concludes with this tribute:

'It is, nevertheless, Nyerere's moral example which made him so exceptional, the image of a President standing patiently in a queue waiting to make his confession at the cathedral in Dar: a humble, intellectually open and ascetic teacher, the true Mwalimu.

Unlike almost all the other successful political leaders of his generation in Africa, he was uncorrupted either by power or wealth....

Gentle, humorous, radical, persistent, he remained the icon of a truly ecumenical Christian approach to politics and human development.'"

Although Tanganyika won independence peacefully and was therefore no longer under British colonial rule, not everything changed overnight.

There were some whites who did not accept the change

and refused to treat black Africans and other non-whites as equals even in public places. They were a minority but they did exist.

Incidents of racial injustice during colonial rule demonstrated, in a very tragic way, how vulnerable and helpless we were at the hands of our colonial masters. They also demonstrated the utter futility in trying to seek justice under a judicial system that did not treat blacks and whites as equals. And many people in East Africa even today can tell similar stories about their bitter experiences with the British and other Europeans who settled in our region in large numbers in order to turn it into a white man's homeland as if we did not even exist. However, we must also understand that not all whites mistreated Africans. In many cases, race relations were good even if Africans and Europeans did not interact socially.

People in West Africa have similar incidents to talk about, but not as many as we do in East Africa. And probably there is more bitterness in East Africa about the white man's oppression than there is in West Africa for the simple reason that we were subjected to direct humiliation than our brethren were in the western part of the continent because of the daily contact we had with Europeans in a region where they had settled in large numbers. Just remember Mau Mau and what it was all about.

Also remember the Maji Maji uprising in Tanganyika from 1905 to 1907 during German colonial rule. It was a mass insurrection that covered the entire southern half of the country and almost drove the Germans out until they sought immediate reinforcements from Germany to contain and eventually quell the "rebellion."

It was more of a revolution than a rebellion. It was a war of resistance against imperial rule. It was a liberation war. And it transformed the people into true nationalists transcending tribal loyalties.

Many different tribes took part in the uprising as one people, Africans, fighting alien invaders. The Germans, like the British, also came to East Africa to settle permanently.

I remember what our teachers used to say when they taught us African history in secondary school in the sixties. They used to say the mosquito was the best friend of West Africa because it kept the white man out of there: it stopped Europeans from settling permanently and in large numbers as they did in East Africa, especially in Kenya, and to a smaller degree in Tanganyika.

It was a common saying in Africa, as it probably still is today, especially among people of my generation or older.

When Tanganyika won independence in 1961, it had more than 20,000 white settlers, mostly British; a significant number of Germans, some Dutch including Boers from South Africa and others. Kenya had about 66,000 whites, mostly British including members of the British aristocracy, at independence in 1963. Kenya also had a significant number of Boers, or Afrikaners, from South Africa who founded the town of Eldoret in the Western Highlands in the Great Rift Valley.

Robin Johnson, whom I mentioned earlier, was typical of the British settlers who had established themselves in East Africa determined to make it their permanent home as civil servants working for the colonial government or as farmers or something else. In fact, a significant number of them were born in Kenya and Tanganyika.

Some of them came from as far away as Australia and New Zealand. And many, or their children and grandchildren, are still there today living in different parts of Kenya and what is Tanzania today.

Some of the settlers who acquired large tracts of land were members of the British aristocracy, probably the last people who would think of relinquishing power to Africans one day.

Johnson himself gave up his job as a civil servant and took up farming. He was the District Commissioner (D.C.) of Kongwa in the Central Province in Tanganyika during

160

the ill-fated groundnut scheme that was intended to produce groundnuts on a commercial scale. The scheme was a disaster. He was later assigned to Arusha in northern Tanganyika, what was then called the Northern Province:

"Robin himself was becoming increasingly interested in Tanganyika's long-term future. He felt if he became a farmer, like his father before him, and thereby rooted in the soil, he could play a more permanent role in the country's development than permitted to a transitory civil servant.

He had met David Stirling, the founder of the Capricorn Africa Society, and felt that his policy of common citizenship and a multi-racial form of government might well be the answer for the East African states where Africans, though still backward, must soon begin to move politically, and there was a small settled European and Asian community.

He resigned from the Colonial Service in 1951 when he was alloted one of the Ol Molog farms [in Arusha in northern Tanganyika]. His colleagues thought he was quite mad. Surely every diligent Administrative Officer only had one goal in life – to be a Governor finally. How irresponsible of Robin carelessly to throw that chance away." – (Erika Johnson, *The other Side of Kilimanjaro*, op. cit.).

Little did they realise that hard as they were planning to turn East Africa into their permanent home dominated by whites, Africans were at the same time proceeding on a parallel path towards mobilisation of the masses in the quest for independence and did not, for one moment, believe that the multiracial government proposed by some of the more liberal members of the settler community would ever include them as equal partners. Universal adult suffrage, a cardinal principle cherished in every democratic society, was totally out of the question in this

161

dispensation.

In Tanganyika, Nyerere admitted in the fifties that the colonial government and the African nationalist movement were headed in the same direction, but at a different pace. As a UN Trust Territory under British mandate, Tanganyika was supposed to be guided towards independence by the colonial government. But the colonial rulers had a different timetable. It would have taken decades before the country won independence. Nyerere and his colleagues wanted independence much sooner.

Many of the settlers were, of course, aware of the political awakening and agitation that was taking place but did not believe that the people of Kenya and Tanganyika under British tutelage would demand or win independence within a decade or so.

The British colonial office suggested that if independence ever came to Tanganyika, it would be in 1985. Britain had to have some kind of time table since Tanganyika was not a typical colony, like Kenya, but a trusteeship territory under UN mandate, with Britain playing the role of "Big Brother" or guardian to guide the country towards independence on terms stipulated by the United Nations.

Yet the UN itself was not seriously concerned about freedom and independence for Africans without being pushed by our leaders who included Julius Nyerere as the pre-eminent African leader in Tanganyika.

In fact, political awakening among Africans had already been going on for quite some time long before the "halcyon days" of colonial rule in the 1950s. And Julius Nyerere played a critical role, at a very early age, in galvanising his colleagues into action, despite his humility. As Chief Abdallah Said Fundikira, who became one of the first cabinet members after independence, said about what type of person Nyerere was in those days:

"If you want the truth, one did not particularly notice

Nyerere." – (Abdallah Said Fundikira, *Africa News Online*, November 8, 1999).

He was talking about the time when Nyerere entered Makerere University College at the age of 22 after attending secondary school in Tabora in western Tanganyika, the hometown of Fundikira, chief of the Nyamwezi, one of the largest ethnic groups in Tanzania with more than one million people.

But in spite of such incidents (barring black people from white hotels, bars and other establishments, openly insulting them in other ways), and they were rare after independence, race relations were good in general, in fact very good sometimes, as they were before independence in spite of overt racism in a number of cases during the colonial era.

For the vast majority of Tanganyikans of all races, including non-citizens, life in general went on as before as if no major political changes had taken place in the country ending colonial rule.

Even during the struggle for independence, indignities of colour bar experienced by Africans now and then, here and there, did not fuel animosity towards whites among Africans to make them rebellious.

There was potential for revolt just like in any situation, anywhere, when people are demanding basic human rights and those demands are not met. But in the case of Tanganyika, conditions were no close to what they were in apartheid South Africa; nor was land alienation as serious or widespread as it was in Kenya, especially in the Central Province where the Kikuyu revolted against the British and launched Mau Mau.

There were, however, incidents in Tanganyika which clearly showed that fundamental change was needed if the different races were to live in harmony.

As I showed earlier, Nyerere himself was involved in one such incident in 1953 at the Old Africa Hotel in Dar es Salaam – invited by Colin Legum – when he and three of his black African colleagues were denied service just before he formally began to campaign for independence. He was already, even by then, the most prominent African leader in Tanganyika as president of the Tanganyika African Association (TAA) which was transformed into TANU in 1954. And there were other incidents of racial injustice involving many other blacks in different parts of the country including Dar es Salaam.

Yet the incident involving Nyerere and his colleagues demonstrates one simple truth about Tanganyika in the fifties and throughout the entire colonial period under British rule.

It was not a rigidly segregated society; and whatever racial separation existed was in most cases voluntary and not strictly enforced even by convention.

There were no laws against racial integration. Had there been such laws, Colin Legum would not even have thought about going to the white manager to protest against what happened to his African colleagues whose glasses of beer were taken away by an African waiter at the Old Africa Hotel in Dar es Salaam.

Had this been apartheid South Africa, or had Tanganyika been a segregated society in the legal sense, separating the races, Nyerere and other Africans who were with him on that day would not have entered the Old Africa Hotel without being arrested. And their sympathetic friend, Colin Legum, who had invited them, would have been arrested as well, not only for defying convention but for breaking the law.

But the incident also showed that without fundamental change in the system, there would be trouble in the country even with Nyerere as the leader of those campaigning for independence.

And racism did exist in Tanganyika during colonial rule. It was experienced by many Africans and other non-whites. Probably the worst part of race relations was that black people – who constituted the vast majority of the population – knew that white people in general did not see and treat them as equals. And the majority of the whites also felt that black people were not equal to them.

All that was the result of the conquest of Africa by Europeans – the conquered are not equal to their conquerors. And it "legitimised" assumptions and beliefs of racial superiority and inferiority which were codified into law in apartheid South Africa and sanctioned by practice and convention in Tanganyika and other white-ruled countries across the continent.

After independence, Nyerere remained restrained in the conduct of national affairs and earned a reputation as a tolerant leader. But he also had a reputation of being tough and uncompromising on matters of principle especially involving equality.

One of his major achievements was containing and neutralising radical elements in the ruling party who wanted to marginalise racial minorities in national life, forcing them to live on the periphery of the mainstream.

There were even those who would have resorted to outright expulsion of racial minorities, if they had the power to do so, the way Idi Amin did in Uganda ten years later – after Tanganyika won independence in 1961 – when he expelled Asians including Ugandan citizens of Asian origin. Nyerere was the only African leader who publicly denounced and condemned Amin and called him a racist because of what he did.

Fortunately, there were no racial tensions in Tanganyika after independence, earning the country a reputation as one of the most stable and most peaceful on the continent and tolerant of racial minorities.

But although the people celebrated independence and were glad to be masters of their own destiny as a nation, they did not see any dramatic improvement in their lives as many of them had expected.

Such changes don't come overnight. Yet there were

165

many people who had very high expectations, thinking that their lives would dramatically improve soon after colonial rule ended. That was not the case.

However, this was offset by the fact that there was a major achievement in one area, "overnight." The prophets of doom who had predicted racial conflict or some kind of civil strife soon after independence were proved wrong.

I remember a few years after independence that there were still some signs on toilets saying "Africans," and on some hotels saying "Europeans" even in the capital Dar es Salaam.

I remember one very well on a toilet for Africans at the bus station of the East African Railways & Harbours Corporation in the town of Mbeya. No one took it down. It was simply ignored. And the toilet was filthy, as expected for Africans who had the worst facilities in general.

When I moved to Dar es Salaam a few years later, I also remember seeing one sign on a hotel saying "Europeans."

Although the sign at the bus station in Mbeya – it was the first apartheid-type sign I saw in Tanganyika – reminded me and other Africans of a bygone era and symbolised our subordinate status during colonial rule when we were not welcome in some places including a few hotels and clubs which had signs saying "Europeans," it did not inspire the kind of outrage – if any – some people might have expected from Africans after Tanganyika won independence.

There were Africans who simply accepted the status quo during colonial rule; there were those who simply ignored it; and there were, of course, those who were determined to change it.

But even those who sought change in the status quo were no more hostile towards whites than those who did not after the country won independence. And that was one of the biggest achievements of the independence struggle, making it possible for people of all races to live in peace and harmony.

Many whites who left Tanganyika after independence did so for economic reasons mainly because of the economic policies which deprived them of their property and even means of livelihood especially after the country adopted socialism in 1967 and not because they were targeted as whites.

Many Africans who owned a lot of land and even more than one house for rent also lost most of their property and were equally bitter because of such stringent measures which were designed, rightly or wrongly, to reduce income disparities and social inequalities – gaps between the rich and the poor – in the quest for socialist transformation of the country.

It was the most ambitious exercise in social engineering in the history of post-colonial Africa launched only five years after Tanganyika won independence. But it also proved to be a disastrous failure in terms of economic development as the economy virtually came to a grinding halt in the mid- and late seventies, less than 10 years after the government enunciated its socialist policies embodied in the Arusha Declaration of February 1967.

Socialism and Africanisation were some of the main reasons many whites – as well as Tanzanians of Asian origin mostly of the mercantile class – left or were forced to leave Tanganyika and later Tanzania.

Africans welcomed those changes because they transcended race and served as an equaliser. Socialism sought equality. It was also intended to protect the poor and vulnerable members of society from exploitation by the rich and powerful. Africanisation gave Africans access to opportunities they had been denied before purely on the basis of race. And Experience had taught them that even some of the most "liberal" members of the settler community did not really believe black people should participate in a multiracial government as equal partners.

The multiracial Legislative Council, known as

LEGCO, which existed during colonial rule was dominated by whites. And whatever was proposed by the colonial authorities for the future would have proceeded along the same lines. Universal adult suffrage, a cardinal principle cherished in every democratic society, was totally out of the question in this dispensation.

Many of the settlers were, of course, aware of the political awakening and agitation that was taking place but did not believe that the people of Kenya and Tanganyika would demand or win independence within a decade or so. Even some of the African leaders themselves said their countries would not win independence – or would have to wait – until the 1980s because they were not ready to manage their own affairs. Nyerere believed exactly the opposite: Africans were ready for independence even if achieving the goal would take longer than expected.

It was when he was a student at Makerere University College that his leadership qualities came to be noticed. He formed the Tanganyika Welfare Association intended to help the small number of students from Tanganyika at Makerere to work together as a collective entity for their own wellbeing. It was not a political organisation but had the potential to become one.

The welfare association soon forged ties and eventually merged with the Tanganyika African Association (TAA), an organisation founded by African civil servants in Tanganyika in 1929, to address their problems. But they had to operate within prescribed limits, as defined by the colonial authorities who said the association could only deal with welfare problems; nothing political.

Nyerere and his colleagues wanted the association to fight discrimination against the African civil servants who were being paid less than their European counterparts. It was a "welfare" problem, but with profound implications, hardly indistinguishable from political demands. He later described these "welfare" demands as "the politics of sheer complaints" which did not address the fundamental problem of inequity of power between Africans and Europeans.

He wanted the colonial authorities to pay attention to demands by Africans in order to bring about fundamental change in this asymmetrical relationship that had existed since the colonialists took over Tanganyika before he was born. As he recalled those days:

"When I was born, there was not a single person who questioned why we were being ruled. And if my father had heard that we wanted changes, he would have asked me, 'What do you think you can do, you small silly boy?'" – ((Julius Nyerere, quoted in *Africa News Online*, 8 November 1999).

But nothing could dissuade him from his commitment to justice, no matter what the cost. And much as his father would have been apprehensive of the situation, had he lived long enough to discuss the matter with his son after he became mature, Nyerere knew that nothing was going to change until Africans themselves did something to bring about change. His mother was equally apprehensive and probably even more so. She was quoted as saying:

"I began to know about Julius' activities when he was teaching at Pugu College [St. Francis College] in 1952. Everyday, a man called Dossa Aziz came to our house and he would talk with Julius for a long time. One day I overheard them talking about taking over the government from Europeans.

I became afraid. Later I asked Julius if what I heard was true. When he said yes, I became more frightened. I told him what he was doing was bad. God had given him a good job and now he wanted to spoil it. But he said that what he was doing would benefit not only us but everyone in the country." – (Julius Nyerere's mother, Christina Mgaya wa Nyang'ombe, his father's fifth wife, quoted in

169

*Africa News Online*, 8 November 1999).

Nyerere had just returned to Tanganyika in October 1952 after three years at Edinburgh University in Scotland where he was admitted in October 1949. He earned a master's degree in economics and history and also studied philosophy.

The fifties was a critical decade in the struggle for independence in Tanganyika. It was not only the decade when TANU (Tanganyika African National Union), the party that led Tanganyika to independence, was formed; it was also the time when mobilisation of forces in the struggle for freedom from colonial rule began in all parts of the country.

It was also the decade in which the colonial government tried to neutralise TANU, as much as the British colonial authorities tried to do to KANU (Kenya African National Union) in neighbouring Kenya when they arrested and imprisoned Jomo Kenyatta and other leaders in 1952 It was also the last decade of colonial rule in both colonies.

Before the 1958 – 1959 general election in Tanganyika, the British colonial government launched a harassment campaign to discredit and if possible destroy TANU. Nyerere was banned from making public speeches. He was accused of libel and put on trial. And twelve branches of TANU were closed down.

The banning of Nyerere came after a highly successful campaign across the country to get support for TANU and for his campaign for independence. He travelled to all parts of Tanganyika, to every province, in a battered Land Rover which belonged to his compatriot Dossa Aziz who gave the vehicle to TANU to help with the independence campaign, and was able to build, with his colleagues, the party's membership to unprecedented levels. Just within a year, TANU had 250,000 members.

It was during one of those campaign trips that I saw

Nyerere for the first time when he came to address a mass rally in Tukuyu in the late 1950s; riding in the same Land Rover that had taken him to all parts of Tanganyika before.

I remember that day well. He wore a light green short-sleeved shirt and rode, standing, in the back of the Land Rover, waving at the crowd that had gathered to welcome him when he first arrived to address a mass rally at a football (soccer) field in Tukuyu one afternoon.

Although he was committed to non-violence, the colonial authorities claimed that some of his speeches were highly inflammatory; but to the people of Tanganyika, they were highly inspiring and patriotic. And because of this he was banned, in early 1957, from making public speeches.

Yet he remained unperturbed. As he told a correspondent of *The New York Times* in Dar es Salaam on 31 March 1957:

"I am a troublemaker, because I believe in human rights strongly enough to be one."

Earlier in the same year he had written an article published in the Tanganyika *Standard* which two District Commissioners (DCs, as we called them, and as they called themselves) complained about, claiming Nyerere had libelled them. Twelve years later, I became a news reporter of the same newspaper.

Nyerere also said although TANU was committed to non-violence, the nationalist movement would resort to civil disobedience to achieve its goals; and, by implication, to violence if necessary, should there be no other options to pursue independence. And his trial gave the colonial authorities the opportunity to learn more about him.

The trial was a turning point in the history of TANU and of the country as a whole. A reporter of *Drum* magazine was one of those who covered the trial. He wrote the following in the November 1958 edition when the proceedings took place in Dar es Salaam:

"The sun has not yet risen but hundreds of people are already gathered round the small courthouse in Dar es Salaam.

Some have come from distant villages, with blankets and cooking utensils as if for a camping holiday. They have been in Dar es Salaam for more than a week at the trial of the president of the Tanganyika African National Union (TANU), Julius Nyerere, on a charge of criminal libel. It was alleged that Nyerere wrote an article in which two district commissioners were libelled.

Police constables line the streets round the court and a riot squad stands ready nearby in case of trouble. As the time draws near for the court to open, the crowds jostle and shove for the best positions.

The trial has been a mixture of exciting arguments, explosive surprises and hours of dullness.

Mr. Pritt – Nyerere's counsel – insisted that the two commissioners should be called to give evidence. He accused the government of prosecuting Nyerere without investigating his allegations. The government was telling the world that if anybody said anything against a district commissioner, he could be put into prison for saying what was true.

When Nyerere gave evidence, he took full responsibility for the article and said that he had written it to draw the attention of the government to certain complaints. He was followed by three witnesses who spoke of 'injustices' they had suffered at the hands of the the two district commissioners.

Halfway through the proceedings, the attorney-general appeared in court in person to announce on behalf of the Crown that it would not continue with the counts concerning one of the commissioners.

Now, on the last day of the show, the stars begin to

172

arrive: Mr. Summerfield, the chief prosecutor; Mr. N.M. Rattansey, defence counsel who is assisting the famous British QC, Mr. D.N. Pritt. Mr. Nyerere, wearing a green bush shirt, follows later. He smiles and waves as members of the crowd cheer him.

The curtain goes up with the arrival of Mr. L.A. Davies, the magistrate. The court is packed. Everyone is tense and hushed.

The magistrate sums up then comes to judgement – Nyerere is found guilty!

The magistrate, in passing sentence, says he has formed the impression that Nyerere is an extremely intelligent and responsible man. He fines Nyerere Pounds 150 or six months. The money is raised by locals and the Kenya defence fund."

In the election that followed in 1958 – 1959, TANU won a landslide victory. It won 29 seats out of 30 in the general election. As Nyerere said after the victory:

"Independence will follow as surely as the tick birds follow the rhino."

In March 1959, Sir Richard Turnbull, the last governor of Tanganyika, appointed to his 12-member cabinet five TANU members who had been elected to the Legislative Council (LEGCO), the colonial legislature which was established in 1926.

In 1958 Sir Richard Turnbull had succeeded Sir Edward Twining as governor of Tanganyika. He had previously served as chief colonial secretary in Kenya during the Emergency, which was during the Mau Mau uprising, and had witnessed firsthand the violence and bloodshed which resulted from the colonial government's refusal to address the grievances of the masses over land and working conditions and from its unwillingness to accept demands by Africans for freedom and independence. He did not want to see that happen in Tanganyika when he became governor.

Initially, the colonial government in Tanganyika wanted only three ministerial posts to be filled by LEGCO members, but Nyerere insisted on having a majority from his victorious party, TANU.

During the election, TANU had sponsored an Asian and a European for each seat, besides its own African candidates. The two also won.

Governor Turnbull conceded and appointed three Africans, one Asian and one European to the cabinet to represent TANU and the majority of the voters who had voted for TANU candidates.

It was also in the same month, March 1959, that Nyerere was interviewed by *Drum* and spoke about the future of Tanganyika after it won independence, which was almost three years away:

"Tanganyika will be the first, most truly multiracial democratic country in Africa.

When we get our freedom, the light of a true multiracial democracy will be put high upon the top of the highest mountain, on Kilimanjaro, for all to see, particularly South Africa and America.

Tanganyika will offer the people of those countries free entry, without passports, to come and see real democracy at work.

As long as we do not have a popular government elected by the people on democratic principles, we will strive for freedom from any kind of domination.

We regard the [UN] Trusteeship as part of a scheme to keep Tanganyika under the British Crown indefinitely. The greatest enemy of our vision is the Colonial Office.

But Tanganyika cannot be freed by drawing up resolutions or by tabulating long catalogues of the evils of colonialism. Nor do we find it enough to tell rulers to quit Tanganyika. It will be freed only by action, and likewise the whole of Africa.

Continued colonialism is preventing investment in this country. Germany, for example, cannot invest money as long as the British are still here.

I agree that the country lacks technicians. So what? Shall we give the British another 40 years to train them? How many have they trained in the past 40 years?

As far as money for a self-governing Tanganyika is concerned, Tanganyika has not been receiving much money from the British taxpayer at all. For the past 11 years, Tanganyika has only received Pounds 9 million. I can raise 100 times that within a year if it becomes necessary.

I believe that the continued, not existence, but citizenship of the European would be taken for granted had not the white man created a Kenya, a Central Africa [the Central African Federation of Rhodesia and Nyasaland], a South Africa and other similar places and situations.

African nationalism is not anti-white but simply anti-colonialist. When George Washington fought the imperialists, he was fighting for the divine right of Americans to govern themselves; he was not fighting colour.

The white man wants to live in Africa on his terms. He must dominate and be recognised by the rest of the inhabitants of this continent as their natural master and superior. But that we cannot accept. What we are after is fellow citizenship, and that is exactly what is frightening the white man.

The question is not whether we must get rid of whites, but whether they must get rid of themselves. Whites can no longer dominate in Africa. That dream is gone. Africa must be governed by Africans in the future.

Whether an immigrant African will have an equal part to play in this free Africa depends upon him and him alone. In Tanganyika, we are determined to demonstrate to the whole of Africa that democracy is the only answer.

We are being held back, not by local Europeans, but by the Colonial Office and, I believe, by Europeans in neighbouring countries, who are frightened of the possibility of success in Tanganyika."

A month later in April 1959, after the interview with *Drum*, Nyerere went to Zanzibar to attend a meeting of the Pan-African Freedom Movement of Eastern and Central Africa, popularly known as PAFMECA when I was growing up in Tanganyika, and of which he had previously been elected president.

In fact, it was on his initiative that PAFMECA was formed. It was he who called a meeting of the representatives of all the nationalist parties in the countries of East and Central Africa to mobilise forces and coordinate the struggle for independence in those countries: Tanganyika, Kenya, Zanzibar, Uganda, Nyasaland, Northern Rhodesia, and Southern Rhodesia.

Representatives from Tanganyika, Kenya, Uganda, Zanzibar and Nyasaland attended the meeting. It was held in the town of Mwanza on the shores of Lake Victoria in northern Tanganyika from 16 to 18 September 1958 and PAFMECA was born.

One of the most prominent Tanganyikan leaders of PAFMECA was John Mwakangale from my home district, Rungwe. He was also one of the TANU members who was elected as a member of the colonial legislature, LEGCO.

While in Zanzibar, Nyerere played a critical role in forging unity between some Africans and some Arabs, bringing their political parties closer together in the struggle for independence and for the sake of national unity.

Speaking at a meeting of PAFMECA in Nairobi, Kenya, in September 1959, he made it clear that Europeans and Asians as well as others were welcome to remain in Africa as equal citizens after independence was achieved.

In the following month, October, he gave a speech in the Tanganyika colonial legislature (LEGCO) in which he uttered these famous words:

"We will light a candle on mount Kilimanjaro which will shine beyond our borders, giving hope where there is despair, love where there is hate, and dignity where before there was only humiliation."

In December 1959, Britain's new Colonial Secretary Ian McLeod announced that Tanganyika would be given virtual home rule towards the end of 1960 under a constitution that would guarantee an African majority in the colonial legislature, LEGCO. However, Nyerere criticized the retention of income and literacy qualifications as eligibility criteria for voters and for membership in the legislature.

He was also critical of the reservation of a specific number of seats in LEGCO for the European and Asian minorities. But he saw the concessions by the British colonial rulers, including new constitutional provisions guaranteeing a legislature with an African majority, as a step towards independence in the not-so-distant future.

In the elections of August 1960, TANU again won by a landslide, 70 out of 71 seats, its biggest victory so far and less than a year before independence.

Nyerere was sworn in as chief minister of government under a new constitution, but the governor, Sir Richard Turnbull, continued to hold certain veto powers, although rarely exercised, if at all, since it was now inevitable that Tanganyika would soon be independent.

Nyerere's status as the leader of Tanganyika was formally acknowledged even outside the colony, for example, when he attended a meeting of British Commonwealth prime ministers in London in March 1961, although Tanganyika was still not independent.

But in his capacity as prime minister of Tanganyika since the colony won internal self-government, hence *de facto* head of government in lieu of the governor, he joined other African leaders in denouncing the apartheid regime of South Africa and its racist policies and declared that if South Africa remained a member of the Commonwealth, Tanganyika would not join the association; a position he had articulated earlier in August 1960 when he said:

"To vote South Africa in, is to vote us out."

South Africa withdrew from the Commonwealth. Many people attributed that to Nyerere's uncompromising stand on the apartheid regime and his threat to keep Tanganyika out of the Commonwealth if South Africa remained a member.

Following a constitutional conference in March 1961, Colonial Secretary Ian McLeod announced that Tanganyika would have internal self-government on May 1, and full independence in December in the same year.

On 9 December 1961, Tanganyika became independent. A few days later, it was unanimously accepted as the 104th member of the United Nations. Nyerere was 39 years old and, at that time, the youngest national leader in the world.

On 9 January 1962, Nyerere resigned as prime minister and appointed Rashidi Kawawa, minister without portfolio, as his successor.

He said he resigned to rebuild the party which had lost its focus and to give the country a new purpose now that independence had been won.

But with independence came responsibilities. It was no easy task. So much lay ahead.

# Part Two

# Our colonial experience and our destiny

MY LIFE under British colonial rule was not a unique experience. It was only a part of the cumulative experience we Africans had to endure under colonial rule.

I was born a colonial subject like millions of other Tanganyikans. Therefore, the story of my life is, in general and in some fundamental respects, a microcosm of the experience of other Tanganyikans who were also born during the colonial period.

It is the story of other Tanganyikans not only in terms of colonial domination and but also in terms of racial injustices perpetrated against them.

Racial injustices had the biggest impact on the lives of black people – far more than they did on the lives of other non-white Tanganyikans. And that was for one simple reason. Black people constituted the vast majority of the population. They were also at the bottom of the social hierarchy in a society structured like a pyramid, with whites on top.

But it is also a story of racial accommodation in which racial minorities had plenty of room to continue living their lives without fear of the black majority who were to assume power after the end of colonial rule. It is also a story of racial harmony in a country where members of different races got along well even if they were socially distant from each other, as was indeed the case.

But my life under colonial rule is also my story, very personal in many respects, in spite of its wider relevance as an individual's experience reflective of what other Tanganyikans also experienced as colonial subjects, each of them also with a personal story to tell about that experience.

Growing up in the 1950s, I experienced a form of apartheid and racial segregation my fellow countrymen and women also experienced even if I did not fully understand it, the way adults did, because of my age. I spent my first twelve years under British colonial rule in a decade when agitation for independence was at its peak, finally leading to independence for Tanganyika, the first country in East Africa to emerge from colonial rule.

Yet my story and the individual stories of other Tanganyikans – Africans in general across the continent – is one story set in the broader context not only of the imperial conquest of Africa but also of its impact on our wellbeing and destiny as a people. We are still an integral part of the Western world in terms of influence and domination.

Our dignity has been wounded and identity imperiled by constant bombardment from the cultural forces unleashed by Western civilisation with the full backing of its imperial might even in the cultural arena in a world where Western influence is becoming increasingly dominant in this era of globalisation and has, in fact, been that way even before then. It seems to have conquered other cultures in many areas even if in limited ways.

That has been our fate since colonisation. It includes the policy of assimilation – although it never really worked for the vast majority of the people, especially the masses – in the French and Portuguese colonies which was one of the most brazen and worst attempts to de-Africanise

Africans.

All that has put conscious Africans – those who are aware of and care about our vulnerable position in these culture wars – to be on the defensive by respecting and protecting our cultures and values and by taking an uncompromising stand against the propagation of alien ideas which pollute and pervert African minds and threaten our identity and integrity. There is no better way to undermine Africa.

Our identity, indeed our very being, is rooted in traditional Africa. Take that way, or ignore it, the African renaissance we talk so much about is impossible. It is suicidal for us to help our conquerors denigrate traditional Africa in this "clash of civilisations" – to borrow Professor Samuel Huntington's phrase – whose foot solders on the side of our conquerors include Westernised Africans some of whom have been so brainwashed that they have ceased to be African in thought and spirit.

Conquest does not give conquerors the moral authority to denigrate and rule others; nor does it give them the right to think for them and to shape their destiny. It only gives them the immoral authority to abuse them; hardly grounds for claims of moral superiority by conquerors over their victims.

The "right" to abuse is derived from the power conquerors have to subjugate others. Such power has no moral constraints on it, not even from the morality of individuals who exercise it even if they rebel against authority and refuse to fulfill their obligations.

Only power has the power to restrain itself – which is not in its nature to do so. Its only antidote is counterpower if it is enough to defeat or extract concessions from those in power. This has to come from organised resistance by the oppressed; which we did not have when our conquerors – European invaders – came until we mobilised forces of *unified* resistance later.

Ironically, we used the same institutions they brought

to rule us – constitutions, judiciaries, legislatures and so on – to press and articulate our demands but which had only replaced our traditional institutions of authority, governance, representation and conflict resolution and were not superior to ours; only different in the way they – ours and theirs – operated but with the same purpose and objective of achieving social order and justice.

These traditional institutions of authority over ethnic groups – tribes – across our continent constituted states.

It is not true that Africa was stateless – did not have states – before the advent of colonial rule. They existed in different parts of the continent in varying degrees of organisation and success.

Some were more centralised than others. And there were those which were more decentralised, especially if they administered large territories inhabited by different ethnic groups which were united in a confederation or a highly decentralised form of federation such as the Fanti Confederation in what is now Ghana.

Some of the most centralised traditional states included Buganda, a kingdom which formed the nucleus of the modern nation of Uganda. Other traditional kingdoms – hence states – in Uganda included Bunyoro, Ankole, and the princedom of Busoga, although Buganda became the dominant kingdom.

In Ruanda-Urundi, what is now Rwanda and Burundi, the Tutsi established a centralised kingdom in which they became the dominant group over the Hutu majority. The kingdom was ruled by a *mwami* (king or queen).

There were similar kingdoms in the region including one ruled by a female, Mwami Theresa Ntare VI, queen of the kingdom of Heru in Buha, western Tanzania.

There was, in the same East African region, the Karagwe kingdom in what is now Tanzania. It was located in an area that is now northwestern Tanzania bordering Rwanda.

There were other kingdoms in the Great Lakes region

including the Kitara empire also known as Bunyoro-Kitara or the kingdom of Bakitara. It was a product of the fragmentation of the Chwezi empire which led to the emergence of a number of autonomous states in the region with strong traditional rulers and well-established governments.

There was also the Busongora kingdom located between what is now Rwanda and the kingdom of Bunyoro in what is now southwestern Uganda.

Further fragmentation of some of these states led to the emergence of strong chiefdoms, another form of institutionalised authority prevalent in many parts of Africa among various ethnic groups; testament to the fact that well-organised government and law and order was the norm rather than the exception even among smaller political and social entities formed by members of different "tribes" – ethnic groups.

In what is Ghana today and before it became the Gold Coast, there was the Ashanti kingdom. It was ruled by a king, the *asantehene*, and was one of the most powerful in Africa before the advent of colonial rule.

Determined to remain independent, the Ashanti fought the British in one of the bloodiest wars in the continent's colonial history.

There were other kingdoms and states in precolonial Gold Coast in the north, east and west, not just in the central region inhabited by the Ashanti. They included the Mamprusi kingdom covering northern and northeastern Ghana and parts of Burkina Faso; the **Dagbon kingdom** founded by the Dagomba people in what is now the Northern Region; the Gonja kingdom established by the Gonja also in the Northern Region; the Akuapem and Akropong states in what is now southeastern Ghana which later united and formed the Akropong-Akuapem kingdom; and the Denkyira kingdom which was the first and largest among the Akan people until it was conquered and replaced by the Ashanti kingdom.

Those are just some examples. There were other states and kingdoms in the precolonial period in the region which includes an area that became the Gold Coast.

There were also well-established states and kingdoms in what came to be the countries of Gabon – the kingdom of Orungu which was the most powerful in the area; Dahomey – the Fon kingdom whose founders, the Fon, were also the main founders of the kingdom of Dahomey; Chad – the Kanem-Bornu empire which also covered parts of northeastern Nigeria; Upper Volta (Burkina Faso) – Mossi kingdoms; Ivory Coast – the Kong empire and the states of Gyaman also known as Jamang and Baule; Guinea – it was a part of the Ghana, Mali and Songhai empires; Mali – Mali kingdom; Senegal – Jolof or Wolof empire.

The Hausa of Nigeria and other parts of West Africa established also a number of well-governed states which collectively constituted the Hausa kingdom, with Kano being the most powerful city state in the kingdom which existed as a confederation without a central government.

In an area that became Guinea and beyond its borders, Samori Ture, a Malinke ruler and the great-grandfather of President Sekou Toure, waged a successful guerrilla war with his well-disciplined army against the French and established the Mandinka empire, also known as the Wassoulou empire.

It was a testament to his leadership qualities and military skills that he was able to establish such an empire when the imperial powers were busy destroying traditional kingdoms and other powerful states which had been built in different parts of the continent before colonial rule.

He defeated the French in many battles including a heavily armed French army which used heavy artillery against his soldiers before he was finally captured and exiled to Gabon where he died in captivity.

There was also the Toucouleur empire in what is Mali today. It was a federation of chiefdoms, a form of union

184

that was prevalent in many parts of the continent which did not have highly centralised states such as the Buganda kingdom and others.

There was also the Bamana empire in what became the country of Mali. It was formed after the collapse of the Mali empire and was a centralised state.

In what is Nigeria today, there were highly organised kingdoms among the Yoruba – the Oyo empire being one of the most powerful; it even dominated the kingdom of Dahomey in what is now Benin. The Yoruba were well-known for their city states long before Europeans came.

Among the Hausa-Fulani and the Kanuri and others in Northern Nigeria, there were strong states under traditional rulers including emirs and the Sardauna of Sokoto who wielded so much power that he became the most powerful leader in Nigeria even after the country won independence because the federation was dominated by Northern Nigeria which was under his control.

The Igbo were the exception among the three largest ethnic groups which constitute Nigeria's triad – the Hausa-Fulani in the north, the Yoruba in the west, and the Igbo in the east. They did not have central authority.

The imposition of colonial rule on the Igbo was the first time state formation took place among them, uniting them under the British administrators, unlike in other parts of Nigeria where the people were already united under their traditional rulers.

There was also the kingdom of Benin, or the Edo empire, in what is now southern Nigeria, one of the most powerful in precolonial Africa. The king of Benin ruled as an absolute monarch, thus leading one of the most centralised states in precolonial Africa.

There were others in different parts of the continent.

In the former Belgian Congo, the Bakongo were organised in a powerful kingdom, one of the best organised on the continent, and after which two countries were named.

It covered a vast expanse of territory not only in what is now the Democratic Republic of Congo (the former Belgian Congo) and the Republic of Congo (Congo-Brazzaville) but also a part of Angola in northern Cabinda.

It was ruled by one king, *Mwene Kongo*, and exerted influence on other kingdoms in the region. And it was not the only kingdom or state in that part of Africa before Europeans came.

What came to be known as Angola under Portuguese rule also had kingdoms – well-organised states – before Africa was invaded and conquered by Europeans. Some of the most well-known were Ndongo and Matamba.

In the western part of what came to be Northern Rhodesia, now Zambia, in a region called Barotseland, the Lozi built a kingdom in precolonial times.

It was one of the most successful on the continent in the precolonial era, having united at least 25 different ethnic groups including members of the northern Sotho tribe of South Africa who migrated there and were assimilated by the Barotse and became Barotse themselves.

Members of other tribes who became Barotse migrated from Congo, Namibia, Angola, Zimbabwe and South Africa. The original founders of the kingdom came from Congo, what became the Belgian Congo during colonial rule.

During its heyday, the Barotse empire stretched into South West Africa, now Namibia, and into Angola as well as other parts of what is now Zambia. The king of Barotseland was known as *litunga*.

In modern Botswana, formerly Bechuanaland when it was ruled by Britain, there were a number of states before colonial rule. One of the most well-known was the Bamangwato whose hereditary rulers – kings – included Seretse Khama who became the first president of Botswana after the country won independence. He became *kgosi* (king) of his people before independence. He was the grandson of Khama III, king of the Bamangwato.

There was the Swazi kingdom in precolonial times which continued to exist during colonial rule. After independence, it continued to be known as the Kingdom of Swaziland and is now officially called Eswatini or the Kingdom of Eswatini.

In what is now Mozambique, the Gaza kingdom, also known as the Gaza empire, covered a large area in the southern part of the country and southeastern Zimbabwe and extended in the northern part of South Africa.

The Yao of northern Mozambique in Niassa Province built some of the most powerful kingdoms and states in East Africa. They straddle the Tanzanian-Mozambican border. They are also found in large numbers in Malawi where two presidents, Bakili Muluzi, and Joyce Banda who was the country's first female president and one of the first in Africa, were Yao.

The Maravi kingdom, after which the country of Malawi is named, covered a vast expanse of territory in the areas of what is now Malawi, Mozambique and Zambia. It was a confederacy, a form of union in which constituents parts enjoy extensive autonomy.

In South Africa was the Zulu kingdom established by Shaka. It became one of the most powerful and best organised, militarily, in the history of precolonial Africa.

There was also the kingdom of Zimbabwe in southern Africa, a kingdom founded by the Shona and other ethnic groups which covered a vast expanse of territory extending beyond the borders of what is now the country of Zimbabwe, formerly Southern Rhodesia.

There were other states in the area of modern Zimbabwe including the kingdom of Mapungubwe located south of the kingdom of Great Zimbabwe and which played a major role in the formation of the kingdom of Zimbabwe.

There was also the Bukalanga kingdom which, like many others on the continent, was multi-ethnic composed

187

of the Bakalanga of what is now northeastern Botswana, the Karanga of western Zimbabwe, and the Venda of the northeastern part of modern South Africa.

Like other Africans, the indigenous people of what is now Zimbabwe, the Shona and the Ndebele, fiercely resisted the imperial forces when Southern Rhodesia was being formed as a colony,

The Ndebele established a powerful state in the southern part of what is now the country of Zimbabwe. It was a highly centralised state under the leadership of Mzilikazi, its founder. He broke away from Shaka in what is Kwazulu-Natal Province today and fled north with his people, finally settling in what became the British colony of Southern Rhodesia.

During their last resistance against the British, the Ndebele were led by Lobengula, the son of Mzilikazi and their last king, who summed up the duplicitous nature of their conquerors in these poignant words:

"Do you know how a chameleon catches a fly?

It gets behind the fly, remains motionless for some time, then advances very slowly and gently, first putting forward one leg and then another. At last, when well within reach, it darts its tongue and the fly disappears. England is the chameleon and I am the fly."

Those are just some examples of the traditional states which existed in precolonial Africa. And where no complex systems of government in the form of a state existed, there were chiefdoms or other forms of central authority uniting the people under one leadership; which was also a form of government even if it did not fit the definition of government the way the colonial rulers defined it.

It was government, nonetheless, and served Africans well. Africans were not happy they were conquered and colonised. And they were not happy they had to pay taxes to be ruled by other people – from Europe or anywhere else.

Some of the kingdoms and empires in different parts of the continent disintegrated but later evolved into other political units, highly organised states comprising different ethnic groups under one leadership as multi-ethnic entities or as individual ethnic groups.

Many ethnic groups simply had chiefdoms including some of the most powerful in their regions. They included the Hehe of Tanzania whose chief, Mkwawa, led his people in a fierce war against the German colonial rulers in his homeland in the Southern Highlands. It was one the most heroic wars in the history of the country, together with the Maji Maji war of resistance from 1905 to 1907 which almost ended German rule.

In 1891, Mkwawa's army of 3,000 soldiers overpowered the German colonial force and killed its commander, Emil von Zelewski. In retaliation, the Germans launched a major attack on Mkwawa's fortress at Kalenga in 1894 but could not capture him. He escaped and continued to wage guerrilla warfare against the colonial forces until 1898 when he shot himself. He vowed he was not going to be captured alive. He is nationalist hero in Tanzania.

The Germans also cut off his head and took the skull to Germany. It was returned to Tanganyika in 1954, coincidentally in the same year the nationalist campaign for independence started in earnest when the party that led the independence struggle, the Tanganyika African national union (TANU), was formed.

All these examples of precolonial states, empires, kingdoms and chiefdoms clearly show that Africans did not learn from Europeans how to form nations and governments. They already existed when Europeans arrived.

Still, a case can be made that colonisation, or colonial rule, was responsible for state formation in Africa – but *only if* it is acknowledged that the colonial rulers destroyed what we already had and replaced it with theirs; not that they built states because none existed before they came.

An argument can also be made that the colonised got some benefits *not* from colonialism but from the things the colonisers did to facilitate imperial rule; which is not a defence of colonialism.

The colonial rulers were responsible for state formation which led to the creation of the countries we have in Africa today. They united different ethnic groups – smaller tribal states – to form larger administrative entities we inherited at independence and on which we continued to build our nations.

There was no Tanganyika or Nigeria or any of the other countries on the continent ruled by Europeans before the advent of colonial rule.

That does *not* mean the colonisers formed those countries to help or benefit Africans. They created them to facilitate imperial rule and help themselves and their mother countries.

Yet, Africans benefited from the creation of those nations – the ones we have today – which did not exist before but instead had tribal units which for all practical purposes are the units they identified with and to which they pledged allegiance as their nations.

Most Africans don't want to break up the countries we have today and return to precolonial days to live under tribal authorities which constituted states of their tribal nations during those days.

What they demand is inclusive government, meaningful participation in decision making and in the political process, and democratic representation in institutions of authority without excluding some groups; an exclusion which has led to demands for extensive autonomy or devolution of power and even secession.

But they prefer to live in the larger political units and

be members of the nations we have today –  Ghana, Zambia, Kenya, Nigeria and so on – which were formed by the colonial rulers.

That does not mean those political units – colonial territories, now our countries –  were created to help Africans pursue unity in the name of Pan-African solidarity.

They were created to facilitate colonial rule, in most cases by centralising authority and by administering through indirect rule, a system introduced by Lord Lugard in Northern Nigeria. Yet Nigeria was not created to benefit Africans living within the boundaries of  what came to be the Nigerian federation. It was created for the purpose of exploitation to benefit the colonial power: Britain.

Still, Nigerians benefited from the existence of Nigeria as a single political entity they inherited at independence instead of breaking it up into smaller political units – the tribal states – which existed before colonial rule. And that was the case in all the other former colonies across the continent.

None of them decided to break up and return to tribal rule, with each tribe or ethnic group having its own authority as an independent and separate political unit. African leaders agreed in May 1963 when they met in Addis Ababa, Ethiopia, and formed the Organisation of African Unity (OAU) that they would maintain the boundaries they inherited at independence. It was Nyerere who presented that resolution.

With state formation by the colonial powers came other developments including the establishment of schools, hospitals, transport networks – roads and railways – and other institutions and facilities of modernisation. Again, this was done mainly to facilitate colonial rule more than anything else.

The colonial rulers did not even build many hospitals and clinics. Post-colonial governments in some countries – such as Ghana under Nkrumah and Tanzania under

Nyerere – built more hospitals and other medical facilities than the colonial rulers did.

Some countries also expanded the transport network and built other infrastructure which did not exist before colonial rule. Some of them also built factories to manufacture import-substitution items and other products. The colonial rulers never intended to build them because they wanted all manufactured goods imported from their home countries – Africa being used only as a market for imports from the metropolitan countries – and from a few "favoured" colonies such as Kenya whose exports went to neighbouring Uganda and Tanganyika.

The schools the colonial governments built were also not enough to train the required number of people our countries would need to meet their manpower requirements after they won independence. They built only enough to meet their needs – educate a limited number of Africans to work for the colonial governments even though the money to fund those schools came from the Africans themselves: the taxes they paid and the money the colonial governments earned from cash crops grown by African farmers but for which they were grossly underpaid by the colonial rulers.

Also, the limited higher education Africans were able to obtain was mainly a product of their effort. They demanded to be educated while the colonial rulers wanted to provide only lower education for clerical work and other services needed to maintain colonial rule.

Even church schools – established by European missionaries – were funded by the Africans themselves from the contributions they made to their churches yet did not get their money's worth in terms of education and other services.

After African countries won independence, they built far more schools and trained far more people in a much shorter period than the colonial rulers did during a much longer period they ruled those countries. As Nyerere stated at a meeting with World Bank officials in Washington, D.C., in 1997:

"We took over a country with 85 per cent of its adults illiterate. The British ruled us for 42 years. When they left, there were two trained engineers and 12 doctors. When I stepped down, there was 91 per cent literacy and nearly every child was in school. We trained thousands of engineers, doctors and teachers." – (Julius K. Nyerere, quoted by Godfrey Mwakikagile, *Nyerere and Africa: End of an Era*, op. cit., p. 76; Julius Nyerere, quoted in *Sunday Times*, London, October 3, 1999; R.W. Johnson, "Nyerere: A Flawed Hero," *The National Interest*, June 1, 2000, Washington, D.C., p. 73. See also, "Farewell to the Father of Tanzania," in the *Mail and Guardian*, Johannesburg, October 15, 1999; "Julius Nyerere of Tanzania Dies; Preached African Socialism to the World," in *The New York Times*, October 15, 1999, p. B10; "Former Tanzanian President Julius Nyerere Dies at 77; African leader Led Independence Movement and Worked to Unify Nation, Continent," in *The Washington Post*, October 15, 1999, p. B-06; "Julius Nyerere: Former President of Tanzania Led Country to Independence," in the *Los Angeles Times*, October 15, 1999, p. 30).

That was great achievement within 24 years he was president. He stepped down in November 1985.

Even the way the roads and railways were built clearly showed they were intended to facilitate exploitation of African resources in the interior and other parts of the colonies. They went straight to where the resources were. The resources – minerals and other commodities such as tea, coffee, cocoa and forestry products – were transported from the interior to the coast to be shipped to Europe. Areas which had no resources to be exploited were ignored in terms of "development." They hardly had any roads or modern facilities built by the colonial governments.

When our countries won independence, they inherited the transport network and other infrastructure although none was built to benefit Africans – in fact, it was African labourers who built all the infrastructure, earning meagre wages and sometimes nothing.

State formation – the creation of modern institutions of authority as well as the countries we have today in Africa – by the imperial powers also facilitated our integration into the international community. We effectively became an integral part of it unlike before when we were virtually isolated.

The educational system – schools built by the colonial rulers and European missionaries – also played a major role in laying the foundation of our modern sates even though the primary purpose of building those schools was to train Africans to work for the colonial governments and facilitate imperial rule.

Imposition of imperial rule on us meant we were no longer the owners of our own homeland. For all practical purposes, Africans no longer owned Africa.

We not only became captives in our own motherland, of all places; we lost the only place that was home to us.

We were even given new names by our conquerors – Gold Coast, Ivory Coast, Rhodesia, Nigeria, Niger, Central African Republic, Sierra Leone, Cameroon, Guinea, Deutsch-Ostafrika (German East Africa), Deutsch-Südwestafrika (German South West Africa), Transvaal, Natal, and so on.

Even some of our lakes and mountains were named after our European conquerors, replacing indigenous names: Lake Victoria instead of Nyanza; Lake Albert; Victoria Falls; Livingstone Mountains; Drakensberg Mountains, Murchison Falls; so were towns and cities: Leopoldville, Stanleyville, Elisabethville, Albertville, Brazzaville, Libreville, Livingstone in Northern Rhodesia, Francistown in Bechunaland, Grahamstown, Eldoret,

Salisbury, Lagos, Durban, Cape Town, Port Elizabeth, Pretoria, Johannesburg, Bloemfontein, Blantyre, Lourenço Marques, Beira, Walvis Bay, Windhoek, Cape Coast, Broken Hill in Northern Rhodesia, Neu Langenburg in Deutsch-Ostafrika, and by doing so erased the history of many places which was preserved and transmitted by the use of indigenous names.

Colonisation also not only robbed us of our natural right to live free and think for ourselves; it also robbed us of our dignity and self-esteem. We were reduced to being mere objects of ridicule and contempt for our conquerors. In their eyes, we ceased to be full human beings – if we ever were, to them.

There is no question that the colonisation of Africa has had a profound impact on the personality of Africans as individuals and as a collective entity in a way no other external force or form of invasion has had on the continent. And its effects are still felt, and manifested in many ways, even today.

Conquest of our ancestors by the imperial powers can be attributed to one thing: weakness. This weakness can also be attributed to something else: lack of technological development. Without technology, Africans could not make advanced weapons to defend themselves against the superior firepower of the invaders from Europe.

The invaders had guns – Africans did not – enabling only a few European soldiers and adventurers to conquer vast expanses of territory inhabited by millions of people. Simply firing a few bullets or a single cannon, with its "sonic boom," was enough – in fact more than enough – to scare and scatter the "natives" and send them running for their lives with their spears, bows and arrows.

The conquest of Africa was that simple in terms of firepower. Africans fighting Europeans was a mismatch. The imperial order prevailed, thanks to European guns. This is what Professor Kenneth Minogue, in his book *Nationalism*, calls the technological theory of imperialism, expressed in jingoistic terms: "We have got, the Gatling gun, and they have not."

The Gatling gun played a major role in intimidating, subduing and conquering Africans during the era of colonisation; its firepower best demonstrated during the Anglo-Ashanti wars in the Gold Coast, the Anglo-Zulu wars in South Africa, and against the Ndebele in Southern Rhodesia. And it happened the same way in other parts of Africa where our Europeans conquerors used guns, or the mere threat of it, to subjugate the "natives."

The rest of the Africans in those regions got the message which spread fast farther afield, itself as a weapon of psychological conquest of the people. They were conquered even before they could think of resisting invasion or they simply surrendered, knowing the odds against them, because of European guns whose use was the best expression of imperial might. And that had a profound impact on us as a people. We were emasculated.

The psychological wounds inflicted on us by our conquerors caused enormous and incalculable damage in terms of self-esteem and even personality formation and development among some of our people who came to believe that our conquest could be best explained in terms of natural differences between blacks and whites; that whites were more technologically advanced and more powerful than we were because they were naturally superior to us. For, how else could we explain our defeat and humiliation by a mere handful of whites, here and there, when they invaded us? Even if this could be explained in terms of guns, why were we not able to make them before they came and when we were fighting them if we had the same mental capacity to do so? And why are they so far ahead of us even today?

While some of us – including me in my book *Africa is in A Mess* – do concede there have indeed been some benefits from the interaction that has taken place between Africa and Europe through the centuries, and that the benefits have been reciprocal not just one-sided as our conquerors and their supporters amongst us claim that we have been the biggest beneficiaries because of the Western material civilisation that was brought to us, history is not on the side of our conquerors and their admirers among us.

It took Europe hundreds of years to develop and get where they are today; much of that development attributed to other cultures including Africa.

Europeans did not invent the wheel on which many civilisations have rolled forward since its invention. They did not develop arithmetic critical to scientific progress and technological development; nor did they invent gunpowder which was vital to Europe's conquest of other cultures and civilisations.

Even Africa's contribution to Europe's development in terms of material and labour – the two being the most obvious from the time they conquered us although our intellectual contribution before then and after cannot be ignored – far exceeds what Europe contributed to the development of Africa.

Yet Africa's contribution to the development of Europe and Europe's role in the underdevelopment of Africa is hardly acknowledged by our conquerors because they were the beneficiaries of both. And they still are in this era of globalisation.

There is little in Europe's argument – that European countries initiated and fuelled their own development – which can refute or undermine Walter Rodney's thesis of his work, *How Europe Underdeveloped Africa*.

Europe's contribution to Africa's development has been extraction: building extractive industries – for minerals and other resources – to benefit Europe. And that still goes on today. Look at who benefits the most from the exploitation of Africa's natural wealth including land, not just minerals and others resources.

By its very nature, colonisation is exploitative – and oppressive to facilitate exploitation. Oppression goes hand in hand with degradation to strip the colonised of their dignity in order to make it easier to dominate them.

Recolonisation of Africa has become the norm in this era of globalisation and is even lauded by some brainwashed Africans as our only salvation from the misery and suffering, and grinding poverty, tens of millions of our people have to endure all their lives.

Even during colonial rule, the disadvantages of colonisation far outweighed its advantages. Most of the advantages have been the result of mutual cooperation between the two – Africa and Europe – although in a lopsided way, with Europe benefiting more than Africa has from this interaction.

But because we were conquered and subjugated, it is difficult if not impossible for some of our people to acknowledge all that even if they know it is true.

Europe has not been our saviour; very much to the contrary. Our very African-ness has been sorely tested by this European invasion whose impact continues to shape the destiny of many Africans including entire nations despite years of "independence" from alien rule.

Yet we know who and what we are, the essence of our very being, rooted in traditional Africa. It is this essence of African-ness which is acknowledged even by some Westernised or brainwashed Africans in rare moments of nostalgia when they say: That is how we lived before the coming of Europeans; that is how our ancestors lived; that is what our ancestors did; not everything was good back then but they were good old days; our communal and family ties were stronger then than they are now; that is how we lived as Africans – an that is what it meant to be African. Sadly, those days are gone.

It was an essence, of African-ness, that was not contaminated or threatened in its pristine beauty, by foreign influence, because there was no such influence. When Westernised Africans acknowledge this essence, they are invoking the essence of their very being. Yet, they

198

at the same repudiate it when they embrace Westernisation or any other foreign influence and identity because they think it is better than being African.

It does not mean we want to isolate and even insulate ourselves from the rest of the world. We can continue to be active members of the global community, learn from others as much as they can learn from us, and benefit from modernisation without losing or compromising our identity and essence as Africans. And that means reclaiming the spirit and values of traditional Africa and its institutions as well as indigenous knowledge to enable us to chart our way forward and navigate in the treacherous waters of globalisation which threaten the integrity and wellbeing of Africa in terms of identity and personality.

We have to be what we are. Otherwise we are going to copy everything from other people and become a product of other cultures as if we did not have our own essence and identity before we came into contact with them. It would be as if we never even existed before.

We cannot abandon or denigrate our cultural identity. Without culture, our own culture, we are nothing as a people. Culture is a vital force and source of life for a nation, any nation, and for Africa as a collective entity even if it is not a monolithic whole. But Africa is organic in essence, with a vital force of its own that animates it and gives it a distinctive identity.

By turning against traditional Africa, modernised Africans have not only turned against themselves; they have lost their soul since it is traditional Africa which is the essence of their very being.

There is no question that cultural imperialism has had a devastating impact on many Africans in terms of identity. Many of them prefer to be anything else – and everything else – but African. That is because they are ashamed of who they are and what they are. They are ashamed of their "primitive" African heritage; they are ashamed of Africa's "backwardness" – and even the food our people eat in villages and prefer European food because they are "civilised."

Some of them are even proud to say they have "forgotten" their native languages after living outside Africa, especially in Europe, the United States and other non-African countries, preferably "white," for only a few years; sometimes for only two to three – let alone five or more.

They say they can no longer speak Kiswahili; they can no longer speak Gikuyu (Kikuyu), Chinyanja, Shona, Mende – the list goes on and on. They can only speak English, French, German, Dutch, Swedish, Polish, Spanish or some other European language. Many of them have not even mastered those languages. Yet they are so proud of them simply because they are not African languages.

There are even those who anglicise their African names or spell them in some other European language they speak. Why not? It makes them "sophisticated," "civilised," "educated," "Europeanised" – and no longer "backward," "primitive" or "uncivilised."

Many Africans also like to mix English, French or Portuguese – the languages of our former colonial masters – with the native languages they speak as a sign of being "sophisticated" and "educated," a phenomenon which, in East Africa, has led to the evolution of what we call Kiswanglish, a hybrid of Kiswahili and English especially in Kenya and Tanzania.

That is very common among the elite, most of whom are a product of Western education. That is the case even in local schools in terms of intellectual preparation from primary school patterned after the colonial educational systems we inherited and are therefore Western because that is where our rulers came from.

Even our countries are described as "English-speaking," "French-speaking" or "Portuguese-speaking" even though the vast majority of our people in those countries don't even understand or speak those languages.

Many of them don't even want to learn those languages. They are satisfied with what they already know – their own native languages.

Africans themselves describe our countries in terms of being "Anglophone," "Francophone" and "Lusophone" instead of describing them as being multi-lingual African-speaking countries since most of the people in those countries speak their own native languages, not European languages.

They don't even want to become "European" like many of their educated brethren who try to be more "European" than the Europeans themselves by desperately trying to shed or run away from their African identity.

"Uneducated" Africans and those who live in villages are more African than their educated brothers and sisters – some of whom don't even know what they really are, caught between two worlds, African and non-African. They are caught between being a part of Africa or Europe, Africa or America and so on.

And the less African they become, by identifying with and becoming a part of the non-African world and deliberately distancing themselves from their African identity and heritage, the prouder they are.

That has been one of the devastating results and consequences of our being colonised – subjugated and brainwashed by our conquerors into believing that any other place, especially Europe and any other part of the "white" world, is better than Africa.

Cultural imperialism also has been very destructive in terms of indigenous knowledge.

Our indigenous knowledge has been lost through the suppression of our native languages which are the repository of knowledge transmitted from one generation to the next.

It is a tragedy that the languages of our conquerors who ruled us are the preferred languages in our countries, especially by the elite and government officials and leaders. They are still given priority at the expense of our native languages even decades after independence as if we want to remain under European control and are proud of being an extension of Europe.

In most African countries, very little or nothing is being done to give native languages priority and the status they deserve as vital tools for the preservation and dissemination of indigenous knowledge and as a vital part of our identity while, at the same time, continuing to use the languages of the former colonial powers – English, French and Portuguese – out of necessity.

It is as if our native languages are irrelevant to our wellbeing as Africans, reinforcing the notion, and the attitude, that nothing good comes out of Africa except gold, diamonds and other minerals and resources. And nothing good – not even indigenous knowledge and institutions – ever came from Africans except labour, especially manual labour extracted from Africans in conditions which amounted to virtual slavery and even outright enslavement to serve our conquerors.

Although we have benefited from the knowledge that we have obtained from the West through schools established by our colonial rulers and missionaries, there is no question that Western education was also intended to de-Africanise Africans.

Even educated Africans deliberately attempted to de-Africanise themselves by turning against their own indigenous cultures and traditional ways of life and values – and therefore turned against their own very being – in order to become "British," "French," and "Portuguese," the colonial powers which ruled Africa.

Western education was also intended to alienate educated Africans from their own people – the more educated they were, the less African they became – and turn them into loyal servants of our conquerors to perpetuate imperial domination of Africa even after the end of colonial rule; a goal that was achieved in most cases as has been demonstrated by the existence of neo-colonial governments and institutions in all parts of the continent since independence, making a mockery of the sacrifices we made to end colonial rule.

There were only a few exceptions where neo-colonialism faced stiff resistance. That was in Ghana under Nkrumah, Tanzania under Nyerere, and Guinea under Sekou Toure. The three leaders were also ideological compatriots who earned Africa a respectable place in the global arena as relentless and uncompromising champions of African liberation, unity and independence. And they never wavered even when the positions they took were challenged by the leaders of powerful nations, especially Western, on a number of vital and fundamental issues affecting the wellbeing of Africa and the Third World as a whole.

They made genuine attempts to achieve true independence. But even in those countries, there were subversive elements within the government and elsewhere in society who collaborated with the imperialist powers to undermine the leaders  and subvert institutions of authority in order to sabotage their efforts to achieve true liberation from foreign domination, especially Western.

In fact, we have witnessed a sad spectacle since the end of colonial rule in the sixties when most African countries won independence: the collapse of a number of states in different parts of the continent because of bad leadership around which everything else revolves.

The vast majority of the leaders we have had since independence have been corrupt, incompetent, despotic and tribalist – a liability imperial powers have effectively exploited to establish and support neo-colonial governments.

So, we see that the colonial rulers never really left Africa; they only changed faces. There is no other way to look at it unless we want to delude ourselves into believing that we achieved genuine independence and are truly free today, while the rest of the world laughs at us for being so stupid to believe that – as if we are a bunch of idiots to whom naïveté is a virtue to be glorified and celebrated.

And that would justify the psychological defeat we also suffered at the hands of our conquerors when they conquered our minds as well.

We have been victims of imperial conquest from the beginning when our conquerors invaded our continent for the first time as soon as they arrived from Europe to colonise us. We are still their victims even today. And we were conquered in more than one way.

We lost our land. We lost our freedom, We lost our dignity and self-esteem. We even lost our mind when we were brainwashed by our conquerors into believing they were superior to us in terms of intelligence and everything else. Not all of us believed that. But many of our people did and still do. We lost terribly. The list goes on and on.

But we did not lose our humanity and our intrinsic worth of being humane more than our conquerors were.

Still, we were conquered. Our capacity to be humane did not save us; in fact, it was a liability and our downfall in many areas when dealing with our invaders who did not care about morality except when it benefited them. We also fought back, of course, and still lost mainly because of our technological inferiority. Let us admit.

But it was conquest of the mind where we suffered the ultimate defeat. Conquest of the mind was the worst form of imperial subjugation whose impact is still felt today. Many of our people have been thoroughly brainwashed by our conquerors.

Even when we try to find solutions to our problems, we look to Europe and America – or some other non-African country – for guidance and assistance instead of looking within Africa itself to find those solutions from our own people. We are so dependent on other people – they even have to build buildings for us including the headquarters of the African Union (AU) – that we even refuse to think for ourselves, and don't want to think for ourselves, to find solutions to our own problems. Yet these are African problems, within Africa itself, and should and *do* have African solutions.

But because we are a conquered people, even mentally and psychologically, we have to turn to our conquerors – of all people – to help us as if they are a part of us and we are a part of them. And this didn't just start. It started from the beginning when they conquered us and consolidated their rule over us through the years when we were under colonial rule.

It has been a tragic history for us as a conquered people. Our subservience to our former colonial masters and other powers we always beg to help us has been ruthlessly public – in the international spotlight – for decades since independence.

Even our annual budgets have to be approved by them although most of the money does not come from them but comes from our own resources within. Our leaders worry about what the leaders of powerful nations think about our condition and the problems we face instead of worrying about our own people – what they think and what have to say.

That is the history of conquest and the psychology of conquered people.

In many cases during colonial rule, the conquered even ended up identifying with their conquerors. They emulated them. They not only tried to be more British than the British themselves, or more French than the French themselves; they wanted to be "white."

They glorified our conquerors as if they were the best specimen of mankind in spite of all the suffering and humiliation they inflicted on them.

That also has been the case with many of our people since independence, including those who were born after independence. Many of them look to the West – where our conquerors came from – for guidance; although this can also partly be attributed to rotten leadership across Africa during the post-colonial era because our leaders have failed to address our problems the way they should have.

The psychological defeat we suffered at the hands of our conquerors turned many of our people against themselves, against their African-ness.

Many of them even today want to be "white" in every conceivable way. Some of them even bleach their skin in a desperate attempt to change their physical appearance and shed their African identity. The lighter, the better – that is the "whiter" the better.

It is sad, depressingly sad, that many Africans have also chosen our former colonial rulers to be their "kith-kin" instead of embracing their own people, fellow Africans, as their true kith-and-kin.

They identify themselves with their former colonial masters more than they do with fellow Africans who were ruled by other colonial powers. For example, Guineans, Malians and Senegalese identify with the French more than they do with Ghanaians, Nigerians and Sierra Leoneans who were ruled by the British, further reinforcing the racist notion that Europeans are superior to Africans – it is better to be a part of them than it is to be a part of fellow Africans.

This political and cultural divide between Francophone and Anglophone Africa is evident even in the African Union (AU), an umbrella organisation who primary objective is to foster African solidarity and cooperation in solving and finding solutions to African problems including disunity among ourselves. Yet it has done exactly the opposite in terms of fostering unity. Despite professions to the contrary, the African Union is operating under the banner of "us versus them" when Pan-African solidarity and unity is being pursued.

There is rivalry and even mistrust between member countries which were ruled by the two colonial powers:

France and Britain. And that has been the case since the Organisation of African Unity (OAU) – which preceded the AU – was formed in Addis Ababa, Ethiopia, in May 1963 whose only achievement was in supporting the African liberation movements fighting to end white minority rule in the countries of southern Africa and Portuguese Guinea in West Africa. It was a tragic failure in conflict resolution, let alone in pursing the goal of continental unity under one government.

In terms of Franco-British – or British-French – rivalry in post-colonial Africa, the most tragic case and glaring example within a country is the civil conflict – which has been bloody – between Anglophone Cameroon and Francophone Cameroon in a nation where the former colonial power, France, still wields enormous power and influence, and is virtually the final arbiter on all matters, to the detriment of English-speaking Cameroonians of Southern Cameroons who constitute what should at least be an autonomous entity in a genuine federation or confederation or even an independent state if that is the only way the conflict can be resolved.

It is not unusual for the former colonial powers to intervene in conflicts in their former colonies or simply to interfere in their affairs because they still consider them to be their spheres of influence.

Imperial control of Africa is manifested in many other ways, making a mockery of independence Africans are so proud of. It is as if our struggle for independence amounted to nothing and we want to return to the status quo ante and be a part of the old colonial empires.

One of the tragedies that befell Africa was that to many Africans, our conquerors – European colonial rulers and settlers – not only became their role models; they emulated them in many ways and and as much as they could. By doing so, they ended up destroying themselves. It was diminution of African identity and a brutal attack on the African personality. And it still goes on even today, as many Africans try to run away from themselves and be what they are not.

All that is clear victory for cultural imperialism. Evidence is everywhere, not only in terms of language – English and French are the main official languages in Africa – but also in terms of cultural imitation with many Africans adopting European manners and mannerisms as well as culture. It is also a victory in terms of ideas propagated by the West to our detriment as if we cannot think for ourselves.

Yet that is exactly what we fought for: not only to end colonial rule – only to invite our former rulers back – but to rule ourselves and think for ourselves for our own wellbeing. And let the people decide.

We never had the opportunity to decide for ourselves during colonial rule on a wide range of issues affecting our wellbeing and destiny as one people constituting a nation; our colonial masters did that for us. Sadly, even today, most of our leaders across the continent don't allow the people to decide for themselves decades after colonial rule ended.

The end of colonial rule came with responsibilities. The main responsibility was for us to be responsible for ourselves and for our wellbeing. That is still the case today. Nobody is going to help us. We should not even want or expect other people to solve our problems. We have to help ourselves. Otherwise our independence is meaningless. And that seems to be the case.

We should not expect other people to come to our rescue or solve our problems. We are on our own. The rest of the world does *not* care about us. And it shouldn't when we don't care enough about ourselves and don't do enough to help ourselves to solve our own problems. As Nyerere said in his speech at the University of Dar es Salaam, Tanzania, which was conversational in tone and style, not long before he died:

"You wanted me to reflect. I told you I had very little time to reflect. I am not an engineer (reference to the vice-chancellor of the University of Dar es Salaam who identified himself as an engineer in his introductory remarks) and therefore what I am going to say might sound messy, unstructured and possibly irrelevant to what you intend to do; but I thought that if by reflecting, you wanted me to go back and relive the political life that I have lived for the last 30, 40 years, that I cannot do.

And in any case, in spite of the fact that it's useful to go back in history, what you are talking about is what might be of use to Africa in the 21st century. History's important, obviously, but I think we should concentrate and see what might be of use to our continent in the coming century.

What I want to do is share with you some thoughts on two issues concerning Africa. One, an obvious one; when I speak, you will realise how obvious it is. Another one, less obvious, and I'll spend a little more time on the less obvious one, because I think this will put Africa in what is going to be Africa's context in the 21st century. And the new leadership of Africa will have to concern itself with the situation in which it finds itself in the world tomorrow - in the world of the 21st century. And the Africa I'm going to be talking about, is Africa south of the Sahara, sub-Saharan Africa. I'll explain later the reason why I chose to concentrate on Africa south of the Sahara. It is because of the point I want to emphasise.

It appears today that in the world tomorrow, there are going to be three centres of power: some, political power; some, economic power, but three centres of real power in the world. One centre is the United States of America and Canada; what you call North America. That is going to be a huge economic power, and probably for a long time the only military power, but a huge economic power. The other one is going to be Western Europe, another huge economic power. I think Europe is choosing deliberately not to be a military power. I think they deliberately want to leave that to the United States. The other one is Japan. Japan is in a different category but it is better to say Japan, because the power of Japan is quite clear, the economic power of Japan is obvious.

The three powers are going to affect the countries near them. I was speaking in South Africa recently and I referred to Mexico. A former president of Mexico, I think it must have been after the revolution in 1935, no, after the revolution; a former president of Mexico is reported to have complained about his country or lamented about his country. "Poor Mexico," said the president, "so far from God yet so near the United States." He was complaining about the disadvantages of being a neighbour of a giant.

Today, Mexico has decided not simply to suffer the disadvantages of being so close to the United States. And the United States itself has realised the importance of trying to accommodate Mexico. In the past there were huge attempts by the United States to prevent people from moving from Mexico *into* the United States; people seeking work, seeking jobs. So you had police, a border very well policed in order to prevent Mexicans who *seek*, who *look* for jobs, to *move* into the United States. The United States discovered that it was not working. It *can't* work.

There is a kind of economic osmosis where whatever you do, if you are rich, you are attractive to the poor. They will come, they'll even *risk* their own lives in order to come. So the United States tried very hard to prevent Mexicans going into the United States; they've given up, and the result was NAFTA. It is in the interest of the United States to try and create jobs in Mexico because, if you don't, the Mexicans will simply come, to the United States; so they're doing that.

Europe, Western Europe, is very wealthy. It has two Mexicos. One is Eastern Europe. If you want to prevent those Eastern Europeans to come to Western Europe, you jolly will have to create jobs in *Eastern* Europe, and Western Europe is actually *doing* that. They are *doing* that. They'll help Eastern Europe to develop. The whole of Western Europe will be doing it, the Germans are doing it. The Germans basically started first of all with the East Germans but they are spending lots of money also helping the other countries of Eastern Europe to develop, including unfortunately, or *fortunately* for them, including Russia. Because they realise, Europeans realise including the Germans, if you don't help *Russia* to develop, one of these days you are going to be in trouble. So it is in the interest of Western Europe, to help Eastern Europe including Russia. They are pouring a lot of money in that part of the world, in that part of Europe, to try and help it to develop.

I said Western Europe has two Mexicos. I have mentioned one. I'll jump the other. I jump Europe's second Mexico. I'll go to Asia. I'll go to Japan. Japan - a wealthy island, *very* wealthy indeed, but an *island*. I don't think they're very keen on the unemployed of Asia to go to Japan. They'd rather help them where they are, and Japan is spending a lot of money in Asia, to help create jobs *in* Asia, prevent those Asians dreaming about going to Japan to look for jobs. In any case, Japan is too small, they can't find wealth there.

But apart from what Japan is doing, of course Asia *is* Asia; Asia has *China!* Asia has *India*, and the small countries of Asia are not very small. The population of Indonesia is twice the population of Nigeria, your biggest. So Asia is virtually in a category, of the Third World countries, of the Southern countries; Asia is almost in a category of its own. It is developing as a power, and Europe knows it, and the United States knows it. And in spite of the *huge* Atlantic, now they are talking about the Atlantic *Rim*. That is in recognition of the importance of Asia.

I go back to Europe. Europe has a second Mexico. And Europe's second Mexico is North Africa. North Africa is to Europe what Mexico is to the United States. North Africans who have no jobs will not go to Nigeria; they'll be thinking of Europe or the Middle East, because of the imperatives of geography and history and religion and language. North Africa is part of Europe and the Middle East.

Nasser was a great leader and a great *African* leader. I got on extremely well with him. Once he sent me a minister, and I had a long discussion with his minister at the State House here, and in the course of the discussion, the minister says to me, "Mr. President, this is my first visit to Africa." North Africa, because of the pull of the Mediterranean, and I say, history and culture, and religion, North Africa is pulled towards the North. When North Africans look for jobs, they go to Western Europe and southern Western Europe, or they go to the Middle East. And Europe has a specific policy for North Africa, specific policy for North Africa. It's not only about development; it's also about security. Because of you don't do something about North Africa, they'll come.

Africa, south of the Sahara, is different; *totally* different. If you have no jobs here in Tanzania, where do you go? The Japanese have no fear that you people will flock to Japan. The North Americans have no fear that you people will flock to North America. Not even from West Africa. The Atlantic, the Atlantic as an ocean, like the Mediterranean, it has its own logic. But links North America and Western Europe, not North America and West Africa.

Africa south of the Sahara is isolated. That is the first point I want to make. South of the Sahara is totally isolated in terms of that configuration of developing power in the world in the 21st century - on its own. There is no centre of power in whose self-interest it's important to develop Africa, *no* centre. Not North America, not Japan, not Western Europe. There's no self-interest to bother about Africa south of the Sahara. Africa south of the

212

Sahara is on its own. *Na si jambo baya*. Those of you who don't know Kiswahili, I just whispered, "Not necessarily bad."

That's the first thing I wanted to say about Africa south of the Sahara. African leadership, the coming African leadership, will have to bear that in mind. You are on your own, Mr. Vice President. You mentioned, you know, in the past, there was some Cold War competition in Africa and some Africans may have exploited it. I never did. I never succeeded in exploiting the Cold War in Africa. We suffered, we suffered through the Cold War. Look at Africa south of the Sahara. I'll be talking about it later. Southern Africa, I mean, look at southern Africa; devastated because of the combination of the Cold War and apartheid. Devastated part of Africa. It could have been *very* different. But the Cold War is gone, thank God. But thank God the Cold War is gone, the chances of the Mobutus also is gone.

So that's the first thing I wanted to say about Africa south of the Sahara. Africa south of the Sahara in those terms is isolated. That is the point I said was not obvious and I had to explain it in terms in which I have tried to explain it. The other one, the second point I want to raise is completely obvious. Africa has 53 nation-states, most of them in Africa south of the Sahara. If numbers were power, Africa would be the most powerful continent on earth. It is the weakest; so it's obvious numbers are not power.

So the second point about Africa, and again I am talking about Africa south of the Sahara; it is fragmented, fragmented. From the very beginning of independence 40 years ago, we were against that idea, that the continent is so fragmented. We called it the Balkanisation of Africa. Today, I think the Balkans are talking about the Africanisation of Europe. Africa's states are too many, too small, some make no logic, whether political logic or ethnic logic or anything. They are non-viable. It is not a

213

confession.

The OAU was founded in 1963. In 1964 we went to Cairo to hold, in a sense, our first summit after the inaugural summit. I was responsible for moving that resolution that Africa must accept the borders, which we inherited from colonialism; accept them as they are. That resolution was passed by the organisation (OAU) with two reservations: one from Morocco, another from Somalia. Let me say why I moved that resolution.

In 1960, just before this country became independent, I think I was then chief minister; I received a delegation of Masai elders from Kenya, led by an American missionary. And they came to persuade me to let the Masai invoke something called the Anglo-Masai Agreement so that that section of the Masai in Kenya should become part of Tanganyika; so that when Tanganyika becomes independent, it includes part of Masai, from Kenya. I suspected the American missionary was responsible for that idea. I don't remember that I was particularly polite to him. Kenyatta was then in detention, and here somebody comes to me, that we should break up Kenya and make part of Kenya part of Tanganyika. But why shouldn't Kenyatta demand that the Masai part of Tanganyika should become Masai of Kenya? It's the same logic. That was in 1960.

In 1961 we became independent. In 1962, early 1962, I resigned as prime minister and then a few weeks later I received Dr. Banda. *Mungu amuweke mahali pema* (May God rest his soul in peace). I received Dr. Banda. We had just, FRELIMO had just been established here and we were now in the process of starting the armed struggle.

So Banda comes to me with a big old book, with lots and lots of maps in it, and tells me, "Mwalimu, what is this, what is Mozambique? There is no such thing as Mozambique." I said, "What do you mean there is no such thing as Mozambique?" So he showed me this map, and he said: "That part is part of Nyasaland (it was still

Nyasaland, not Malawi, at that time). That part is part of Southern Rhodesia, That part is Swaziland, and this part, which is the northern part, Makonde part, that is *your* part."

So Banda disposed of Mozambique just like that. I ridiculed the idea, and Banda never liked anybody to ridicule his ideas. So he left and went to Lisbon to talk to Salazar about this wonderful idea. I don't know what Salazar told him. That was '62.

In '63 we go to Addis Ababa for the inauguration of the OAU, and Ethiopia and Somalia are at war over the Ogaden. We had to send a special delegation to bring the president of Somalia to attend that inaugural summit, because the two countries were at *war*. Why? Because Somalia wanted the Ogaden, a *whole* province of Ethiopia, saying, "That is part of Somalia." And Ethiopia was quietly, the Emperor quietly saying to us that "the whole of Somalia is part of Ethiopia."

So those three, the delegation of the Masai, led by the American missionary; Banda's old book of maps; and the Ogaden, caused me to move that resolution, in Cairo 1964. And I say, the resolution was accepted, two countries with reservations, and one was Somalia because Somalia wanted the Ogaden; Somalia wanted northern Kenya; Somalia wanted Djibouti.

Throw away all our ideas about socialism. Throw them away, give them to the Americans, give them to the Japanese, give them, so that they can, I don't know, they can do whatever they like with them. *Embrace* capitalism, fine! But you *have* to be self-reliant. You here in Tanzania don't dream that if you privatise every blessed thing, including the prison, then foreign investors will come rushing. No! No! Your are dreaming! *Hawaji!* They won't come! (*hawaji!*). You just try it.

There is more to privatise in Eastern Europe than here. Norman Manley, the Prime Minister of Jamaica, in those days the vogue was nationalisation, not privatisation. In those days the vogue was *nationalisation*. So Norman Manley was asked as Jamaica was moving towards independence: "Mr. Prime Minister, are you going to nationalise the economy?" His answer was: "You can't nationalise *nothing*."

You people here are busy privatising not *nothing*, we did *build* something, we built *something* to privatise. But quite frankly, for the appetite of Europe, and the appetite of North America, this is privatising nothing. The people with a really good appetite will go to Eastern Europe, they'll go to Russia, they'll not come rushing to Tanzania! Your blessed National Bank of Commerce, it's a branch of some major bank somewhere, and in Tanzania you say, "It's so big we must divide it into pieces," which is *nonsense*.

Africa south of the Sahara is isolated. Therefore, to develop, it will have to depend upon its own resources basically. Internal resources, nationally; and Africa will have to depend upon Africa. The leadership of the future will have to devise, try to carry out policies of *maximum* national self-reliance and *maximum* collective self-reliance. They have no other choice. *Hamna*! (You don't have it!) And this, this need to organise collective self-reliance is what moves me to the second part.

The small countries in Africa must move towards either unity or co-operation, unity of Africa. The leadership of the future, of the 21st century, should have less respect, less respect for this thing called "national sovereignty." I'm not saying take up arms and destroy the state, no! This idea that we must *preserve* the Tanganyika, then *preserve* the Kenya as they *are*, is nonsensical!

The nation-states we in Africa, have inherited from Europe. They are the builders of the nation-states par excellence. For centuries they fought wars! The history of Europe, the history of the *building* of Europe is a history of war. And sometimes their wars when they get hotter although they're European wars, they call them *world wars.* And we all get involved. We fight even in Tanganyika here, we *fought* here, one world war.

These Europeans, powerful, where little Belgium is more powerful than the whole of Africa south of the Sahara put together; these *powerful* European states are moving towards unity, and you people are talking about the atavism of the tribe, this is nonsense! I am telling *you* people. How can anybody think of the tribe as the unity of the future? *Hakuna!* (There's nothing!).

Europe now, you can take it almost as God-given, Europe is not going to fight with Europe anymore. The Europeans are not going to take up arms against Europeans. They are moving towards unity - even the little, the little countries of the Balkans which are breaking up, Yugoslavia breaking up, but they are breaking up at the same time the building up is taking place. They break up and say we want to come into the *bigger* unity.

So there's a *building* movement, there's a *building* of Europe. These countries which have old, old sovereignties, countries of hundreds of years old; they are forgetting this, they are *moving* towards unity. And you people, you think Tanzania is sacred? What is Tanzania!

You *have* to move towards unity. If these powerful countries see that they have no future in the nation-states - *ninyi mnafikiri mna future katika nini?* (what future do you think you have?). So, if we can't *move*, if our leadership, our future leadership cannot move us to bigger nation-states, which I *hope* they are going to try; we tried and failed. I tried and failed. One of my biggest failures was actually that. I tried in East Africa and failed.

But don't give up because we, the first leadership, failed, no! *Unajaribu tena!* (You try again!). We failed, but the idea is a good idea. That these countries should come together. Don't leave Rwanda and Burundi on their own. *Hawawezi kusurvive* (They cannot survive). They can't. They're locked up into a form of prejudice. If we can't move towards bigger nation-states, at least let's move

217

towards greater co-operation. This is beginning to happen. And the new leadership in Africa should encourage it.

I want to say only one or two things about what is happening in southern Africa. Please accept the logic of coming together. South Africa, small; South Africa is very small. Their per capita income now is, I think $2,000 a year or something around that. Compared with Tanzanians, of course, it is very big, but it's poor. If South Africa begins to tackle the problems of the legacy of apartheid, they have no money!

But compared with the rest of us, they are rich. And so, in southern Africa, there, there is also a kind of osmosis, also an economic osmosis. South Africa's neighbours send their job seekers *into* South Africa. And South Africa will simply have to accept the logic of that, that they are big, they are attractive. They attract the unemployed from Mozambique, and from Lesotho and from the rest. They have to accept that fact of life. It's a problem, but they have to accept it.

South Africa, and I am talking about post-apartheid South Africa. Post-apartheid South Africa has the most developed and the most dynamic private sector on the continent. It is white, so what? So forget it is white. It is South African, dynamic, highly developed. If the investors of South Africa begin a new form of trekking, you *have* to accept it.

It will be ridiculous, absolutely ridiculous, for Africans to go out seeking investment from North America, from Japan, from Europe, from Russia, and then, when these investors come from South Africa to invest in your own country, you say, "a! a! These fellows now want to take over our economy" - this is nonsense. You can't have it both ways. You want foreign investors or you don't want foreign investors. Now, the most available foreign investors for you are those from South Africa.

And let me tell you, when Europe think in terms of investing, they *might* go to South Africa. When North

America think in terms of investing, they *might* go to South Africa. Even Asia, if they want to invest, the first country they may think of in Africa *may* be South Africa. So, if *your* South Africa is going to be *your* engine of development, accept the reality, accept the reality. Don't accept this sovereignty, South Africa will reduce your sovereignty. What sovereignty do you have?

Many of these debt-ridden countries in Africa now have no sovereignty, they've lost it. *Imekwenda* (It's gone). *Iko mikononi mwa IMF na World Bank* (It's in the hands of the IMF and the World Bank). *Unafikiri kuna sovereignty gani*? (What kind of sovereignty do you think there is?)

So, southern Africa has an opportunity, southern Africa, the SADC group, *because* of South Africa.

Because South Africa now is no longer a destabiliser of the region, but a partner in development, southern Africa has a tremendous opportunity. But you need leadership, because if you get proper leadership there, within the next 10, 15 years, that region is going to be the ASEAN (Association of South-East Asian Nations) of Africa. And it is possible. But forget the protection of your sovereignties. I believe the South Africans will be sensitive enough to know that if they are not careful, there is going to be this resentment of big brother, but that big brother, frankly, is not very big.

West Africa. Another bloc is developing there, but that depends very much upon Nigeria my brother (looking at the Nigerian High Commissioner - Ambassador), very much so. Without Nigeria, the future of West Africa is a problem. West Africa is more balkanised than Eastern Africa. More balkanised, tiny little states.

The leadership will have to come from Nigeria. It came from Nigeria in Liberia; it has come from Nigeria in the case of Sierra Leone; it will have to come from Nigeria in galvanising ECOWAS.

But the military in Nigeria must allow the Nigerians to

exercise that vitality in freedom. And it is my hope that they will do it.

I told you I was going to ramble and it was going to be messy, but thank you very much." (Julius Nyerere, in his speech at the University of Dar es Salaam, Tanzania, 15 December 1997. Translation of Kiswahili words, phrases and sentences in Nyerere's speech into English in the preceding text, done by the author, Godfrey Mwakikagile. Reprinted in Godfrey Mwakikagile, *Nyerere and Africa: End of an Era*, Pretoria, South Africa, 2010, pp. 553 – 560).

Globalisation is not going to solve our problems. It is controlled and dominated by the big powers, especially Western, including our former colonial masters, and is intended to benefit them.

We are now losing land and other natural resources everyday under globalisation as if we are still under colonial rule.

I have written about life under colonial rule – including racial injustices – in Tanganyika when I was growing up to show how life was during those days from the perspective of colonial subjects. We hardly had any rights in our own country ruled and dominated by whites. Africans were lowest in the racial hierarchy, with Asians and Arabs ranked next to whites, partly to facilitate imperial rule but also because our rulers saw that to be the natural order of things.

This brings up another point why I wrote the book. I wrote it also to show how the colonial rulers profoundly affected the destiny of our people.

The impact they had on us still reverberates today, manifested in many ways including the belief among some of our people that colonial rule was better than our traditional institutions of governance; that it had more advantages than disadvantages, and that the people who

220

ruled us were superior to us – as if they had divine mandate to rule us.

They are defending the indefensible. As Walter Rodney stated in his book, *How Europe Underdeveloped Africa*:

"The only positive development in colonialism was when it ended." – (Walter Rodney, *How Europe Underdeveloped Africa*, Dar es Salaam, Tanzania: Tanzania Publishing House, 1973, p. 414).

Sadly, the liberation of Africa is not complete, especially in this era of globalisation dominated by Western powers, although China is also flexing muscles in the international arena and has become a major player in Africa.

Although we are not completely free, we won something when colonial rule ended.

The first thing we got back when we won independence from our colonial rulers was dignity, what in Swahili we call *utu*. It is rooted not only in our humanity as equal human beings but also in what we are as a people with our own identity and history. It is rooted in our African-ness. As Nkrumah said:

"I am not African because I was born in Africa but because Africa was born in me."

It will take a lot of pride in what we are as a people and in seeing Africa as one for us to move forward.

# Part Three

## Administrator in Africa

### 1951 – 1956: Tanganyika

#### David Brokensha

I SPENT nearly five years in the Colonial Service in Tanganyika, serving in seven different districts. Government policy was not to leave officials for long in any one district: usually the longest period one could hope for was one 'tour', which averaged two and a half years. The rationale behind this policy was that a long stay would lessen objectivity, the officer becoming too closely identified with the local people. The result was that few officers learnt any local vernacular language: we all became proficient in Swahili, which sufficed for most occasions, but it was by no means the lingua franca then that it is today. My being both junior and a single man, when most of my colleagues were married, meant that I was transferred even more frequently than the average. Relatively short postings meant that I had few opportunities to make anthropological enquiries; these would have needed both longer postings, and more 'free' time.

Tanganyika had been ruled as German East Africa for nearly thirty years, until the end of World War 1 when it became a protectorate of the League of Nations, with Britain being the administrative body. After World War 2 it became a United Nations Trusteeship Territory, still administered by Britain. This UN status differed only a little from the 'regular' British colonies: Tanganyika was under the Colonial Office, and periodic inspections by UN teams were meant to ensure that the rights of the local people were upheld.

## Tanganyika, 1950s

Unlike in neighbouring Kenya, with its more fertile land, there was only a handful of white settlers, concentrated in two or three of the higher parts of the country. A few Germans had remained, and there were a small number of Afrikaners from South Africa, as well as Greeks, Indians and Lebanese, the last three being mainly in trade.

In preparation for coming out to Tanganyika I was advised to visit a colonial outfitter in London, where I was given mostly inappropriate advice. I bought a sun helmet and a red flannel 'spine pad' (supposed to protect one's spine from the harmful effects of the tropical sun), neither of which I used. I also bought a portable hip-bath with a wicker basket inside, which proved useful for packing small, fragile items on safari; a small canvas washbasin was, however, invaluable. My maroon cummerbund, when bound around a white shirt, was adequate for formal evening wear. I also bought, on the advice of well-meaning friends, a .22 rifle ('you can shoot guinea-fowl') and a recorder ('you should have a musical instrument to play'), neither of which lasted long. I declined to buy a white tropical uniform with a white helmet; in the event I never really needed one. I was thankful though that the colonial outfitters persuaded me to buy an elegant pair of boots, made of light leather and covering the legs up to the

224

calves, providing excellent protection against the abundant evening mosquitoes.

I set out for Tanganyika in July 1951, routing myself via South Africa so that I could see my father in Durban. Ouma and I had a good voyage out to South Africa, arranging to travel on the same Union-Castle mail ship as the Evans-Pritchard family: E-P, Ioma and their six children. I taught the twin five-year-old boys to swim, and I had long conversations in the late evenings with E-P, walking on the deck while he told me about his days in Cairo, in the Sudan, and later in North Africa among the Sanusi. Another memorable passenger was my Durban High School English teacher, Neville Nuttall, so I was able to introduce two of my three most important mentors to each other (the third was Monica Wilson). I served daily mass, in the dining room, for the Provincial of the Jesuits in Southern Africa. And I became friendly with one of my first gay couples, returning from a holiday in Morocco, which they had chosen because they wanted to visit a country with a predominantly dark population where being white had no particular advantage.

We arrived in Cape Town in September 1951, three years after the National Party had taken power, and had begun implementing apartheid. On disembarking, I wanted to telephone a college friend, and I noticed that the telephone booths at the docks were all marked Europeans Only or Non-Europeans Only. Wishing to make a protest, I used one for 'non-Europeans'; when I emerged, I realised that I had been using the only telephone for non-Europeans, and that my futile protest had merely served to inconvenience an old coloured man, patiently waiting for me to finish, and not daring to use the 'whites only' telephone.

We disembarked in Durban, and Ouma settled herself in a flat there. I had a good reunion with my father; then boarded an intermediate Union-Castle liner, bound for England via the East Coast. We made one stop, at Isla do

225

Mozambique, a charming old Portuguese colonial city, where my fellow colonial cadet Bill Tulloch and I had a happy day, having to be summoned by sirens to catch the last ferry to our boat. I disembarked at Dar es Salaam, the capital city of Tanganyika, staying a few days at the New Africa Hotel, enjoying the new tropical sights, and practising my Swahili. I presented my visiting card ('Mr. D. W. Brokensha, Provincial Administration') at the Governor's residence and also at the Office of the Chief Secretary, who warned me not to be too hard on white settlers or prospectors, telling me that South African officials tended to compensate for their country's discriminatory policies by being unduly harsh with the white settlers and traders, who, as he pointed out, also had rights.

After a few days in Dar es Salaam I boarded the train for the two day journey to Tabora, the headquarters of the Western Province. The journey on the slow, wood-burning train was my real, exciting introduction to rural tropical Africa. In the 1950s communications, including railways and postal services, were slow, but reliable.

During my short stay in Tabora, the District Commissioner (DC) invited me to join the hunt for a lion, which had been killing the pigs of a white farmer. Being no hunter, I was not thrilled at this assignment, but I thought it best to comply. Another cadet (as newly-arrived district officers were called) and I spent most of the night crouching in long grass, with our borrowed rifles, waiting for the lion, which, I am happy to say, did not appear.

I was only once again involved in a hunt, when I was visiting Kigoma, on Lake Tanganyika, and local people had asked the DC to kill a hippo that had been destroying their crops. I joined a small party of hunters, including the Belgian consul, an avid hunter, who fired at the hippo, but, to my relief, he missed. I appreciated that it was our duty to see that the crops were not damaged, but I thought that there must be other ways than by slaughtering this great animal.

# Kahama

There were fifty-six districts in Tanganyika, and in October 1951 I was posted to Kahama, north of Tabora, where the local people were Nyamwezi. Cadets were not eligible for a loan for a personal vehicle during their probationary period, so I travelled on an administration truck. I spent three months in Kahama, becoming familiar with the duties of a district officer.

I lived in a tumbledown house where I slept on the verandah, supposedly protected against insects by netting which was broken in many places. At night I was often disturbed by strange noises, and I looked them up, using my torch, in R Lydekker's The Game Animals of Africa. This fine 1908 volume enabled me to identify my nocturnal visitors, including civet cats and genets, porcupine, hyena and once a magnificent leopard. When I had identified my visitor, I would return to sleep, despite the flimsy protection of the netting. I soon learnt, too, that in the mornings, before putting on shoes, I needed to tip them up and shake them, to dislodge any lurking scorpions. It was an adventure for me, I expected to be in strange and exotic locations, and I was prepared to put up with what was offered: it was all part of the romance.

My colonial homes varied greatly, most being better than this first one. Few of my early stations had electricity: we depended on Tilley or Aladdin paraffin lamps for illumination, and we had paraffin refrigerators. Hot water was provided, quite satisfactorily, by a boiler consisting of two 44-gallon drums, the lower one for firewood, the top one for water.

During my five years in Tanganyika, the period of my short stay in Kahama was my only unhappy experience because the DC and I did not get on. Almost as soon as I arrived, I was told, as a 'third-class magistrate', with limited powers, to take a court case in which a man was accused of cutting down a *mninga* tree (Pterocarpus bussei), a valuable hardwood tree and a protected species. I asked the DC what sentence I should give, and he replied, pompously, 'Oh, I could not possibly discuss this case with you, it would be most unprofessional.' At all my other stations, the DC and DO cheerfully discussed cases and appropriate sentences.

This case was my first personal experience of the vast gulf between ruler and ruled, of the myriad cultural misunderstandings. Forestry laws protecting certain species had been passed, but the accused had almost certainly not heard about the new regulations. He lived in a remote area, and his people had for generations been accustomed to using the mninga hardwood for furniture and for building. He readily admitted that he had cut down the tree, to make a chair; the prosecuting police officer (with whom I was friendly, we played tennis together) suggested a fine of twenty shillings or ten days in jail. I worried about the stoical young man, and I visited him in prison every day, to make sure that he was alright – which he was. Both he, and the sergeant in charge of the small prison, thought that my behaviour was odd.

A more serious conflict arose when I was invited to dinner at the DC's house. Seven of us had dinner on the veranda, others including the senior District Officer (the DO1), and his wife, together with three bachelor officials – the police officer, the agricultural officer and myself. All were 'Europeans' and all were dressed formally, the men in jackets and ties, even in that tropical heat and humidity. It was the time of the 1951 general election in Britain when the Tories (the Conservative Party, under Winston Churchill) defeated the Labour Party and regained power. When we heard the news on the radio, the DC stood up and proposed a toast to the new government. I declined to stand, saying that as colonial administrators we should not

228

be involved in British politics. I was correct, but the pompous DC never forgave me and after that we were barely on speaking terms. Probably most of my colleagues voted for the Conservative Party, but I never felt obliged to hide my own views – I have always voted for the Labour Party in Britain, even today when I have many reservations about Labour policy. I managed, with the help of the DO1, to minimise contact with the DC and I found congenial company with others.

I soon got used to dealing with court cases, which concerned minor offences, when the accused, as often as not, admitted guilt. I had been told that one of my duties might be to witness a hanging, if an accused person had been sentenced to death. To my great relief I was never called on to do this fearsome duty: I am not sure whether in conscience I could have done so. (My father, a judge in the Natal Native High Court in South Africa, had pronounced the death sentence many times; he and I never talked about this.) In one of my court cases a twelve-year-old boy was accused of stealing from a storeroom. With some reluctance, I sentenced him to three strokes. I had to witness the punishment, which was administered by a sergeant of the police, who carefully placed a cloth soaked in antiseptic over the boy's buttocks. I had been tempted to ask the sergeant not to make the strokes too hard, but that proved unnecessary.

On Saturdays I made my regular round, inspecting the small clinic, the market, the shops and the prison, to make sure that all was in order. Prisons in the stations where I was posted were small and well run. I saw no brutality in these prisons, which had no resemblance to the terrible overcrowded prisons in many countries today. Besides inspecting trading licences, and ensuring that litter was cleared away, the important part of the walkabout was chatting with the shopkeepers (mostly Indian) and to the Native Authority officials.

In Kahama I made my first acquaintance with

missions, which played an important role in Tanganyika, providing many of the schools, hospitals and clinics. The missions varied in their effectiveness; most of my contemporaries would agree that generally the Roman Catholic and the UMCA (the Anglican 'Universities Mission to Central Africa') were the most effective, partly because the staff remained at the same mission for many years – sometimes as long as forty years. They spoke the vernacular language fluently, and knew much more about local history and society than we could ever hope to learn, in our short stays. However, we had to be careful not to rely too much on the missionaries' interpretation of people and events, which, understandably, tended to give prominence and sympathy to their own adherents. Although relations between missionaries and colonial administrators were generally cordial, sporadic quarrels did occur – for example concerning the use of child labour by the missions. It was common practice at mission schools for the pupils to help with cleaning the classrooms and the school compound. But some enthusiastic missionaries ordered schoolchildren to do an increasing range of tasks, such as helping with building, or the upkeep of roads – until officials felt bound to step in.

I had to take care not to allow being a Catholic to influence any of my official decisions. Protestants and Catholics competed over permission to open schools, the rule being that different denominations could not have schools within five miles of each other. One Catholic missionary told me that he preferred to deal with Protestant officials, because Catholics like me tended to be hard on Catholic applications, just to show that we were not biased.

The nearest Catholic church – a mission church – was eight miles away, and I had no motor car, but the Senior District Officer, Major Mitchell, was a Catholic and took me to mass with his family. We were the only white people in a congregation of several hundred Nyamwezi, and the

French-Canadian priest would give his sermon in kiNyamwezi. Sitting immediately below the pulpit, the Major would impatiently and ostentatiously tap his watch if the sermon went on too long, and the priest would hurriedly wind up. Although embarrassed by this, I never remonstrated with my colleague because I had had a problem with this priest. I used to play tennis with his junior priest, Jean-Michel, also French-Canadian, and like me new to the country. We enjoyed this as a welcome Saturday afternoon break, but the senior priest decided that Jean-Michel and I were becoming too friendly, and told him to stop seeing me. So I put up with the Major's peremptory curtailing of the Sunday sermons.

Tanganyika, like most of the British colonies in Africa, had adopted the policy of 'indirect rule'. We really had little choice, because the few hundred British administrators could not possibly have used any form of direct rule. We confirmed the appointment of chiefs, whom we paid, and in return they were obliged to undertake many duties, the main one being the collection of taxes. Many African societies (including those in Handeni, where I later spent over a year) had never had traditional chieftaincy, so there were initially serious problems in getting the people to accept the authority of the government-appointed 'chiefs'.

While I was at Kahama, I had my first thrilling experience of safari, a term that could mean any journey, but usually referred to an overnight stay. The Governor, Sir Edward Twining, decreed that all rural administrative officials should spend at least ten nights per month out in the district. He maintained, validly, that we could not understand the people if we spent all our time in the boma (the administrative headquarters). By making regular safaris to all parts of the district, we came to know the people better. This suited me very well, although some of the married officials missed their families. When on safari I sometimes slept in the open, but usually in one of the small mud and thatch rest houses available at each of the Native Authority locations. I had neither a weapon, nor an armed escort, and I never felt any fear when I was in the bush.

Once I put up my camp bed under a tree, on the outskirts of a collection of huts. I was awakened in the middle of night by a stinging sensation in my legs, accompanied by distressed squawks from the village chickens. On shining my torch, I discovered that we had been invaded by a column of safari ants, and soon all the villagers were stamping, swatting and cursing as we all tried to get rid of these tenacious and fierce insects.

On one of my first safaris, I was approached at night by a clearly frightened man who said that his name was Omari, and that the game ranger, who employed him as a cook, and who was camped nearby, had beaten him. In the morning I had an unpleasant interview with the ranger, who angrily told me that he wanted to charge Omari with desertion. I told him that there would be a counter-charge of assault causing grievous bodily harm. He then withdrew his charge and said that he would not employ Omari again. At the time I had no cook, so I employed Omari, who was a sweet man but a hopeless cook, and I was relieved when I was transferred a little later to Kasulu, because this gave me an excuse to leave Omari behind. I felt bad, but not for long.

I met a few other Natural Resource officials who had little sympathy with Africans, being concerned only with the resource (game, forests, or water) they were charged to protect. However, most of them eventually came to recognise that local people did have rights, and that compromises were in order.

During my first months in Kahama I tried to play my recorder, but after struggling, excruciatingly, with Bobby Shaftoe's gone to sea … he'll come back and marry me, and getting nowhere, I gave up.

Tennis was a favourite occupation, tennis courts being

found at most stations. I recall one Saturday afternoon when several visitors were present, a young African girl, about fifteen years old, walked behind the tennis court, on her way home from fetching water at the river. She was not self-conscious, singing sweetly and softly, water from the pot on her head having spilled on to her kanga, so that her beautiful young figure was clearly silhouetted. Both players and spectators turned to watch her, the men gazing spellbound, while the wives sadly watched their men.

I took my .22 rifle on a few late afternoon walks, seeing many guinea-fowl but not managing to shoot any. My heart was not in it, so I disposed of both recorder and rifle, and set about living my own life, not one imposed on me by the expectations of others. I reminded myself of my POW resolve not to be 'pushed around'. I slowly got used to alternating periods of elation and excitement, with fewer times of loneliness and doubts. Whatever my mood, I was never bored: there was always so much to do, so many new experiences.

## Kasulu

After three months at Kahama I felt discouraged, largely because of the hostile and unhelpful attitude of the DC. By one of the many happy coincidences of life, John Beattie, my friend from Oxford, came to see me on his way to do anthropological fieldwork among the Bunyoro of Uganda. John had spent eight years in the Tanganyika administrative service, and (without my knowledge) communicated my doubts and misgivings to the Provincial Commissioner (PC). The PC apparently decided that I was worth saving, and sent his administrative assistant to see me. The result was that I was transferred to Kasulu, another district in the Western Province, which bordered with the then Belgian-administered territory, Urundi, now Burundi. As far as I was concerned, the PC could not have made a better decision.

My new DC, John Leslie, was experienced, kind, and humorous. He and his wife Elizabeth immediately made me feel welcome and useful; I could not have wished for a better guide in my new career. The DC's home was an old German fort, dating from 1906 – very romantic in a Beau Geste way – where I was entertained hospitably on many occasions. Although it was certainly romantic, with grand views over the countryside, the house was not very practical: when the Leslies went on leave, the new DC, who had a family, opted to live in a new bungalow: his wife was afraid for the safety of their children, with the fort's unprotected stairs, terraces without railings and a generally inconvenient design. Because the DC did not live in the fort, I was able to move in and enjoy it in solitary splendour for a few months.

It was at this time that a colleague discovered the new 33 rpm 'long-playing' gramophone records, and sold me a hundred of his old 78s. The forestry officer, who also liked classical music, and I had some happy evenings, sitting on the terrace, a glass of Tusker beer in hand, taking it in turn to wind the gramophone, and gazing out at a grand expanse of Africa.

John Leslie and I alternated going out for a week's safari, so that we saw each other only at weekends. John knew the district well (its population was then about 200 000) and encouraged me to see as much of it as I could. As a DO, I was known as Bwana Shauri, which meant that I looked after the shauris or problems of local people. John encouraged me to settle as many of the complaints as I could. When I asked him what I should do if a man wished to see the DC personally, but had nowhere nearby to stay, John told me that I could accommodate people like that in the prison for a few days. One man complained that the chief had fined him unjustly, and he wished to appeal to the DC, whom he insisted on seeing personally. He had no relatives with whom he could stay, so I took him to the prison – and I forgot all about him. When John was inspecting the prison, later, he asked the man (who by then had served two weeks, without hard labour) what he was doing there he was told, 'Bwana Shauri said I should wait here until you came.' John laughed when he told me this, but advised me to keep a note in my diary in future.

The alternate weeks, spent at the boma (administrative headquarters), were occupied by attending to the many people, mainly men, who came with complaints or questions. We set aside a stipulated time for these petitioners; each one took a long time to settle. By the time I arrived at the boma, at 7 a.m., there would be a line of men, and occasionally a few women, waiting for me. The clerk would already have done a preliminary sorting, deciding which people I needed to see. The role of clerks, like that of the chiefs, was difficult, demanding exquisite tact if they were not to become unpopular, and even risk being bewitched. They acted as gatekeepers or brokers, a difficult balancing act.

Part of the week was set aside for hearing court cases. I had authority to try minor criminal and civil cases, with a maximum sentence of three months' imprisonment. During this probationary period all my court reports were reviewed by a High Court judge. I was glad that my father did not see some of the judge's scathing comments: none of my sentences was altered, but I was often reproved for my sloppy court procedure. For example, I might neglect to write (court records were hand-written) and sign, at the appropriate section, 'ROFC', indicating that I had 'Read Over (to the witness) and Found Correct' a witness' statement. John Leslie, always kind and helpful, encouraged me to master such details, and I gained confidence.

The week at the boma also involved dealing with correspondence, the most important being that with the PC, who was usually understanding about our problems, having invariably been a 'bush' DC himself. There was

235

also contact with Departments (Prisons, Public Works, Police, Tsetse Fly, Water, Game, Forestry, Health, Education) at Dar es Salaam, where many officials had no idea of the constraints under which we worked, often making unrealistic demands on us. This 'periphery/centre' conflict is a universal one, and we – like soldiers at the front – were convinced that we knew what was best to do, and what was possible. The office clerk, in those days always an African man, typed the correspondence, and looked after the yellowing files. My relationship with the clerks was always close, particularly during my first year, when I relied heavily on their experience and advice. Even experienced officers, when arriving in a new district, were careful to listen to the clerk, who might well have been in that job for many years, and who would know certain details, especially about the local people, and their relationships and past histories, that would not appear in the ' Handing Over Notes', which the outgoing DC would have written for his successor.

I had a happy time at Kasulu, improving my Swahili and learning more about the district. I was intrigued by Teresa, Paramount Chieftainess of the Buha, the main group in the district. Mwami Teresa belonged to the minority Watusi cattle owners, who lorded it over nearly 300 000 WaHa, (spread over both Kasulu and Kibondo Districts) in a situation similar to that of the Tutsis and Hutus in Belgian-administered Ruanda-Urundi. Fortunately, Tanganyika's independence was not followed by the tragic conflicts that occurred in the neighbouring territories though both Kasulu and Kibondo now have large concentrations of refugees. Mwami Teresa was an educated, confident and forceful young woman, who handled her elders – and us, the colonial officials – with great skill. Anthropologists have examined the difficult 'interstitial' or broker role of African chiefs: difficulties would arise because of the chiefs having to balance two often-conflicting demands and expectations, those of their

236

own people, and those of the Administration. Another important player – or 'stakeholder' in today's parlance – was the local White Fathers' Catholic Mission; one of the old Dutch priests had known Teresa's father, and had taught Teresa at school. Teresa was superb in maintaining an appropriate balance between the conflicting demands.

I loved the safaris, usually travelling in a GT (Government Transport) three ton lorry. When I accompanied Richard, the Agricultural Officer, who had a Land Rover, we were glad of each other's company. We would go about our respective business at each chieftaincy, then meet in the evenings, learning from each other's experiences. Of all the other departmental officials, I invariably found the agricultural officers the most congenial; they knew the most about the local people, and did not seek blindly to impose their views.

Once, Richard and I were dropped off in the western section of the district, and walked for two days, near the Gombe Chimpanzee Reserve (later made famous by Jane Goodall's pioneering long-term research among the chimpanzees), to Lake Tanganyika, where we had arranged to be collected by the official launch, Imara. We felt grand, enjoying a gin and tonic under the awning, with the Union Jack fluttering in the breeze, while the Imara headed for its home port of Kigoma. We justified this marvellous safari to our superiors by pointing out that the admittedly small lakeside population had seldom been visited, and indeed we were able to recommend some much needed improvements.

A remarkable German lady, with an extensive knowledge and love of English literature, ran the Dar es Salaam Bookshop, which dispatched parcels of books all over Tanganyika. She soon got used to my tastes, so I could leave the selection to her; each month she posted a batch of six to eight eagerly-awaited books. They arrived regularly, coming by train from Dar es Salaam to Kigoma, then by railway bus to Kasulu.

One day, when I was at the boma, I heard excited voices outside; a young man had brought in an adolescent female chimpanzee who clung to him nervously. The man told me that he had found the animal in the forest; possibly her mother had been shot, or captured by poachers, in the Gombe Chimpanzee Reserve. The elders had told him that he should bring it to the boma. I was unable to look after it – I was looking after a colleague's dog and also I was away on safari for much of the time. I remembered John Leslie's advice about using the prison as a temporary home for strangers, so I walked with the young man and the chimpanzee to the prison. The gates were open, with about thirty prisoners waiting for their lunch. The chimpanzee dashed off and threw her arms around one of the older prisoners, Kilungu, who was waiting trial for murder. He accepted his new companion as though he had been expecting her.

Kilungu had walked from his home to the boma two months earlier and told me his story. He had a young wife, and when he was at the market, drinking beer, he heard the young men joking about how the wives of elderly husbands always had young lovers. He realised that this was directed at him and he walked home, flung open the door of his hut, and found his wife in a young man's arms. 'I killed him with one blow and then I walked here. I know what the penalty is and you should hang me. I had to do this and I have no more to say.' Kilungu was astonished at what seemed to him a very cumbersome procedure. First he had to make a voluntary statement before me, and then I told him there would be a Preliminary Inquiry (PI) when witnesses would be called and a judge would review the record and decide if he had to go to trial at the High Court. Kilungu said, slowly and distinctly, 'I killed that man. I told you why I did it. Now you must hang me.' The PI lasted several days, because we had to call many witnesses – the men present at the beer drink; the dresser who testified about the wound made by the spear; the chief, the clerk, the messenger, the policeman – everybody who knew anything about the case had to come to court to give evidence. After hearing each witness's testimony, Kilungu was asked whether he wished to cross-examine any of the witnesses, or ask any questions. He bore all this with dignity and patience but also with scarcely concealed disdain.

Kilungu's meeting with the chimpanzee changed his life; he ceased being impatient and bored and took a great interest in his new companion, making sure that she had bananas and fresh maize, and the chimpanzee slept at his feet at night. Knowing that Kilungu would not attempt to escape, we allowed him out for an evening's walk, when he and the chimpanzee would take a gentle stroll, hand in hand, a poignant pair, but I knew that their happiness could not last for long.

A game warden who was fond of orphaned animals agreed to take the chimpanzee. I arranged that Kilungu and she should travel together to Tabora, the provincial capital, he to face his trial, she to be met by my friend. The last I saw of them was Kilungu, composed and grave, sitting at the back of the GT three ton truck, with his companion sitting close to him and firmly clasping his hand for reassurance, while looking out eagerly from her solemn brown face. The chimpanzee settled down with the game warden, and the judge found extenuating circumstances at Kilungu's trial, sentencing him to two years' imprisonment.

Once a year, all the District equipment, which was meticulously inventoried, would be inspected by a 'Board' of three colonial officers, two of whom came from other departments – not from the Administration. At a large station, a Revenue Officer would come from provincial headquarters, specially for this important annual check. A rigorous physical inspection of each item ensued, to ensure that the inventory was correct. The Board was empowered to 'write off' any items that were clearly beyond repair. If nothing else, our administration was frugal: it was only the thinnest hoe blade, the leakiest karai – a metal bowl used for many purposes – the most threadbare tunic, or the wobbliest chair, that was ever written off. Visiting Kenya and Tanzania after independence, Bernard and I were shocked by the profligate waste – Land Rovers would be left by the roadside after they had been damaged in a minor accident; typewriters abandoned when there was a malfunction. When I remarked on this, a clerk at the University of Dar es Salaam told me, 'Oh it is alright, the Swedes will give us a new typewriter.'

I was awoken one night, before I had moved into the fort, by a violent shaking of my bed, with pieces of the ceiling tumbling down around me – fortunately the mosquito net draped over the bed protected me. At first I thought that some of my colleagues had had a jolly evening, and were shaking my bed, then I realised that it was an earthquake. Slipping on a dressing gown, I peeped outside, not being sure what the drill was: I did not wish to appear nervous. However, my neighbour, the DO1 and his wife, with her young baby, were outside and clearly alarmed, so I joined them, waiting until the aftershocks subsided. In the light of day, I could see that our houses had not suffered serious damage, but I had to move out, to the rest house (for visiting officials) for a few weeks, while repairs were being done. I shared the rest house with an American missionary and his wife, whose house had been destroyed in the earthquake. Seeing me practising my Swahili one morning (I did this to escape boring conversation with him), he told me that he did not need to learn Swahili, because he 'spoke in tongues'. He could not have been very proficient, because when his house had been rebuilt, he moved back and a short time later his congregation burnt it down. It was difficult for me not to feel some schadenfreude.

At this time I was confused about my sexual identity, although that phrase was not then in use. I had had a few sexual encounters with other young men at university, but I was also attracted to women, and on the voyage out I had met, and been attracted to, a young woman, M, whom I invited to Tanganyika, where she stayed with my District Commissioner and his wife. (In those days, it was unthinkable that she could have stayed with me.) I had asked her to marry me, and been accepted, and ironically it was my religion that doomed the affair. M came from a devout Anglican family (she later married an Anglican priest) and she could not accept the ruling of the Church that any children would have to be brought up in my faith. At that time (1952) the Church did not encourage 'mixed marriages'. Looking back, I regard the breaking off of our relationship as providential: I now know that I am basically and irrevocably homosexual; I would not have made a good husband, and it would have been terribly unfair on M. Ironically, she would have made an outstanding District Commissioner's wife, being competent at almost everything, with a sunny temperament, socially easy with all whom she met, enjoying the simple safaris, calm in herself, and brave, patient, resourceful and resilient.

## Safari

What did I do when I went on safari? The main purpose was to check on the Native Authority (the chief and other staff) and the Native Treasury, which was responsible for collecting tax (a major source of revenue) and for paying employees. Other routine checks were made on schools, clinics, building works, roads, markets and shops. We often stayed at mission stations; sometimes it was difficult to get away from the hospitable missionaries; they saw few people from the outside world and were reluctant to let us go on our way.

Here, based on a surviving letter to Ouma, are some of

my other tasks:

Attesting contract labourers for the coastal sisal estates – labour recruiters were allowed to enlist young men prepared to make the long journey to the coast and to do the arduous work of cutting sisal, in order to earn money. Many of them were illiterate, so it was my responsibility to read the contracts, and to make sure that the labourers understood what lay ahead for them.

Authorising tax exemption for older men, and enrolling young men who were old enough (18 years old) to be on the tax register.

Arranging for porters to be supplied to carry sleeping sickness patients to the clinic.

Discussing any personal problems of the staff – who included game scouts, forest guards, school teachers, road foremen and 'dressers'. These men (or, occasionally, women) often had queries or complaints about pay, allowances or housing, requests for transfers, for new uniforms or bicycles.

Finding two men to look after a roadblock to serve as a tsetse fly picket – they would search all vehicles for tsetse flies, which had to be captured with a net and destroyed.

Asking the chief to find a beekeeper, prepared to go to provincial headquarters for a month-long course.

Checking up on equipment, including bicycles, and road-building tools.

Calling on Asian traders and also on missionaries – the former would offer a welcome cup of tea, made with sugar and condensed milk and tea leaves, all boiled up together.

## Malagarasi safari

The Malagarasi River rises seven miles from Lake Tanganyika and runs in an enormous loop for five hundred miles, passing through both Kasulu and Kibondo Districts, then entering Lake Tanganyika. I was intrigued by the

242

course of this great river, particularly after reading two articles in Tanganyika Notes and Records (TN&R). This journal was published twice a year by the Tanganyika Society, founded in 1936 'to promote the study of ethnology, history, geography, natural history and kindred sciences in relation to Tanganyika'. The journal included a marvellous Victorian miscellany, with articles on seashells, seaweed, salt, iron, canoes, bark, ships, Arabs, Germans, churches, Indians, Islam, witchcraft, music, vegetation, tsetse flies, snakes, railways, volcanoes, rock paintings, and famine. Many administrative officers contributed accounts of their safaris, two concerning the Malagarasi. TN&R also carried ethnographic articles, mostly written by colonial officials, with a few by professional anthropologists, including Philip Gulliver and Hans Cory. (My first 'publication' – a footnote to an article, Mwariye: a Sacred Mountain of Tanganyika – was written when I was stationed at Kibondo, and was published in TN&R No 36, in January 1954).

In August 1942, JP Moffett, then District Commissioner at Kibondo, set out to determine whether the Malagarasi was navigable between the ferry on the Kasulu–Kibondo road and the railway line. In his TN&R article, A Raft on the Malagarasi, he described the large herds of game, and the hippos which were a 'constant menace' on his trips on his home-made raft. Although he wrote 'I am far from being a good shot', he did regularly shoot game with his 'heavy .425 rifle'. He concluded that the river was not navigable, but he clearly enjoyed his safari, writing that 'the best moments of the day are the start in the early morning, and in the evening, when bathed and refreshed, one emerges from one's tent and sees all round the friendly flickering fires of the porters, a cosy little island of security in this wilderness of bush … [and] one forgets the maddening tsetse.' Moffett also had to 'arrange for the removal of the last 350 families to sleeping sickness concentrations'. He was delighted to encounter some of the little-known and shy people, the Wakiko wa Wanyahoza, whom he named 'the Water Gypsies'.

In 1947 Captain CHD Grant wrote, also in TN&R, The Valley and Swamps of the Malagarasi river, Western Tanganyika Territory. He noted 'numerous water birds, sitatunga [marshbuck], hippo, crocs, zebra, topi [tsessebe], buffalo, roan antelope and reedbuck'. Grant also mentioned that the river was eighty feet wide when it reached the railway at Malagarasi Station.

As well as reading these articles in TN&R, I spoke to many people who had been moved from this area because of sleeping sickness, which had taken a heavy toll. Sleeping sickness, or trypanosomiasis, is caused by the bite of a tsetse fly. Its incubation period is two weeks, and, if untreated, most cases end in death. Early treatment, involving a painful lumbar puncture, is effective. Because of the rising death toll, the government decided to relocate all the people living in the area. The move, though unpopular, was reluctantly agreed to, largely through the efforts of the patient Sleeping Sickness Officer, the only American citizen in government service in Tanganyika. The tsetse fly was believed to depend on its main host, game animals, so the only other way to tackle sleeping sickness (which affects both domestic livestock and people) was thought to be the devastating slaughtering of all game in the affected area. This approach was adopted in the 1920s in the Umfolozi area in South Africa, culminating in the killing of 100 000 animals in 1947. After this doubts set in and the process was halted.

I was eager to see this wilderness for myself and I proposed that I do a three week safari to investigate the feasibility of a road through this area, going to some lengths to show the potential benefits of such a road. The Provincial Commissioner, to my joy, agreed to my making the trip, although he later told my DC that he knew that the road was impracticable, but that because I was doing a

244

good job, he had been prepared to humour me.

The logistics of such a safari require two porters to carry food for everyone carrying other loads. I had no difficulty enlisting porters, because the men who had been resettled, both young and old, were keen to see their ancestral homes. Not wishing to appear arrogant, I wanted to keep to a minimum the loads being carried for me, foregoing a tent (it was dry season), and proposing to leave Kayanda, my old cook, behind. But he told me that I could not manage on my own, and insisted on coming with me. As a veteran of many foot safaris, including some with pre-WW1 German administrators, Kayanda also insisted, to my eventual relief, that I take a folding chair, and a canvas wash-basin. Kayanda himself, not about to give up any luxury, ended up with more porters than I did.

Many of the African officials also wanted to join the safari, and I was happy to allow the game scout and a dispenser to accompany us, even though each additional person meant engaging more porters. We set out with a total of thirty-seven men, who, in their eagerness to see their old homes, set off singing happily, with me feeling very 'Sanders of the River-ish'. I am glad to have had the privilege of seeing this part of 'the old Africa' with all its wildlife; I tried to reconstruct in my mind the lives of the local people, and what their interactions with the game had been.

Before World War 2, foot safaris were common: good roads were rare and walking was accepted as the best way to see one's district. But by the time that I arrived in Tanganyika in 1951, a long foot safari was quite unusual and I count myself extremely fortunate to have been allowed to do this – it was an unforgettable experience. The game scout shot 'for the pot', ensuring a good supply of meat. But the porters could not understand why I, a white official, who was permitted to shoot almost everything in sight, not only had no rifle, but restrained the game scout from killing more game than we needed. The porters started telling me early on 'this is where Bwana Moffett shot his first buffalo … this is where Bwana Moffett shot his first roan antelope …' If their stories were true, Bwana Moffett must have done a great deal of killing. However, I suspect they were exaggerating, hoping to goad me into allowing more shooting.

We soon got into a routine, breaking camp at dawn and walking in the cool of the day, stopping in the early afternoon when it was hot and the porters were getting tired. Guided by the older men, who knew the area well, we always camped at well-wooded and well-watered locations. We saw huge herds of buffalo as well as elephant and almost all the antelopes, including the water-loving sitatunga antelope, and at night we would hear lion and hyena. At no time did I feel in danger – I was in the company of such knowledgeable men, and I had the game scout as protection. In camp there was also the comfort of the 'flickering fires'. Looking back, I am mortified that I had no special interest in birds, for the bird life was prolific.

As Moffett wrote, the early morning and the evenings were the best time of the day. We saw the remains of small villages, which the older men would excitedly point out to their younger relatives, explaining who had lived there. Eventually we reached the Malagarasi River, where we had arranged to meet our lorry at Malagarasi Station – a few miles away, on the other bank of the river. The river was certainly more than 80 feet wide and I asked the men whether Bwana Moffett had swam across. Bwana, haiwezikani, ni hatari sana … ('No sir, it is too dangerous, there are crocodiles and hippopotamus'). With boyish bravado I stripped, told them to tell the next traveller that this is where Bwana Brokensha swam across, and I plunged in. I was relieved to see that a canoe had set out from the other bank to accompany me, but I was not prepared for my welcome: as I climbed out, naked, on the other bank, I was greeted by a group of ululating women. I clutched a bunch of leaves as covering and greeted them as solemnly as I could.

The rest of the group was ferried across the river in canoes, the lorry was indeed waiting, and after many dusty hours, we reached home, the men keeping their spirits up until the end. What made this safari so special was partly that the mood of the porters was so cheerful, they were delighted to have the opportunity to visit their old homes again – normally this was a closed area, because of the real danger of sleeping sickness. I had to do no dragooning, nor persuading; it was more a matter of selecting the strongest men, but ensuring that I included some older men, because of their experience of the area. Afterwards the dispenser urged the men to report to the clinic if they noticed any threatening symptoms, such as headaches, fever or joint pains: we had all been bitten, many times, by the tsetse flies. We told the men that Dr Taylor, a specialist in the treatment of sleeping sickness, who worked at the Seventh Day Adventist Hospital, could cure them if they reported in time. I also checked myself, a little anxiously, but fortunately none of our party became infected with sleeping sickness. As far as the projected road was concerned, it was clear – to no-one's surprise – that it would have been far too costly.

Soon after this epic safari, a new cadet came out from Britain and, on one of his first walks near the boma, was unfortunately infected with sleeping sickness. He was cured, however, after some painful injections. Since there was no permanent doctor in Kasulu, Dr Taylor supervised our Native Authority dispensaries; he was a most impressive man. I accompanied him on safari once, watching him treat yaws, ulcers and leprosy, as well as seeing the patients whom the 'sleeping sickness scouts' had brought in, with suspected sleeping sickness. At one of our stops, at a market, a madman emerged from the small crowd, brandishing a panga (machete) and threatening Dr Taylor, who remained composed, talking quietly to his assailant in kiHa, the local vernacular. While Dr Taylor kept the conversation going, his assistant crept behind the man, deftly throwing a blanket over his head, and restraining him. Dr Taylor paused only to make sure that the madman was taken to hospital, and not harmed by the now angry crowd. He seemed surprised when I congratulated him on his bravery. (Fifty years later, I was delighted to meet his son, Bill Taylor, a dentist and writer, in Bulawayo.

## Kibondo

After spending nearly a year in Kasulu and beginning to understand the district and its problems, I was disappointed to be told that I was to be transferred a hundred miles to the north to neighbouring Kibondo, a district similar both physically and socially to Kasulu.

There was again a Catholic Mission five miles away, but no Catholic colleague to drive me, so I used to walk to mass. It was a rewarding experience. As I walked, I joined an ever-growing throng of men, women and children, all happily talking to each other, and to me – although the older people spoke no Swahili, only kiHa.

Some of the faces of the older women, especially, were radiant with joy, and I thought how beautiful they were, wrinkles and all. These times gave me some idea of how the early Christians must have felt. After mass, the Dutch sisters would invite me to breakfast. They were memorable Sunday mornings.

When I arrived at Kibondo, there was a shortage of housing because of the recent earthquake, and I was allocated a large bell tent which had a small annex as a bathroom. Shortly after my arrival, my Cambridge friend Julius Lister stayed with me for three weeks.

Julius' arrival coincided with a visit to Kibondo by a seventy-yearold hunter coming to have his hunting licence endorsed, allowing him to shoot one elephant in the district. He invited Julius and me to accompany him. First, to ensure that Julius and I knew how to handle a rifle, the hunter set up small targets (the bases from tins originally containing fifty cigarettes) and carefully watched our shooting: we passed the test. I think the old hunter wanted us to cover his back. Both Julius and I were glad to have had this brief experience of a hunting safari, which included two days tracking the elephants in thick bush, before the hunter found and shot his elephant. I was saddened by the death of the elephant, but we had had requests for 'something to be done', because the elephants were raiding and destroying the crops.

While Julius was staying with me, I took local leave, so that we could go on the hunting safari, and also to allow us to visit neighbouring Urundi. We had a hair-raising journey with an Indian trader, who drove furiously on the rough winding mountain roads, but were rewarded with a few days at Bukavu, then a calm and beautiful small town on Lake Kivu, which in recent years has witnessed many bloody killings and conflicts. We stayed with an Indian businessman who had the most complete collection of classical records I had seen. 'What shall I play?' he would ask, and he was delighted when he could meet most of our requests.

Julius had arranged to board a lake steamer at Mwanza, a port on Lake Victoria, two hundred miles to the north, from where he would cross the lake, and go by train from Kisumu to Nairobi, to board an aircraft for Britain. Public transport on the road to Mwanza was scarce, and I was still relying on government transport, which I could not use for personal trips. (Later, in independent East African states, Bernard and I were shocked to see how both government officials and development aid workers blithely used 'official' vehicles for personal trips to night-clubs, game parks or beaches. It was a different culture, when the rules were 'internalised', and one did not dream of breaking them.) One chief, with whom I was friendly, and who had liked Julius, insisted that I borrow his 1938 Chevrolet car, one of the very few private vehicles in the district, so that I could drive Julius to Mwanza.

After Julius left, I suffered my first bout of malaria. While lying on my bed in my tent, I had a visit from the medical officer, who was making one of his infrequent visits. When the doctor bent over me to examine me, I commented that his tie – even in the bush some officials, including this doctor, wore a tie – seemed familiar, and I was told that it was a Wadham College tie. I told the doctor that I had also been at Wadham, and he later said to the DC, 'Brokensha must be in a bad way; why, he didn't even recognise his old college tie.'

## Handeni

Soon after I had settled in at Kibondo, I was told to report to Handeni, in Tanga Province, in the north-east of Tanganyika. Handeni was about six hundred miles as the crow flies from Kibondo but more than a thousand miles on the circuitous route that I had to take. From Tabora I went by train to Dar es Salaam and then by road to Handeni. A domino effect had come into play, affecting transfers: if one officer (or his wife) became ill, and needed to be replaced, this often resulted in several men being moved around. As I explained, I was especially vulnerable to transfers being both junior and single.

My disappointment at leaving the Western Province soon changed when I met my new colleagues, Randal Sadleir, the ebullient Irish DC, and John Ainley, the effective Agricultural Officer. Both men later wrote books about their time in Tanganyika, each writing at some length about Handeni. I am still in touch with these two good friends, Randal in London, and John in Yorkshire. As I have indicated above, the personality, knowledge and

250

competence of the DC, and of other colleagues, made all the difference in my various postings. Another favourable factor was that I could now take out a loan to buy a short wheel-base Land Rover – £600 at Gailey and Roberts in Tanga, the provincial headquarters, a hundred miles away. This sum represented my entire year's salary but was well worth it for the flexibility it gave me. Most up-country stations had an inspection pit, so that we could do our own regular vehicle maintenance. This was necessary when garages were often distant, and sometimes inaccessible in the rainy season. It was also good for the non-mechanically-minded such as me to learn, under the patient instruction of the African fundi, the simple tasks that needed to be done.

In another stroke of good fortune, I met and employed a young local man, named Timotheo, to help me in the house. Timo soon became a good companion as much as a servant, and he remained with me until I left Tanganyika. He was relaxed, even laconic: once, I asked him, probably a little testily, why he had not performed some particular task. Sijui, he answered, labda nimesahau ('I don't know … perhaps I forgot'), a useful tension-reducing phrase that Bernard and I frequently used. On another occasion, Timo and I discovered a snake on the veranda. I thought it was a boomslang, a venomous reptile, and asked Timo to dispatch it, saying, 'You are the African, this is an African snake.' With an impish smile, and a hint of mockery, he replied, 'No, you are the bwana, this is your job.' While we were arguing, the snake slithered away.

I was allocated a spacious, pleasant house and immediately tackled the garden. I had remarked, early on, that I saw little point in gardening if I was likely to be moved fairly soon. An older colleague rebuked me, 'In Tanganyika you do not garden for yourself but for your successors … we all hope to find a pleasant garden at our new station.' Even with my meagre gardening skills, I could coax a few of the old stand-bys to grow – zinnias, petunias, and African marigolds.

Although there were basic similarities in the pattern of work (the alternating of safari and desk, and the types of problems encountered), there were also great physical and social differences in the seven districts where I worked. Handeni was occupied by the Zigua in the south and by the Nguu in the more mountainous north. There were also a few nomadic WaKwavi, similar to the better-known Maasai, who wandered in with their herds of cattle, to the alarm of the Nguu farmers. Although the people, many of whom were Muslims, had had longer contact with the outside world than had those in the Western Province, much of that contact had been of an unfriendly nature, including slaving raids. At first I found them reserved and suspicious, but we soon got used to each other. As had happened at Kasulu, the advice and guidance of my DC was invaluable, saving me from many difficult situations. Like Kasulu, Handeni had also been a German boma, with some of the original buildings still standing. Near the boma was a poignant, trim cemetery, maintained by a caretaker paid by the Commonwealth War Graves Commission. It contained about thirty graves of soldiers who had died during World War 1 – both German and British.

Shortly before my arrival, Randal had supervised Tanganyika's first secret-ballot election, which had been a great success. Handeni had a council consisting of nine chiefs, nine elected members and nine nominated members. Such councils were by no means 'rubber stamps', and it was essential for the smooth running of the district that the administrative officers and the council had cordial relations.

A mile away from the boma was the market, a much larger one than I had previously known. The most prominent Indian trader was Kheraj Bhimji, a genial person who carried an amazing range of goods in his small shop, and from whom we bought nearly all our basic supplies. Once I was settled in Handeni, I invited Ouma to stay with me for her first visit to tropical Africa. She was then aged seventy-five, but stood up well to the journey and soon adjusted to the community, getting on well with both the small European community and also with the Africans and Indians whom she met. I was proud of her easy manners and her adaptability, and pleased to see how readily she was accepted.

Ouma once let out a scream from the bathroom, when she found a strange creature in the bath. She was a little impatient when I insisted on identifying the animal (it was an elephant shrew, which I had not seen before) in my invaluable Lydekker. Once the animal had been identified and released, Ouma continued with her bath. (I saw the beautiful elephant shrew on only one other occasion, when Bernard and I were at Diani beach, in Kenya, twenty years later.)

Soon after Ouma's arrival I returned unexpectedly to our home to find an embarrassed Kheraj Bhimji on our veranda, with an African assistant carrying a case of Scotch whisky. When I shook my head, he said, 'Oh no, this is not a present for you, it is just to welcome Mama.' He was not surprised when I told him to take it back, the rules being strict and clear: we were allowed to accept one bottle of whisky at Christmas from our local trader and that was that.

The Universities Mission to Central Africa (UMCA) had a thriving mission, with a school and a hospital, five miles away. There I met the saintly Father Neil Russell, and the devoted Mission sisters, who included a doctor. I have said before that there was great variety in the missions; this UMCA Mission was one of the most effective and it was appreciated by the surrounding populace – who were mostly Muslims.

Randal encouraged me to tour the district and to meet the nine chiefs, and Zumbe (chief) Hemedi Sonyo – whose chieftaincy, Magamba, was only nine miles away – soon became a close friend. I learnt much from him, including a lesson in courtesy: I once drove through Magamba without stopping to greet him, because I was in a hurry to reach a further destination. A few days later he cycled to the boma, on his regular visit. On meeting me, he said, 'People told me that you drove by without stopping to greet me the other day but I said this was not possible, you would not do that.' Duly rebuked, I apologised and I made certain that from then on I always made time to stop for a cup of tea, usually accompanied by Marie biscuits and hard-boiled eggs, and a good chat.

Like countless other junior colonial officials, I benefited greatly from the wisdom and experience of older men such as Zumbe Hemedi, always ready to dispense tactfully conveyed advice. Ouma met Zumbe Hemedi, and became friendly with his senior wife. As a farewell present, Ouma gave a brightly coloured teapot and teacups to the family. When I visited them fourteen years later, the tea set was still in use, as was proudly demonstrated. David Nickol, who had been DC Handeni after I left, visited Handeni in 2005, when he was in his mid-eighties. He wrote to Randal:

"Then at Magamba we were taken to see the grave of the late Hemedi Sonyo, the chief whom we all liked so well. I touched the headstone three times, and thought of you all, almost in tears. A crowd of about 80 soon collected, and I told his grand-daughter, our hostess, how Zumbe Hemedi Sonyo once honoured me by inviting me to an all night ngoma, which culminated at dawn with a rain-making ... and I imitated the way he jogged and jigged down that slope with a club in his hand, shoulders bent, surrounded by his elders and family ... I think they recognised the scene."

Having seen Zumbe Hemedi in this posture, I could easily visualise it too.

Handeni has always been susceptible to drought and famine, and in 1953, after a serious drought, we experienced a grim famine. With forethought, Randal had obtained funds to build grain stores, where we kept maize as a famine reserve. I soon became familiar with terms such as moisture content – a vital factor in storing maize if it was not to rot. For some months Randal and I, as well as John Ainley the Agricultural Officer, were fully occupied in checking the availability of food in our nine chieftaincies, supervising the distribution of grain, and arranging road work as part of a famine relief programme. The Native Authorities co-operated, with the exception of one chief who blocked our efforts and failed to distribute the famine relief food.

There was no telephone then in Handeni, and one Saturday afternoon, when we were playing tennis, a small aircraft – an unusual sight, which stopped play – circled overhead, dropping a metal container which held an urgent message: a Central African Airways Viking aircraft, on its regular trip from Nairobi to Johannesburg, via Salisbury (now Harare in Zimbabwe) was late in its schedule, and would we search for it? Randal and I set out in my Land Rover, the only four-wheel-drive vehicle in the district, while John Ainley searched another route. We drove to the chieftaincy of Kwamsisi in the south of the district, one of the most rugged and least developed. With the help of the chief we located the aircraft, which had crashed in the most remote corner of our district, killing all five crew and eight passengers. Leaving the chief to look after the site, Randal and I drove to the coast, where we were able to send a message, by telephone, confirming our grisly find. This was at Sadani, a small fishing village where we had a most welcome cleansing swim in the Indian Ocean; we felt we were washing away the horrors we had seen. (Forty-five years later, at the University of Cape Town, I supervised a Tanzanian student, Rose Mwaipopo, writing her doctoral dissertation about environmental problems in a coastal village. When I asked her the name of the village she said, 'Oh, you would not know it, it is called Sadani.' Rose was amazed when I told her the circumstances of our visit to Sadani, many years before she was born.)

Soon after our return to the crash site, two accident investigators from Britain arrived.

They were accommodated in a luxury camp, the like of which I had not seen, complete with generator, refrigerator and all manner of luxuries – which we too were able to enjoy. One investigator, who had had twenty years' experience of such accidents, told me that in all his investigations, which had taken him all over the world, he had never met such honesty: the local people brought in everything they found – watches, jewellery, other valuable items, clothing, even money. According to the investigator, at other accident sites local people usually stole such items, either to sell or to keep as gruesome souvenirs. We were proud of 'our people'.

The main witness of the disaster, a local farmer called Musa, had been sheltering under a tree during a thunderstorm, when he heard the aircraft flying overhead. He recognised it as the regular weekly flight, the only one to fly over his farm. He then described, graphically and onomatopoeically, how he heard three loud bangs, reproducing each one with uncanny accuracy; his reproduction was so realistic that, combined with the ground evidence, the investigator conjectured that the three bangs represented one wing falling off, the fuselage cracking, then the other wing breaking away. Months later, Randal, and Musa, who had never seen an aircraft at close quarters, flew to Dar es Salaam for the official enquiry, Randal reporting that Musa was 'cool as a cucumber and greatly enjoyed the flight ... He gave his evidence calmly, clearly and with the utmost conviction ... his brilliant mimicking of the sound of the Viking breaking up proved decisive in the court's finding that metal fatigue was responsible for the disaster.' (Vickers, the manufacturers of the doomed aircraft, had alleged that the cause was faulty maintenance by Central African Airways.)

I often went on safari with John Ainley. One of his main tasks was to persuade the local farmers of the value of planting the mandatory one acre of cassava as a famine reserve. Even though everybody knew that Handeni was famine-prone, there was some resistance by farmers to being told by a colonial official what to do on their own farms. John and his team of twenty-two agricultural instructors had to exercise tact, seeking to persuade rather than to order. The instructors, all local men, were vulnerable to being assaulted, or bewitched, if they were too severe, or overbearing.

When we were on safari in the southern areas, we tried to finish at the end of the week at Kwamsisi (where the aircraft had crashed), so that we could drive the extra few miles to Mkwaja, a fishing village on the coast, where we stayed the weekend at the simple rest house. (Forty years later, John sent me a brochure, advertising a luxury hotel at Mkwaja, 'a beautiful area with pure white sandy beaches, offshore islands and coral reefs'. We considered ourselves fortunate, having enjoyed Mkwaja when it was merely a remote fishing hamlet.) Mkwaja was actually in the neighbouring district of Pangani, whose friendly DC had given us permission to stay there whenever we wished: as neither of us at the time had families to rush back to, we made the most of this opportunity. I subscribed to the airmail edition of The Times, and we appreciated the luxury of having no demands made on us for a day or two, giving us time to read the papers from cover to cover.

One morning I was awakened at 3 a.m. by a messenger on a motorcycle, He had come from Zumbe Musa, a young man who had recently been elected chief of Mgera, two hours' drive to the north. Musa requested that I come immediately because the nomadic pastoralist WaKwavi were threatening the Nguu people. I hastily collected our veteran, impressive and unflappable police sergeant Timothy, and two askaris (policemen), and set out in my Land Rover, arriving soon after dawn. An anxious Zumbe Musa explained that a local farmer had been guarding his crops the previous evening, when he heard a rustling noise, and, thinking it was an animal, shot an arrow. But the noise had been made by a young Mkwavi lad, who had been wounded by the arrow. Fortunately, the wound was not too serious and the local dresser had dealt ably with it. But the WaKwavi men, about fifty of whom were gathered outside the courthouse, with their red cloaks and long spears, were furious. Backed by a very prominent Sgt Timothy and his men, I persuaded the WaKwavi to enter the court, leaving their spears outside. Ranged opposite them were Musa's elders, leaving Musa and me seated at the bench on the platform.

Then followed several hours of discussion. When the WaKwavi started murmuring, like an angry swarm of bees, Sgt Timothy ostentatiously breeched his rifle, to me a most comforting sound. Eventually a compromise was reached: the farmer would pay a goat in compensation to the father of the boy whom he had wounded, and the same father would pay a fine for allowing his son to trespass in the fields at night. Before this incident, Musa and I had been wary of each other, I forget why, but afterwards we became good friends, and trusted each other.

Around this time, Hugh Lamprey, a young game biologist, arrived at Handeni to study baboon behaviour. He was particularly interested in the extent of crop damage by baboons: locals told us that baboons regularly ate one third, or even more, of their maize. We had seen the results of a troop of baboons raiding a field of maize, and this estimate seemed credible; indeed, it was widely accepted. Hugh set up camp in various fields, and meticulously observed what happened. After some months of intensive and careful study, Hugh concluded that baboons destroyed no more than two per cent of the crop. (Hugh later became internationally renowned as director of a training centre for game scouts and game rangers, and our paths crossed again fifteen years later when he visited the University of California, Berkeley.)

When Hugh was leaving, he asked me to look after an orphaned baby baboon, until he could arrange for the Game Department to collect it. But the frightened creature escaped, running up a big tree at the boma, and getting its rope tangled around branches high up in the tree. I looked at the crowd of government employees and bystanders that had gathered; they looked at me, making it clear that this was my business, not theirs, so – watched by the expectant crowd – I climbed the tree, with the baboon piteously shrieking and spraying me with urine, until I disentangled it and put it in a safe place.

The Mau Mau war in Kenya was at its height in 1953, the result of the bitter grievances of Africans, especially the main ethnic group, the Kikuyu. After more than fifty years of colonial rule, land dispossession and discrimination, the Kikuyu had started an armed revolt, which was eventually repressed in 1956, with much brutality on both sides. I was told that I was one of six District Officers in Tanganyika to have been chosen for temporary secondment to Kenya. The 'invitation' was couched in terms designed to make this seem like an honour, but I declined, as delicately as I could, and, fortunately, no pressure was put on me. I could not have faced that scene. (Two years later, when I was at Njombe, I received a telegram: AM INSTRUCTED TO INQUIRE IF YOU WISH TO BE CONSIDERED FOR IMMEDIATE SECONDMENT TO CYPRUS FOR TWO YEARS. I wanted to stay in Africa, and Cyprus was, at that time in the middle of a civil war, so again, I had no hesitation in politely declining.)

Towards the end of my stay at Handeni, a telephone service, that worked intermittently, was installed. By this time Randal had collapsed from nervous exhaustion,

259

leaving me as acting DC. After the trauma of the famine, and of the air crash, I decided to take two weeks' local leave, intending to try to climb Mount Kilimanjaro. While I was finalising arrangements, I had an invitation that I could not resist, from Bill Tulloch, my contemporary on the colonial course at Oxford, who had been transferred to the island of Mafia, south of Zanzibar. Bill, a bluff and larger than life figure, easily persuaded me that I would find a visit to Mafia fascinating, as indeed I did. I was accommodated in the spacious, cool, old German boma, where Bill was DC, and sole administrator.

Bill drove me round the small island in his Citroën, introducing me to the dignified Arab and African notables. I was intrigued by reports in the district archives of early trade with China, and organised an informal archaeological expedition. Waiting for the extra low spring tide, Bill and I set out in the government launch, with a party of twelve prisoners who were happy to have a day out. We visited two beaches, which from the records had good potential, and I supervised the prisoners in searching for pottery on the beaches. At the end of our outing, we had collected nearly a bucketful of promising-looking fragments, which, when I later deposited them at the Museum of Dar es Salaam, were enthusiastically received and identified as Chinese and Persian, some going back to the twelfth century.

Another highlight of my visit to Mafia was my introduction to the excitement of underwater snorkelling, and I managed to view a remarkable variety of colourful tropical fish. Bill and I went in the launch to promising reefs, being wary of the schools of menacing barracuda that sometimes followed us – we asked the boat crew to warn us when they came too close. Bill was an effective and respected administrator, but he saw no point in sitting in his office if there was no work for him (Mafia had a small, and mostly law-abiding, population) when he could have been enjoying himself with me.

# Tanga

After one year at Handeni, I was transferred to Tanga, the provincial headquarters of north-eastern Tanga province. Tanga was a pleasant coastal town, with a good natural harbour, and I was lucky in being allocated a fine bungalow in Ras Kazoni, opposite the entrance to the harbour. The colourful garden had tropical flowering bushes and shrubs, including Pride of Barbados, frangipani, masses of bougainvillea and the ubiquitous Cassia siamea. Ouma was still with me, and I was pleased that the faithful Timo could join us from Handeni.

My first DC was a rather formal, reserved man who, nevertheless, taught me an important lesson in administrative manners. I had on several occasions had long conversations with a man who was both obsessed and confused. He wrote a series of rambling complaints and eventually, irritated, I wrote a terse reply. The DC, who read through all correspondence emanating from the boma, told me to write another letter, apologising for the curt tone, inviting the complainant in to discuss the matter. He told me that I should remember that we were servants of the public, whatever the circumstances were. I duly wrote my letter as directed, ending with the customary 'I am, Sir, your obedient servant', leaving it for the DC to review. When I went to collect the letter, I found that the DC had signed it himself, providing a useful lesson; one that I did not forget.

I continued my duties as a magistrate, soon finding that litigation on the coast was immensely more complex than anything I had hitherto experienced. Worst of all were complicated disputes over palm trees, sometimes involving large plantations, on other occasions just a few trees. There was never agreement about ownership, both

Arab and African witnesses wove intricate webs of stories in which I soon got lost; witnesses could often be bribed, and the whole proceedings were usually observed by a large crowd of critical spectators, who did not hesitate to give their opinions.

Just when I was beginning to despair of ever making sense of these acrimonious disputes, a saviour, in the form of one Shabaan Robert, appeared on the scene. An imposing, gracious Muslim, he was one of the first African administrative officers to be appointed. His official title was 'Township Officer' but he soon unobtrusively took me under his wing, improving my confidence and proving an excellent mentor. Even then he was a published poet, and he later became famous for his classic Swahili poetry. Shabaan Robert has been called Tanzania's national poet, and Randal Sadleir referred to him as 'the great and uncrowned Poet Laureate'.

In addition to guiding me through the labyrinth of coastal litigation, Shabaan Robert constantly and gently corrected my Swahili, insisting that I speak the correct coastal Swahili. On a visit to Tanzania, more than thirty years after my lessons with Shabaan, I was congratulated on my spoken Swahili when I visited Dar es Salaam; one man told me that I spoke an archaic Swahili, which I took as a compliment and I felt that Shabaan would have been pleased. My admiration and respect for Shabaan Robert have coloured my views of Muslims ever since. When I hear some of the hysterical post 9/11 generalisations about evil Muslim fundamentalists, I remind myself of my two wise and kind Muslim friends, Zumbe Hemedi and Shabaan Robert.

I have written above on the influence on me of my DCs, John Leslie and Randal Sadleir. Once again I was in luck, in meeting John Allen, who was the next DC in Tanga. John, who was older than the other DCs, was a man of immense rectitude. Pressure had been put on him to approve a large-scale beach development, including a luxury hotel, which would have necessitated the removal of some fishermen, who would then have been denied the use of the beach, on which their livelihood depended. John, like Randal an accomplished Swahili speaker, knew the fishermen well. He resolutely refused to endorse the development, earning the displeasure of some senior officials (though not the Governor) at the Secretariat in Dar es Salaam. His stubborn refusal to yield probably had negative results on his career, but he later made a second distinguished career as a specialist in Swahili at a British university.

Many years later, in the course of a consultancy on the Kenya coast, I heard of a move by a consortium of developers to build a huge luxury complex at the lovely Diani beach, south of Mombasa. Once more the local fishermen were threatened with removal and losing their access to the beach. I was in no position to make a formal protest, but I did write a letter to the PC. I set out, as fully as I could, the case for the fishermen, pointing out the probable and adverse publicity that the proposed development would have. Although I received no reply to my letter, I was delighted, a few months later, to read a speech which the PC had given to his Provincial Council. He declined to approve of the development, quoting gratifyingly large sections of my letter – without any acknowledgement.

Randal had been involved in a similar conflict in Handeni, where ancestral graves were located in the middle of a large sisal plantation. The managers of the plantation wished to plough across the burial site to make tractor access easier. Once again pressure came from the Secretariat because sisal was one of the mainstays of the economy of Tanganyika, the so-called 'sisal barons' wielding a baleful influence. Randal, like John, stood firm, until eventually the Governor intervened and upheld the rights of the local people. Randal had even invoked the United Nations Charter, which supported the rights of indigenous people in such conflicts.

## Meeting my destiny

Despite my liking the variety and challenges of my administrative duties, and generally enjoying the daily round, I was concerned about my future, and about the direction of my life. Here was I, thirty-one years old and what would become of me? I was still troubled by my white liberal South African guilt and very concerned about the state of South Africa, as a result of the many drastic and cruel apartheid policies.

I had been regularly attending mass at the local Catholic Church, where I was friendly with the priests. By 1954, the National Party had been in power in South Africa for six years, and the horrors of apartheid were already quite clear. I thought that it was time for me to 'do something', but no form of political action in South Africa appealed to me. I wrote to Archbishop Hurley in Durban (a fearless and outspoken opponent of apartheid for many years – he died in February 2004) and was accepted for admission to St John Vianney Seminary in Pretoria. I was to start my training for the priesthood early in 1955.

I resigned from the Colonial Service, giving the reason, and was surprised and flattered to be invited to the capital, Dar es Salaam, where a senior official, both a Catholic and a keen sailor, took me sailing in the harbour and tried to persuade me that I could have a valid vocation in the world by staying on in the Colonial Service. But I had made up my mind, I wished to be a priest in Zululand, learning Zulu and using my anthropological background to become involved in social action in Natal, where I had grown up, as a form of reparation. (I was ahead of my time: as I write this there are occasional debates about whether white South Africans should make reparations, and in what form)....

There had been an outbreak of typhoid in the district, and I had helped a nurse to distribute medicines at Korogwe hospital, where I may have become infected. But I am sure that my mental struggles weakened me and encouraged the illness. Bernard was desperate, later telling me, 'I searched all my life for you and found you, and then I feared that I had lost you.' During the delirium, I remember three visitors, all anxious for my welfare – Bernard bringing me every day a blossom from the 'Tree of Heaven' (bottlebrush or Callistemon), Ouma, and Harry Gill, the Provincial Commissioner.

OnRandal Sadleir's recommendation, the Governor had suspended an African zumbe (chief) at Handeni, for corruption, and the chief had sworn that he would take revenge, threatening that anyone who opposed him would go mad, or become ill. People were afraid, because the chief was reputed to have strong supernatural powers, and witchcraft beliefs were widespread in this district. Shortly after this threat, Randal suffered a nervous breakdown, then his successor collapsed with an internal haemorrhage, and then came my illness. Harry Gill, the PC, urged me to recover and go back to show the flag, which I was keen to do. So when I returned to Handeni, one of my first acts was to drive around in a boyish show of authority, accompanied by one of the Irish priests, and by Sergeant Timothy and some of his policemen. We drove in two Land Rovers to the deposed chief's village, on the outskirts of which three policemen were engaged in rifle practice, running about and shooting into an anthill, to impress the local people. It seems childish now, but I was pleased by my own show of supernatural and secular power.

When I had recovered from my illness, I withdrew my resignation from the Colonial Service....

The Tanga Club was the quintessential colonial club, with a mixture of commercial people (from sisal estates, banks, garages, engineering works) and colonial officials.

All members were white (with an exception made if the doctor were Asian); it had a very proper and memsahib-ish air, which we found stifling. By contrast the Tanga Yacht Club attracted a younger and less formal set, all keen sailors, for whom the large bay offered grand opportunities. It was a congenial place, where – as had happened at the Point Yacht Club in Durban – the few motor-boat owners were much looked down on by the true yachtsmen. My friend Daphne, a nursing sister (who later married John Ainley) had the use of a trim yacht named Dainty, which I sailed when Daphne was on duty, with Bernard crewing for me. We even had the thrill of winning one of the major races....

Twenty years later (in 1974), Bernard and I revisited Tanga, and found the yacht club little changed, and, I noticed, with still exclusively white membership. Sailing apparently does not appeal to Africans or Asians.

As at my other stations, retail trade in Tanga was dominated by Asians, with Popat Kassam owning the leading grocery. Shopping there with Bernard, I spotted some bottles of nondescript wine, and asked Mr Kassam what the vintage "was.

'Yes, please?' he asked.   'When was the wine made?' 'Oh, very new, please, all our stock is very new.'

I balance this tale with one from Rhodesia, where we moved a few years later. Early one morning our friend Maire O'Farrell rushed in to tell us that Haddon and Sly, the main departmental store, was having a great sale. The new (white) manager had told all departments that they must get rid of old stock. In vain did the wine manager plead to be able to keep his choice vintage wines – 'No. Everything must go.' This sale introduced us to Pouilly Fumé, one of the first cases of wine that we had ever bought, because we could afford the sale prices – sixpence a bottle. So Popat Kassam was not alone in his ignorance.

As part of my duties in Tanga, I made an official visit to the eccentric Colonel Boscawen who owned a sisal estate, at Moa, near the coast, where he had built a house, described by John Allen as 'a cross between an English country house and the Wallace Collection'. There was an extraordinary collection of paintings and jewels and objets in the Boscawen home. Unlike other sisal estates, where the crop usually came right up to the front door, the house at Moa was enclosed in a small island of shrubs and flowering trees, with vistas carefully cut to give glimpses of the ocean.

Colonel Boscawen, a bachelor, encouraged me to visit and to bring Bernard. We would dress for dinner, wearing shukas (saronglike garments) and long-sleeved shirts and sandals. We got up before dawn to fish, introducing our host to the excitement of snorkelling.

Bakari, the old boatman, tried to dissuade Col Boscawen from this dangerous sport, telling him, *Je, wewe ni Mzee, usiendelee* (I say, you are an old man, do not continue). At that time the coral reefs abounded in marine life, but since then excessive poaching, including the use of dynamite, has resulted in a drastic loss.

Tanga District included a long stretch along the coast as well as large areas inland, parts of which were in the Usambara mountains, which were cool and attractive. There was a lovely old rest house in the hill station of Amani, where we spent several happy weekends. In 1954, the mountain road passed through thick forests and we used to stop halfway for a skinny dip in a clear mountain stream. When Bernard and I revisited the area twenty years later the stream had disappeared, and the grand indigenous Chloraphora excelsa ( African teak) had all been cut down and replaced by stark stands of exotic trees. Amani had magical associations for us, both because of our stolen weekends at the hill station, and also because it means peace in Swahili. We used the name AMANI on our personalised number plates on our VWs in California, and even now my Audi bears the name, a constant reminder to me of those happy days....

267

Bernard was not happy in the hierarchical structure of the colonial education service and he had an unfair imposition thrust on him, when he was told to mark 1700 examination papers in geography, many of them written in Swahili. Although he had a good basic vocabulary in Swahili, Bernard could not manage this task alone, so he and I spent many evenings poring over the papers. By this time I had passed my Higher Standard Swahili examinations, not a difficult task for me because so much of my working day was conducted in that language. Bernard maintained his Swahili, and, right up to his death, our conversation would be peppered with Swahili expressions. Beginning with his first note to me, Bernard called me pen (his invention, based on the verb penda, to love) and always ended his letters with daima wako ('yours forever'). Twelve years later, Bernard was the first doctoral student in the USA to be allowed to take Swahili as his second language; he was examined by a Catholic priest, fluent in Swahili, who set Bernard the task, successfully completed, of translating a short speech of President Nyerere.

I was due for five months' long leave, and in early December 1954 I went to England, and leased a London flat near Marble Arch, where Ouma soon joined me. Bernard resigned from the Colonial Service but had to stay on an extra month to finish his tour. We were re-united in London early in 1955.

## London

Bernard and I spent several months in England, based at our flat in London but making many trips out to the country – Bernard eagerly showing me his boyhood haunts, in Manchester, Shropshire and Anglesey in Wales. Having sold my Land Rover before leaving Tanganyika, I bought a new vehicle, a Standard Vanguard van. Although

I had been in London for short visits, I did not know the city well and Bernard was happy to show me around. He had spent a year at the University of London, doing his teaching degree and sharing a flat just behind Harrods. During this time he had walked and cycled all over London, and he knew the city well and loved showing me hidden corners.

This was our first experience of what became a lifetime pattern of enthusiastic attendance at concerts, opera, dance, plays and art exhibitions. In those days we queued for the cheapest seats: five shillings to sit in the 'gods' at Covent Garden, and were rewarded by seeing Margot Fonteyn dance, or Joan Sutherland sing. We saw John Gielgud and Lawrence Olivier on the stage and we heard the St Matthew Passion at Southwark Cathedral. We were fortunate in sharing many of the same tastes, not identical, but close enough.

Bernard and I both hoped to stay in Africa, and we considered relocating to Rhodesia, partly because each of us had family connections there. My brother Paul and his family were living in Fort Victoria (now Masvingo) and Bernard's sister, Eileen, and her family, together with his mother, lived in Gwanda. Both our families encouraged us to come, and reports from the new Central African Federation were favourable. Bernard accepted a teaching post at Founders High School in Bulawayo, the only advanced secondary school for coloureds and Asians in the Federation. We decided that he would test the waters and inquire about possibilities of a job for me but I would return to Tanganyika, where I still had a commitment, until the picture was clearer. We had a good voyage to Cape Town, from where we drove in our Standard Vanguard to Durban, giving Bernard his first glimpse of South Africa. He was enthralled by the landscape, and horrified by apartheid.

While we were in Durban, Bernard received an urgent telegram telling him to go immediately to Founders High

School. So he flew to Bulawayo, and I drove up in the van. I had only two days with Bernard in Bulawayo, before continuing my journey to Tanganyika. At that time (June 1955) the roads were good and there were many comfortable small hotels on the way. It was much easier then to make this two thousand mile road journey than it would be today; border posts did not involve the agonisingly long waits and the brusque, corrupt officials that they so often do today.

## Njombe

Back in Tanganyika, I had been posted to the Southern Highlands province, with its headquarters at Mbeya. I reported to Geoffrey Hucks, the PC (also a South African), who invited me to stay the night at his home, asking me whether I minded sharing the guest room. My room-mate proved to be Chief David Makwaia, whom I had met briefly when we were both studying at Oxford University.

A few years later David became one of the first four African members of the Tanganyika Legislative Council.My new station, Njombe, was considered a desirable posting because it was at a high altitude, malaria-free, cool, even offering trout-fishing in the high areas. I lived in a pleasant stone house situated near the river, half a mile from the township with the usual line of Asian-owned shops. Timotheo joined me, although it involved a harrowing week-long journey, from Handeni, in different forms of transport. I was delighted to see him again, and we soon organised a happy and comfortable household. I thoroughly enjoyed my short – nine months – stay there.

At Njombe I encountered a new phenomenon. This was a period when the Colonial Office was embarking on a series of development projects, many of them, notably the notorious 'Groundnut Scheme' in southern Tanganyika, being complete disasters because they were so ill-conceived. The Colonial Development Corporation (CDC) had acquired forty thousand acres in Njombe for the planting of wattle trees. It was intended to be a co-operative venture, with local people contributing their labour and eventually receiving some benefits. Like so many of these projects, the main weakness was that the local people had not been adequately consulted and they were, with justification, suspicious, and reluctant to participate. One of my duties was to liaise between the CDC and the local Bena people; I was relieved when a full-time official was later appointed to do this job.

Njombe had the usual up-country colonial club which, by the time I arrived, was dominated by CDC officials and their wives and was far too 'colonial' for my tastes. Going on safari as usual provided a welcome relief and I often travelled with Robert, the bright young Agricultural Officer. Several times we stayed overnight at a Benedictine mission where we were welcomed by the two Dutch priests, who persuaded us to play bridge with them after supper. They were puzzled when we told them that we did not take advantage of our opportunities to play bridge every evening.

Going to the western part of the district involved a long downhill drive at the foot of which was a large Benedictine mission complete with school and clinic. When the Sisters saw our vehicle in the distance, they would start preparing our welcome, and when Robert and I reached the mission to greet them, they would offer us a hearty and welcome breakfast. As good Benedictines, they followed the rule that all guests are to be 'treated as Christ'.

My new DC was fair and efficient but also aloof and remote from the people. He was more interested in the local birds than in the problems of the local people, writing two articles about the birds of Njombe for TN&R. I was glad when he was transferred and I was appointed as acting DC, which gave me a new perspective. After my appointment the Provincial Commissioner wrote to me, in his copperplate handwriting:

"I know you will be kind to the deserving. I depend on you to be hard hearted to the undeserving and impervious to cajolery or threat – both of which are often tried on the new D.C."

One of my main duties was to promote the local council, chairing its annual meeting, which determined the budget. We had to work within strict guidelines: a maximum of forty-five per cent could be spent on 'personnel emoluments', and there was, of course, a limit to expenditure. I spent three challenging but ultimately rewarding days considering a variety of proposals – for expenditure on schools, clinics, cattle dips, water supply, housing, offices and bicycles. We listed all proposals together with estimates of their cost and then had to decide which ones we would select within our defined budget. Discussions were lively but amiable and, as DC and chairman, I was never able to push through my own pet projects if they were not popular with the council. This is another area where I noticed a great contrast after independence, when the central government became much more authoritarian with little participation from local councils. This seems, sadly, to be almost a universal trend, certainly prevailing in South Africa today.

When I was acting DC, a new cadet, Roger Clifford, arrived. He was very different from the usual rather buttoned-up young Englishman: having no car, he walked (about two miles) to the Njombe Club, itself unusual, but – even stranger – he was accompanied by an African friend. Consternation. No-one dared to say that Africans were not welcome, but I was asked to 'speak to Roger'. Instead, I wrote a letter of disapproval to the Club committee, and resigned from the Club. What a relief. The Committee made a formal complaint about my action to the Provincial

Commissioner, who ignored it. Roger was a great companion to me in those lonely days, when I was missing Bernard. I enjoyed his mocking and critical eye, and he teased me unmercifully. Yet, when tasks needed to be done, Roger was quick, bright and effective.

Ouma came from South Africa to join me in Njombe in November 1955, and shortly after her arrival a delegation from the newly-formed Tanganyika African National Union (TANU) visited the district, led by its charismatic and then little-known leader, Julius Nyerere. I hosted a reception for them, the most unusual and exhilarating party I had ever given. I invited my colleagues, and Nyerere arrived with an entourage of about fifteen people, young and old, Muslim and Christian, educated and illiterate. When I introduced Nyerere to Ouma, he sat next to her and conversed courteously with her for several minutes, following the general African custom of honouring older people, and not minding that Ouma had come from South Africa. While most of the older TANU members sipped their Coca-Cola, some of the young men much enjoyed my whisky. It was a lively party, which included any number of serious conversations. As a result of this party, a general circular was sent from the Secretariat, telling administrative officers that they should not entertain any politicians from the new parties. This was a mistake: none of the officials imagined that Nyerere would lead his country to independence only six years after our meeting, and there would have been fewer misunderstandings if we had had more contact with each other.

The Governor of Tanganyika, Sir Edward Twining, visited Njombe twice while I was there. Shortly after my arrival, the DC told me to go to a remote corner of the district and supervise the construction of a 'corduroy' so that His Excellency (HE) could drive over to the next district. I had heard of corduroys but I had never seen one; they are strips of branches and logs which are laid over a

273

swampy area to enable motor vehicles to drive across. Fortunately our experienced African road foreman soon rounded up some young men to cut the branches and lay them in the correct fashion. A few minutes after the corduroy was complete, the Governor arrived in his Armstrong Siddeley. Out sprang the driver and the ADC, and in no time they were efficiently offering HE and me large gin and tonics, complete with ice. I was most impressed by this routine, and even more impressed by HE's enthusiastic interest in, and considerable knowledge of, developments in our district. To my relief the corduroy served its purpose, the gubernatorial car proceeding safely to the next district.

Soon after I had been appointed acting DC, His Excellency visited Njombe again, the main purpose being to open the annual meeting of the newly-formed District Council. As was customary, I vacated my home to allow HE and Lady Twining to stay there. I held a reception for him, inviting leading members of the council, prominent Indian traders and my colleagues. One of these colleagues had an African mistress, Maria, who was very eager to attend the reception. I could not invite her in her own right, but ever-resourceful Timo found the solution, and lent Maria one of his kanzus, the voluminous white robe, commonly worn by servants. Maria borrowed a red fez and passed as an auxiliary waiter, happily handing round drinks and snacks. Only one of my guests realised who she was: Father Russell, whom I had known and admired in Handeni, happened to be visiting Njombe, and smilingly said to me, 'What an attractive new waiter you have, David.'

Before addressing the council on the next day, HE asked me whether I would like to interpret his speech into Swahili or if I would prefer to leave that task to his ADC. As a matter of pride I insisted on doing the interpretation, hoping that I would be able to cope. After preliminary courtesies, HE grinned at me and said to the council, 'Now

274

I am going to put the cat among the pigeons.' While I was beginning, Sasa Mheshimiwa, Bw Gavna, akasema … (Now HE says that …) I was desperately searching in my mind for the appropriate Swahili translation of this idiom. I must have found it, because there were no perplexed faces. The gist of the governor's speech was that the council must assume greater responsibility for looking after local affairs.

I had hoped to spend more time in the mountainous area in the north of the district but I was able to visit it only once. Monica Wilson, my anthropology professor at Rhodes, had done extensive fieldwork among the Nyakyusa of south-west Tanganyika; she had asked me to check on details about the Kinga people and their caves, which they built half underground as a protection against the cold. I was not there long enough to make systematic inquiries but I did call on the fish guard whose job it was to look after the trout in the rivers. He had a lonely life and was glad to see me, insisting that I set up camp by the river and that I do some fishing. When I protested that I had never done any trout-fishing he was delighted and said, 'Now is your chance; I will teach you.' He was a good instructor and I caught a few trout for our supper. Some of my colleagues, who were stationed at dusty lowland districts, could not believe that I did not go fishing every weekend.

At the boma the meticulous Goan cashier, Mr Gomez, took care of the accounts, making my duties much easier. Mr Gomez, a model of honesty, frequently complained about the laxity and corruption among the Native Authority cashiers. Some years later I read an insightful analysis by a Nigerian political scientist who was examining the prevalence of corruption in Africa. According to his analysis – and this made sense to me – most Africans viewed the state as a colonial creation and even after independence it was seen as something alien to them. Most of them regarded their responsibilities to their own families as paramount over any duties to the state. Whatever the explanation, many bright Standard 10 boys who were brought into government service were, sadly, in prison, having been convicted of stealing government funds.

## Tunduru

I was too junior to be left for long in charge of such an important district as Njombe, and in December 1955 I was transferred to Tunduru, a small district three hundred miles to the south. The roads were rough so we – Ouma, Timo and I – stopped the night halfway at Songea, where the DC was expecting us. While we appreciated his hospitality, we did not find it a comfortable evening: first, when the DC came out to greet us he ushered Ouma and me into the house, ignoring Timo. When I asked what Timotheo should do, he said airily, 'Oh, my boys will take care of him.' Leading us into our rooms, he said, 'Because you are travelling, you need not bother to dress for dinner' – which had Ouma and me giggling later. When I asked Timo, the next morning, how he had fared, he grimaced and said it was not too bad. Coming from a distant ethnic group he would have found the local servants inhospitable. In the intervening years, the hundred and twenty different Tanzanian ethnic groups have become much more fused, in large part through the systematic promotion of Swahili as the national language, and there is less ethnic tension in Tanzania than in any of the neighbouring countries.

I was in Tunduru, my last station, for only five months; it was the most remote and least developed of all my postings. On one of my early safaris I visited, on foot, a Yao village near the border with Nyasaland (Malawi), my purpose being to encourage the formation of a local council. After listening patiently to my explanation and urging, one of the elders told me that they were doing very well as they were and they did not need any of this council business. I had to leave that to my successor to sort out. Safaris were exciting in Tunduru because there was always the real likelihood of spotting a lion or a leopard in the early morning or late evening.

One afternoon I had a visit from the liwali (headman) of the village, asking humbly if I would permit them to play the drums that evening, to celebrate the festival of Id ul-Fitr, marking the end of Ramadan. I agreed readily but asked him why he had asked my permission. I was embarrassed to be told that the wife of my predecessor had forbidden any drumming because it gave her a headache – even though the village was a good half-mile away. I asked the liwali if I could join the celebration and he welcomed me; we had a joyful evening.

After heavy tropical rains, our local river, the Muhuwesi, was flooded. On one occasion our three ton GT truck was carrying prisoners, guarded by a policeman with a .303 rifle. When the lorry drove over the bridge on the river, it lurched, causing the rifle to slip out of the policeman's grasp and fall in the turbulent waters. That was the version told me by the policeman, whom I believed. What a fuss that caused. Because of the fear of firearms falling into the wrong hands (the Mau Mau insurrection was still going on in neighbouring Kenya) there was strict gun control. After sending a full report to the Police Commissioner in Dar es Salaam, I was asked whether I had searched the river for the missing rifle. I wish now that I could have emailed a digital photograph of the Muhuwezi river in full flood: there was absolutely no chance of recovering the rifle which had probably been shattered into small pieces. Eventually both the policeman and I were reprimanded, his explanation was reluctantly accepted, and I was able to 'write off' the missing rifle.

While I was at Tunduru, the Secretariat in Dar es Salaam decreed that all stations must observe new office hours: 8 a.m. to noon, and 2 p.m. to 5 p.m. Because it was a busy time in the agricultural cycle, the staff asked if we could revert to the old office hours, 7 a.m. to 2 p.m., which would allow them to do work on their farms in the afternoon. I readily agreed, seeing no need to inform Dar es Salaam of my decision. We were so isolated that we had few visitors, and none who would object – if they noticed – to the unorthodox office hours.

In February 1956 I received favourable news from Bernard about employment prospects in Bulawayo and, being eager to join him, I decided to resign from the Colonial Service, this time with finality. I was offered a post at the Department of African Affairs in Bulawayo which I very happily accepted. In April, I travelled to Dar es Salaam, spending a few days with Randal Sadleir, who had made a complete recovery and who was then working in the Secretariat.

This was the end of my colonial period, a formative and memorable one for me, not least because it had led to my meeting my destiny, Bernard.

## Conclusion

I have made several unfavourable contrasts with contemporary conditions, especially in regard to official attitudes. I do not wish to be too judgmental though: we were working in a different era; in many ways our tasks were easier. The 'Pax Britannica' did prevail, within, and between, the artificially constructed colonial states. Populations, both human and livestock, were much smaller; expectations were lower; societies were very much more local than global; media attention was almost non-existent. (I do not mention this last thinking of atrocities that were hidden, but rather to point out that the media spotlight has many and diverse effects.) In short, ours was a simpler world. From what I have written, it will be obvious that, while not trying to justify or excuse colonial rule, I think that, given the circumstances, we did not do a bad job.

I was later gratified when five of my former students, who had all obtained their doctorates in Anthropology at the University of California, Santa Barbara, and were all engaged in fieldwork in Tanzania or Kenya, contributed to a Special Section, 'Historical Consciousness in Development Planning', in the journal World Development. All of them had started their fieldwork with some degree of the prevalent anti-colonial bias, and all had concluded that a study of the colonial period offered rich lessons for present development planners. They realised that many development problems had already been encountered in colonial times, and that there was a need for studies which should include colonial development as an important part of African History. As Miriam Chaiken wrote: 'we should not throw out the good with the bad in our rejection of the colonial legacy'.

I left Handeni in 1954, seven years before Tanzanian independence, and was able to revisit the district in 1968 – seven years after Independence. I was received graciously, and my path made easier because two men, whom I had helped when they were schoolboys, were now in senior positions. One was an Mbunge (Member of Parliament). The other, the Area Commissioner, whose duties were much the same as the old DC, told me, 'Make yourself at home. You know this place, go anywhere, talk to anyone, and then see me and let us talk.'

I had a happy reunion in 1968 with my old friend Zumbe Hemedi Sonyo, no longer a chief – chieftaincy was abolished in 1963 – but performing many of his old tasks as Development Executive Officer. I saw many changes, many developments, increased staff, twenty Land Rovers instead of just my vehicle, but I also noticed many similarities. The ecological imperative – uncertain rainfall, recurrent droughts and famines, hilly country – still determined much of the development, and many local

279

social institutions were flourishing. I treasure a remark made to me by a policeman, when I told him I had been a DO in Handeni: *Haya, ni nchi yako. Nyinyi mmetangulia, sisi tumefuata.* 'This is your country, then. You people led the way. We followed.'

Source:

David Brokensha, *Brokie's Way: An Athropologist's Story: Love and Work in Three Continents*, chapter 8, Amani Press, 2007.

# 1956 – 1959: Rhodesia

## David Brokensha

On the eve of my departure from Tanganyika, I received a letter from my Oxford mentor, Professor Evans-Pritchard (E-P), who wrote, presciently, 'I hope you won't be too optimistic about Rhodesia. All these countries are variants of a pattern, and in my experience, they are all bloody, not equally bloody, but bloody all the same.' E-P also told me, 'The chap you are going to work with is, Schapera tells me, most delightful. Schapera knows him well.' Rhodesia did indeed prove, eventually, to be 'bloody', and Bernard and I became friendly with Professor Isaac Schapera, a distinguished social anthropologist, during his annual visits to the Ashtons, and again later when we lived in London in the 1990s.

Some brief history: Rhodesia had been occupied for nearly two thousand years by the Shona peoples, who form eighty per cent of the population. The south-western areas are home to the Ndebele, who had fled from the Zulu warrior-king Shaka, arriving in their new territory in about 1840. In 1890, 'pioneers' from Cecil Rhodes' British South African Company arrived, their primary aim being a search for gold. They were followed by white settlers, who, by 1901, numbered 11 000. A rebellion, later known as 'The First Chimurenga' or 'war of liberation', was

281

harshly suppressed. In 1923 Southern Rhodesia became a self-governing British colony, with Britain having rarely-used veto powers, and local whites effectively ruling the country.

In September 1953, the Federation of Rhodesia and Nyasaland was formed, consisting of Northern Rhodesia (now Zambia), Southern Rhodesia (Zimbabwe) and Nyasaland (Malawi), with a population of 6.5 million Africans and 200 000 whites. Despite the valiant efforts of a few liberal leaders, notably the New Zealand-born missionary Garfield Todd, who was Prime Minister from 1953 to 1958, the Federation increasingly fell under the rule of hardliners. When we arrived in Bulawayo (Bernard in 1955, and I the following year) there was still an atmosphere of cautious optimism, which had dissipated towards the end of our stay.

I worked in the African Administration in Bulawayo, where Hugh Ashton was Director. He was an inspirational man to work with, an outstanding administrator who had created the best housing and amenities for Africans in southern Africa. He had been an Assistant District Commissioner in Bechuanaland Protectorate ( Botswana) and was also an anthropologist. He had made a study of the 'Basuto' of Basutoland (Lesotho), and I am sure that he applied his anthropological insights to his administrative duties, in diverse ways.

Bulawayo at this time had a population of about 230 000, with 200 000 of them being Africans, the rest mostly whites, with small numbers of coloureds and Indians. It was a pleasant, sleepy city, always overshadowed by the capital, Salisbury (Harare), three hundred miles to the north-east. Salisbury was referred to as Bamba zonke (takes everything), because the government put significantly more resources into the capital city than into the second city, Bulawayo – and this has also been true of post-independence Zimbabwe.

I was assigned to the new, innovative home-ownership

township of Mpopoma, where I worked under the cheerful and efficient Superintendent, Derek Cleary. The word 'township' refers, in southern Africa, to low-cost housing for 'non-whites', usually Africans; such places are often situated many miles away from places of employment, and public transport is usually rudimentary. Hugh Ashton had persuaded the (all-white) Bulawayo City Council to undertake widespread improvements in housing, transport and recreation for the large African population. Bulawayo was unusual in that it recognised – what should have been glaringly obvious to all – that a large proportion of urban Africans regarded the towns as their permanent homes. In most southern African towns there was an implicit assumption, made devastatingly explicit in apartheid South Africa, that Africans were migrant workers who would eventually return to their rural homes....

Visitors to Mpopoma when we were there in the 1950s included two well-known writers, James Morris (later better known as Jan Morris) and Doris Lessing, whom Bernard and I had so much looked forward to meeting, having read her earlier books, including *This was the Old Chief's Country* (1951), and *The Grass is Singing* (1956).

I took each of them on a tour of our African housing and amenities, and afterwards I invited each to our flat for tea. While James Morris was appreciative and charming, Doris Lessing refused to be impressed. She later wrote a short dismissive account of her tour, in *Going Home* (1957) where she was highly critical of all that she had been shown, including 'my' model Mpopoma township. (Her criticisms led to her being banned from Rhodesia.) Bernard was so irritated by Lessing's blindness that he later said, 'I could cheerfully have thrown her over the [ninth floor] balcony'. I admit that her attitude prejudiced me regarding her much-acclaimed later literary output, but her account (*African Laughter*, 1992) of four visits that she made to Zimbabwe was investigative journalism at its best....

Source:
David Brokensha, *Brokie's Way: An Athropologist's Story: Love and Work in Three Continents*, chapter 9.

# Appendix

## Jennifer Longford

### *The Telegraph*, London, 9 April 2012

Jennifer Longford, who has died aged 82, is thought by many to have been the daughter of the Liberal Prime Minister David Lloyd George by his long-time mistress Frances Stevenson; certainly Jennifer thought so herself, although she did not "discover" her parentage until she was in her forties.

Her mother Frances, who was half Scottish, a quarter French, and a quarter Italian, first encountered Lloyd George when she became governess to his daughter Megan in 1911, and soon became his secretary. She was his mistress from 1912.

Lloyd George's wife Margaret died in 1941, and two years later, when the former prime minister was 80, he and Frances married; she became Countess Lloyd George when he was raised to an earldom in January 1945, two months before his death.

Jennifer Longford was born Jennifer Mary Stevenson in London on October 4 1929. According to her daughter Ruth, who wrote a biography of Frances, Countess Lloyd George: More than a Mistress (1996): "In the late 1920s Lloyd George became temporarily discouraged about his political future, so he thought he would allow [Frances] to have the baby she longed for. She was 40 in 1928, and in

285

previous years she had had two abortions to protect him from scandal."

Jennifer herself would write in an article in 2007: "My mother spent much of her pregnancy in France, where she had relatives, but returned to England for the birth, as things did not go very well, and LG trusted English doctors more than French ones ... As they had agreed, neither of them ever claimed that I was LG's child. On the advice of a solicitor, my mother officially adopted me. I spent my first few months being looked after by a 'minder' who cared for several other children as well. Then I lived for four years in a house my mother had bought in Worplesdon about 20 miles from Bron-y-de [Lloyd George's house in Surrey, where he farmed 1,000 acres], but frequently visited them there. Early in 1935 I moved into a house called Avalon that my mother had built a mile from Bron-y-de, and I visited them there daily when I was not at school."

The little girl called Lloyd George "Taid" (Welsh for "grandfather"), and he lavished her with affection. "He was 66 when I was born," Jennifer wrote, "and I knew that he was not my grandfather, but he was the perfect grandfather-figure. He had responsibility for my discipline or day-to-day care, but he would spend as much time as he wanted or could spare on educating and entertaining me.

"He talked to me as if I was an adult. He entertained me by telling me about the books and music that he liked. When I was eight he took me to Stratford to see my first Shakespeare play, The Merry Wives of Windsor. The following year he took me to London to see Gilbert and Sullivan's Yeomen of the Guard."

Lloyd George also passed on to her his love of the novels of Dickens, while on Saturday evenings she was allowed to watch Westerns in his library, which doubled as a "cinema". In 1938 Frances and Jennifer accompanied him on a trip to Paris, where they visited Napoleon's burial place, Les Invalides. "He was a great admirer of

286

Napoleon," Jennifer recalled, "the foreign upstart who had risen to the top of his world."

Before Lloyd George's death, there had been no suggestion that Jennifer was his child: "Afterwards I was aware that people thought I might be, but my mother kept her counsel until her own death 27 years later, though just before she died she wrote me a curious, ambiguous, letter which may have been meant to acknowledge that the father she mentioned was LG.

"However, for the whole of the 27 years she stuck to her story that she had had an affair with another man, Colonel Tweed, one of LG's political advisers who was already married. Sometimes she even claimed to have married him, though it is certain that their affair never led to marriage, and when she showed me the certificate of her marriage in Guildford Register Office in 1943, the certificate referred to David Lloyd George as a widower and to Frances Stevenson as a spinster."

Jennifer was sent to Penrhos College in Colwyn Bay, but after the school was evacuated during the war to Chatsworth House she caught pneumonia, and her mother moved her to the supposedly more clement surroundings of Headington School in Oxford. She then enjoyed a happy interlude at Le Châtelard in Switzerland, where she perfected her French and became an expert skater.

After taking an English degree at St Andrews, Jennifer Longford decided to become a teacher, and while training at Bristol was persuaded by one of her lecturers to spend a year living with an impoverished family; the father was out of work, the mother a part-time prostitute. In the late 1950s, under the name Margaret Lassell, Jennifer would publish an acclaimed book about this experience, Wellington Road; Malcolm Muggeridge described it as "hell with the lid off".

In 1954 she took up a teaching post at Tabora Girls' High School in Tanganyika, where she met Michael Longford, secretary to the Governor, Lord Twining. They married in 1956, and had three children while living in Africa.

They loved Africa (both spoke fluent Swahili) and when Tanganyika gained independence as Tanzania in 1962, and Michael Longford's job effectively disappeared, the family returned with some sadness to England, settling near Jennifer's mother in Surrey.

Michael joined the Home Civil Service, and Jennifer taught a range of subjects at the secondary modern school at Witley. She took early retirement in her early 50s to care for her mother-in-law, who was suffering from Alzheimer's. Later Jennifer and her husband taught English to foreign students who would lodge at their cottage.

Frances Stevenson died in 1972, and after her death Jennifer discovered a note written in early 1929 by Frances to Lloyd George saying she suspected that she was pregnant and would send him a covert message if that proved to be the case. After Jennifer's birth she had sent him a telegram saying: "The parcel we were expecting has arrived."

On at least two occasions Jennifer Longford considered having a DNA test to establish her parentage, but never followed it through.

She helped Ffion Hague with her book The Pain and the Privilege: The Women in Lloyd George's Life (2008), and AJP Taylor when he edited Lloyd George: a Diary by Frances Stevenson (1971) and My Darling Pussy: the Letters of Lloyd George and Frances Stevenson, 1913-1941 (1975). She was a keen supporter of the Lloyd George Society, of which she became vice-president.

Michael Longford died in 2005, and she is survived by their son and two daughters.

**Jennifer Longford, born October 4 1929, died March 5 2012.**

# Tom Unwin

*The Telegraph*, London, 19 July 2012

Tom Unwin, who has died aged 88, was a Jewish refugee from Czechoslovakia and served in Royal Naval intelligence during the war; afterwards he worked for the Colonial Service and the United Nations, and tried to persuade Alexander Dubcek, exiled leader of the Prague Spring, to defect to the West.

Thomas Michael Ungar was born in Prague in October 25 1923. His father was the controversial writer Hermann Ungar, a protégé of Thomas Mann, who became godfather to Tom. Hermann Ungar died in 1929.

In 1938 Tom Ungar came to London to study agriculture. The following year, after the invasion of Sudetenland, he called his mother and younger brother, urging them to leave Prague and join him. They were all evacuated to Wells, Somerset, where, aged 17 and having anglicised his name, Tom Unwin joined the Home Guard and worked for an aircraft components factory. The rest of his extended family was exterminated at Auschwitz.

His facility with languages led to a transfer to an intelligence unit before, in 1943, he joined the Special Branch of the Royal Navy Volunteer Reserve, later serving on Channel escorts for the D-Day landings and patrolling Norwegian fjords aboard the destroyer Grenville.

In 1945 he was posted to Kiel to participate in the operation to recruit leading German scientists before they were captured by the Soviets. His primary objective was to persuade the inventor of high-speed, hydrogen peroxide fuelled submarines, Hellmuth Walter, to bring his expertise to the West. Unwin's charm and fluency in German proved critical for the mission's success, which resulted in the eventual delivery of a large amount of equipment at the Vickers shipyard in Barrow-in-Furness.

Unwin with President Nyerere and President Houphouet-Boigny of Ivory Coast, on the latter's state visit to Tanganyika in 1963

Unwin married in 1946 and the following year left for Tanganyika to join the Groundnut Scheme, the doomed Attlee-backed plan to grow peanuts in Africa. He and his wife spent their first three years of married life living in tents, surrounded by Dalmatians, wildcats, and Wagogo and Masai warriors.

In 1951, when the scheme failed, Unwin joined the Colonial Service, rising through the ranks to become Permanent Secretary in Foreign Affairs. After Independence he stayed on and worked closely with President Julius Nyerere, setting up the country's first foreign missions in London, Bonn, Kinshasa and Delhi. When the Tanganyika Rifles mutinied in 1964, Unwin hid his friend Brigadier Douglas Sholto from the rebel soldiers under his daughter's bed.

290

He left the country shortly afterwards and in 1965 joined the United Nations Development Programme, where he would spend the next 20 years of his career, in jobs from Malawi to Papua New Guinea. He subsequently took short-term development roles in Cambodia , Darfur , Sabah and Sierra Leone . His final posting, from 1992 to 1997, was in Kyrgyzstan.

In Turkey in the late 1960s he had become friends with Alexander Dubcek, the Czech leader exiled after the Russian invasion that crushed the Prague Spring. Unwin tried to talk his countryman into defecting, but the Czechs detained Dubcek's family and he was forced to return to house arrest as a forester.

Unwin always retained a fondness for his central European roots: Viennese operetta, Strauss waltzes and the songs of Marlene Dietrich were among his passions. Outwardly, however, he seemed the perfect Englishman, complete with monocle and pipe. He is survived by his second wife, Diana, and their son. A daughter from his first marriage also survives him.

**Tom Unwin, born October 25 1923, died 29 May 2012**

# Randal Sadleir

*The Telegraph*, **London,**
**9 September 2009**

Sadleir listening to Nyerere

Randal Sadleir, who died on August 11 aged 85, was a colonial servant in Tanganyika whose friendship with the charismatic Julius Nyerere enabled him to stay on as the last British official in independent Tanzania until 1973.

The two first met in the late 1950s at the Cosy café in Dar es Salaam, when Nyerere, the young leader of the pro-independence Tanganyika African National Union (TANU), made his mark by declaring that the biggest influence on Africans was witchcraft. His account of his

293

early poverty inspired Sadleir, a member of the governor's secretariat, to start a soup kitchen, though it did not last long. Soon the pair were on first name terms, and Sadleir was holding a teatime discussion group for young African civil servants at his home, much to the disapproval of some of his colleagues.

Nevertheless when the governor, Sir Edward Twining, ordered a translation service in English and Swahili for the legislative council in preparation for the multiracial state, then expected to be granted more than decade later (around 1970), Sadleir was appointed to it. He demonstrated such flair that within a year he was seconded to the colonial government's public relations department, participating in Swahili radio broadcasts (which were jammed in nearby Portuguese East Africa to prevent the "contagion" of independence spreading) and starting an eight-page weekly, named *Baragumu* after the cattle horn used to summon people to meetings.

Continuing to be a regular visitor to Nyerere's office, Sadleir would be greeted by a choir cheerfully singing *Englishman Go Home* while the leader of TANU's women's section would tartly say:

"Whenever I see the English flag I want to vomit."

Soon he became the government representative at all of TANU's meetings. He travelled abroad, seeking study grants for young Tanganyikans, and scored a notable success, as a Protestant, in obtaining a £400 scholarship to University College Dublin from the Catholic Archbishop McQuaid.

Whatever its doubts about the enthusiasm with which he went about his work, the colonial government was grateful to Sadleir for his intelligence about Nyerere's difficulties in restraining hot-headed allies, which, it acknowledged, had been gleaned from "remarkable conversations in a tea shop."

By 1960 however, London had abandoned its plans for a slow, organised withdrawal, in favour of an abrupt granting of independence. The change of heart was announced by the new governor, Sir Richard Turnbull, who declared on March 17 1959 that there would be an African majority in the legislative council. This caused a frenzy of excitement. After Sadleir had handed out copies of Turnbull's speech, he joined the jubilant crowd racing through the streets, only to discover that his pocket had been picked.

Thomas Randal Sadleir was born on May 6 1924 at Celbridge, Co Kildare. His father, Thomas Ulick Sadleir, was acting Ulster King of Arms but had his hopes of succeeding to the post dashed when the position was abolished.

Randal was sent to Portrora Royal School at Enniskillen but left early when his father's income from genealogical work halved after the outbreak of the war. He did his first-year exams in Modern Languages at Trinity College Dublin before sailing to England. There he guarded Henley Bridge with the Home Guard before being commissioned into the Royal Inniskilling Fusiliers.

He was subsequently dispatched to join 9th Battalion, King's African Rifles, as it was deployed in Somaliland and Abyssinia. For the next year he enjoyed the constant hardship and occasional dangers, and was impressed by meeting a district officer in the colonial service who held court on his veranda before settling down to a bath, a drink and a five-course meal.

After being transferred to headquarters, where he was responsible for Ethiopian and Somali spies, Sadleir was sent to India in preparation for the invasion of Japan. But the campaign was cancelled by the atom bomb, and he recalled his brigadier the morning after some heavy celebrations twice falling off his horse, relieving himself on the parade ground and then retiring to bed while sending a message that he would not be available to read the lesson at the victory service.

Back in England Sadleir applied to join the colonial service, overcoming the mystification of his interviewers about Portrora Royal School by saying that two famous old boys were HF Lyte, author of *Abide with Me*, and Oscar Wilde – "from the sublime to the ridiculous," as he noted.

After attending a course at Oxford and London and marrying Susan Rickards, a general's daughter with whom he was to have a son and daughter, the young couple arrived by the district lorry at Kahama, in Tanganyika's northwestern province, in early 1948.

Sadleir's first priorities were the maintenance of law and order, and the collecting of taxes on 10-day safaris. But to the Africans he was "Mr Problems" who adjudicated disputes, supervised dam building and inspected schools and hospitals as well as acting as magistrate, coroner, registrar and policeman.

On one occasion he found a body in the bush. Within days he had carried out the inquest; arrested a suspect, and convicted him at trial. In addition he had to work with the illiterate, but important, tribal chiefs while polishing up his language qualifications by reading *King Solomon's Mines* in Swahili.

He also had to cope with two major crises. These were a famine in Hadeni district and a crashed airliner, when the removal of the mangled and rotting bodies led him to suffer a nervous breakdown.

On returning from leave, Sadleir joined the secretariat in Dar es Salaam as assistant secretary for legal affairs, learning such abbreviations as PA (Put Away), BUF (Bring Up on File) and FYC (For Your Consideration) but being stumped by CCL until the governor's secretary explained that it meant: "Couldn't Care Less."

When the Union flag came down in late 1961, Sadleir had no interest in moving to the Foreign Service; "You're neither civil nor servile," Twining told him, in a kindly way, over lunch.

Instead he accepted President Nyerere's invitation to join the new Tanzanian government's ministry of co-operatives and community. His tasks included investigating the co-operative movement behind the Iron Curtain and running the Tanzanian stand at Expo 70 in Osaka; he survived the cull of remaining British government staff because, it was said, the president had mislaid his file.

But while remaining an admirer of Nyerere, Sadleir saw the socialist agenda plunge the economy into chaos and ban the wearing of miniskirts. He was also publicly accused of spying. After retiring from the government Sadleir spent a final two years as a public relations consultant to the tourist department before returning to England.

In his later years he became deputy national appeals officer for the Cancer Research campaign, and read to the blind Sir Anthony Wagner, the former Garter King of Arms, with whom he had played tennis as a boy.

After his wife's death Randal Sadleir wrote *Tanzania: Journey to Republic* (1999) and a memoir of his father (2004), which was well received when he presented it as a lecture in Dublin.

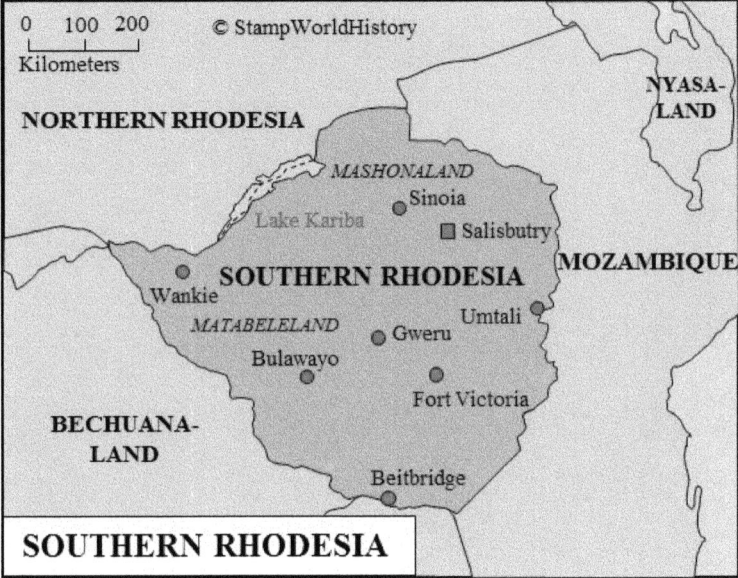

0　100　200　© StampWorldHistory
Kilometers

NORTHERN RHODESIA

NYASA-
LAND

MASHONALAND
Sinoia
Lake Kariba
Salisbutry

SOUTHERN RHODESIA

MOZAMBIQUE

Wankie
MATABELELAND
Umtali
Gweru
Bulawayo
Fort Victoria

BECHUANA-
LAND

Beitbridge

SOUTHERN RHODESIA

Africa

Morocco
Tunisia
Algeria
Libya
Egypt
(Western Sahara)
Mauritania
Mali
Niger
Chad
Sudan
Eritrea
Senegal
Djibouti
Gambia
Burkina Faso
Guinea Bissau
Guinea
Nigeria
Republic of South Sudan
Ethiopia
Somalia
Sierra Leone
Ivory Coast
Ghana
Togo
Benin
Cameroon
Central African Republic
Liberia
Equatorial Guinea
Gabon
Congo
Democratic Republic of Congo
Uganda
Kenya
Rwanda
Burundi
Tanzania
Angola
Malawi
Zambia
Mozambique
Madagascar
Zimbabwe
Namibia
Botswana
Swaziland
South Africa
Lesotho

303

www.ingramcontent.com/pod-product-compliance
Lightning Source LLC
Chambersburg PA
CBHW071408090426
42737CB00011B/1394